KATARIN

BOLD

A new era of strategic HR

empik go

In 2005, there was a famous article titled "Why we hate HR" that shook some corners of the industry and forced many of us to relook and rethink the way we are serving. When I first met Katarina in 2019, I immediately recognised a rebel and a pioneer in her through how she and the amazing HR team at Spotify are redefining our space. Their rock-and-roll approach has been hugely inspiring to many and I'm grateful that we now get an even deeper look into their fascinating methodology.
Ong Chin Yin, Chief People Officer, Grab

Finally! A practical (and entertaining) guide to building the world's best culture-first organisations, as told by the people leaders who have actually done it. Toss out your dusty, antiquated HR playbooks. This book replaces 'best practices' with a renewed sense of inspiration to create the culture you've always wanted!
Katelin Holloway, Founding Partner at Seven Seven Six, People & Culture Exec.

Preface

The seed for this book was planted at the beginning of my career, but the ideas presented here have developed during my many years as an HR professional. I experienced a rigidity in HR education, and that feeling has been exacerbated by the fact that students, in those countries that have an HRM degree, are still learning what HR is from the same textbook that I used many years ago. I have also noticed that those of us who want to think outside the box, who see an opportunity to lead the way and bring the practice into the new century, meet resistance. Is this because of reluctance? Because of a lack of courage? Or perhaps both.

I believe that anyone who wants to work successfully in HR today must dare to stand out. It is obvious to me that many in my professional network, colleagues I meet at conferences and various HR events, have come to the same realisation – unfortunately, however, with the addition of an 'it's not possible' mindset. They believe that in most organisations, HR should only exist as a punching bag – a reactive function. Maintaining this view of HR, which is especially common in the tech industry, means it becomes a suicide mission to stand out, to put your foot down and challenge the organisation, the leadership and the business.

As Global Chief Human Resources Officer (CHRO) at Spotify, I look at my wonderful team with pride. They have all played an important role in the journey towards redefining what an HR department is and by doing so, they have also played a great part in making Spotify a great business. Many people reach out to us and ask us to provide examples of how to work with business-driven HR in practice, and the desire to contribute to real change in this area has grown stronger and stronger within me. The time is ripe. And the team is by my side, fighting and daring to be bold, which has had an incredible impact on the whole organisation. They need to be heard, and they are worth listening to. Together, we are shaping the present and the future of our profession.

The book was not written by me alone but by a large collective of authors consisting of HR leaders and other functional leaders at Spotify. It is partly a response to a high demand for them to share their unique experiences. Together, we have over 150 years of experience in HR – and now, we want to put that experience in your hands. The chapters cover many of the areas a global HR manager works with. It is a book written by practitioners, for practitioners. We describe how we see our profession, and how it can be something extraordinary. This is not my book – it is our book.

Our intention is not to imply that you should now question everything you already know and do. Instead, build on what works! We want to inspire you to pressure test your chosen truths and push yourself out of your comfort zone. There is value in not hiding behind a wall of 'that's how almost everyone does it' or – even worse – that's how we've always done it. Dare to try new things, question old ways of thinking and working, and be *bold*.

We have given theories, data and models some space in the book, but they are not intended to play the main role. We hope to contribute our thoughts and experiences on how to approach HR work in a new era. We will also share some lessons learned, and not only positive ones. Things don't always go as planned, at least not at first. Our hope is that you will be inspired, gain new ideas and, where possible, challenge and develop your own HR approach. So take in what we write, or question it. Smile in recognition, or shake your head sceptically. Even if you don't embrace our philosophy outright, you will almost certainly find something in the book that you like, or something that makes you re-evaluate something you do in your own organisation.

So the question now is: Are you ready to absorb our thoughts, to see where you can be bold, innovative, adventurous – maybe even disruptive?

If the answer is yes, great! Here we go!

Katarina Berg
Stockholm, 2nd January 2023

Contents

**Part 3.
Bread and Butter
– the essence of HR work**   226

Introduction:
A new strategic era in HR
– what does this mean?

All activities undertaken by a company in order to create success fall under one of the three P's coined by the American business leader Lee Iacocca: "People, Product, Profit". The reason "people" comes first in this list is because you can't do much about the product or the profit if you don't have a great team of people. HR is about the culture within the business. It is about the people in the organisation who create that culture.

The role of HR is to develop and challenge the business. No more and no less. To put it in football (soccer for some) terms, HR's job is to make sure that the team has the right players (and a strong substitute bench), that the players are physically and mentally fit, that they continue to develop, that there is a well-rehearsed Game Theory (Theory of Business), and that each individual player takes responsibility for their own personal growth and assumes accountability for the performance as a whole. To borrow football coach and leader Pia Sundhage's words – each player should commit to "play on their teammate's best foot", which results in the whole team improving the individual as well as joint performance, and creates a team that behaves as one. This, of course, assumes that everyone understands the theory of the game; to return to the terminology of the business world: that your organisation has a vision, a purpose, a strategy, goals and core values that are well-founded and well communicated. You dare to be purpose- and value-driven as well as open and transparent with everyone about everything you believe in and intend to accomplish.

Anyone interested in the behind the scenes at Spotify knows that we like to think of ourselves as a 'band'. Because just like a band, we depend on each other to create the best possible audio experience. Just like a band, we need to be in sync. At Spotify, we also put significant focus on our employees, or band members, as we call them.

Those of us who have written this book come from a school of thought where HR works in tandem with the core business. We believe HR's role is to support, think strategically, design, develop, challenge, hold, stretch, invent, question, change and drive. Sometimes, it is our task to challenge the prevailing thought structures, business theories, and the current organisational design. We achieve this by using data, both quantitative and qualitative (employee surveys, tests, workshops, research, etc.). Our HR approach is based on theory, research and data – but also on many years of practical experience in the field.

At Spotify we sometimes talk about the 'HR palette' and the many different colours that make up the HR profession (allegedly 171 different areas of knowledge and expertise). Some believe that HR work can be undertaken by pretty much anyone who has access to data and is attracted to one or more of the colours in the palette. This is not true. You need a deeper knowledge of what happens to the whole picture if you adjust one aspect of an approach, even if that particular aspect may seem insignificant and disconnected from the others.

Just like at any other company, at Spotify, employees sometimes hear about the great things being done by other organisations and wonder: "Hey, why don't we do that here?!" But what works in one organisation won't necessarily work in another. In essence, you should never start from someone else's sketches, or pick the raisins out of someone else's cake. It's essential to begin with your culture, define what you want to achieve, and create a long-term vision and overall picture of the business. Copying and pasting someone else's concept and implementing it quickly and without deeper consideration, simply because it works for them, or because it sounds and looks good, is at best a short-term publicity stunt, and at worst both irresponsible and reckless. When setting your People Strategy, you must always start from your own organisation, its direction and its purpose. Any other approach signifies flying blindfolded, and then HR becomes anxious, not bold.

Our hope is that this book will answer 'everything the CFO always wanted to know about HR but never had the courage to ask' and simultaneously give a picture of what HR at Spotify is, and why we have the approach we have. Our focus is on what we believe drives the business forwards, alongside putting people and culture first. HR is not about trends. And HR's function is not to be the 'cake and balloons department' either. It's about understanding that the company performs best when employee wellbeing is prioritised; that when people develop, so does the business. HR is all about how to achieve such a win-win situation. This is exactly what this book is about too.

Our hope is that this book will help you get the HR side of the business up to speed. It provides strategic advice and suggestions for your teams on all things HR- and business-related – everything we believe is part of the new era of HR. We want to show you how to drive a bolder HR approach, whether you're facing your most challenging change management project ever, dealing with a global crisis, or finding the right successors for key positions. We'll show you how to retain top talent (although some turnover is natural and healthy), and teach you how to test a value-driven compensation philosophy. We hope we will manage to persuade you that the future is not about managing and controlling employees, but rather about supporting, challenging and enabling them to develop.

This book will also discuss how sustainability is becoming increasingly important, as is mental health, diversity, inclusion and community – and why you need to take these topics into account at almost every stage of your design thinking. We will also talk about how labour law is the basis for creativity and innovation, and thus the starting block for HR. It is almost impossible to be anything but reactive, traditional and defensive if you are not aware of the labour code. Understanding the labour code inside out is essential if you don't want to resign yourself to being operational, rarely strategic and never tactical; the labour code affects everything from employment to retirement. If you don't know your stuff in this area, get up to speed as soon as possible!

Another topic we will tackle is the need to see learning as part of your business concept. An organisation that does not continuously invest in the professional development of its people will stop growing and stop developing. Likewise, any organisation that doesn't bring in the right people, at the right time, for the right roles, and adjust its organisational design accordingly, will lose momentum and competitive advantage. Welcome to the era of the employee.

Global HR at Spotify

HR at Spotify is heavily influenced by our rapid growth – rapid for us is between 1,000 and 4,000 new employees a year. We have to work smart as we don't have the luxury to waste a lot of time on the unnecessary administrative tasks internally referred to as 'work around work'. We also have to ensure that all new band members feel welcome and are onboarded in a productive and efficient way. In addition, they should understand our mission (purpose) and stand firmly behind it. Our work is also influenced by the fact that Spotify is a multinational company with +8000 band members, only around 20% of whom are based at the Mothership in Stockholm and most of whom work from home or other locations. This means we practise global HR. Before getting started with the first part of the book, let's describe what we mean by global HR in more detail.

If you are under the impression that all companies with employees distributed around the world work with a global HR model, you are not alone. However, this is not the case in practice. *True* global HR requires a lot of thought and coordination.

The world has never been as small, nor as interconnected, as it is now. Technology enables us to stay in touch with each other wherever we are in the world, and travel is more efficient and faster than ever. The number of both small and large businesses operating in multiple countries has also never been bigger. Therefore, to survive in the market, a business must think globally (although in some cases you have to act locally). That means giving up the old siloed thinking and being willing to blur the organisational boundaries to stay relevant. A company that wants to implement an effective global commercial strategy must have a culture where all employees feel they are working towards the same goal, no matter where they are in the world. HR has an extremely important role to play in order to achieve this.

Research shows that in companies with strong global cultures, teams perform better and have more engaged employees, who in turn stay with the company longer. Perhaps most importantly, employees remain more focused on the company's purpose and goals. Since the very beginning of Spotify's journey, we have strived to create an environment where innovative, resourceful and passionate employees can be their best selves. It has been, and continues to be, incredibly exciting – and challenging – to try to create a truly global culture of constant and rapid growth.

Three things have been particularly important in creating this culture – shared values, a shared mindset and shared leadership criteria.

Our values

We began our values journey with the global Passion Tour, where the executive team established our mission statement – our purpose/why. We then asked our people to define our common values, using a unique approach that we'll explain later in the book. While most companies establish their core values behind closed doors during management meetings – or even outsource that job to external strategists – at Spotify, we believe that core values should be defined by employees, not established by external consultants, or by management alone. Therefore, we involved all our employees in the process. In practice, some of our HR team travelled around the globe and visited all offices to facilitate employee workshops. During the workshops, participants discussed our desired future state (our vision) and our purpose (our mission). Next, they identified the values that were most important to them to be able to do their best work, have fun, and learn and grow while doing so.

Spotify's core values today reflect the values of our employees, globally. We are – as a company and as individuals – *passionate, innovative, sincere, collaborative* and *playful*. Over the years, as we've grown, we've continued to 'test drive' our core values to make sure they still resonate with employees – in every region and in every office. If one of our core values no longer has as much support among employees as it did previously, we are open to making a change – core values are organic, living things, and as such, they should be changeable. If the culture does not evolve, we are not moving forwards as a company. At each new employee induction – Intro Days – we conduct a Passion Tour Encore to test current values and decide if they need to be changed or redefined.

Many companies value a strong culture and therefore want to hold on to what they have created, even when times and the workforce change. The old culture feels comfortable, understandable, rooted. However, we believe it is much more important to have the *right* culture than a *strong* culture, i.e. a *relevant* culture, given who you are and want to be, and where you are going. Employees, especially the veterans, usually need support in order to let go of the 'good old days' and embrace the new. After all, a culture can be strong and dysfunctional or toxic simultaneously. If you believe that people are the culture, and that the culture reflects your people, you cannot cling on to the way it has always been. Doing so can cause three undesirable effects: your culture does not reflect your present, your culture is holding back business development instead of supporting it, and in your eagerness to please a minority, you forget that new employees become demotivated by a constant reminder that things were better in the past.

A global mindset

The basis of our Learning & Development (L&D) philosophy is what is known as a Growth Mindset. This is sometimes referred to as a dynamic mindset, as opposed to a static mindset. At Spotify, we believe that in order to achieve our ambitious goals, we must first create a global culture characterised by such a mindset. The research of American psychologist Carol Dweck, which shows that people with a dynamic mindset are more likely to recognise that they can develop their skills and, through hard work, *improve*, has been an inspiration to us. It's good to be smart, and it's good to be talented, but that's just the starting point.

The concept of this dynamic mindset, together with the notion of the four universal motivators – or drivers, if you prefer – encompasses *autonomy, competence development, belonging* and *benevolence.* This is at the heart of our global learning strategy and, we believe, central to a company culture that encourages employees to be bold, test their limits, dare to fail, learn and try again. We have embedded aspects of this mindset into almost all our development efforts (whether it's leadership development or development opportunities aimed at other groups of employees) and are keen that all our managers understand the impact a Growth Mindset can have on our people and our business.

Our leadership criteria

It's clear that our people managers have played an important role in the creation of Spotify's culture. A global environment is often characterised by complexity and unpredictability, and by polarities – contradictions, paradoxes and major differences in experiences and perspectives between different countries. In our case, it's about managing – and even embracing – those polarities. We accept the fact that it is never or rarely 'either/or', but almost always 'both/and'. Our managers need to accept constant change, be empathetic, be able to adapt their leadership styles, focus on growth, be communicative and convey a thoughtful long-term focus. We realise it is a lot to ask – to be able to embrace and navigate dualities and charter the controlled chaos that is Spotify per design.

When it comes to creating global leadership criteria, a good starting point is to reflect on what your organisation considers to be the core of good leadership. The leadership criteria creates a common language that your organisation can use when expressing what you expect from everyone in a leadership role: it serves as a guideline for your managers. It becomes the framework and compass for those in charge. At Spotify, when we developed our global leadership criteria, we invited all our managers and employees to answer the question: 'What makes a leader successful at Spotify, today and in the future?' We were able to identify a set of principles – and associated behaviours – based on Spotify's values. The work on setting the leadership criteria and the work on the values was therefore done in parallel. Neither leadership criteria nor values can exist in their own world, they must be fully compatible and mutually reinforcing. Nor should they become slogans or feel overly polished. They should come from the organisation – because they are to be used by the organisation.

The criteria will be put to the test, especially when all is not rainbows and unicorns. It will also be an important part of the foundation of your culture building work (and this is an area that is very work-intensive). At Spotify, once we had our values and leadership criteria in place, we created a foundation of leadership training for managers (regardless of their level, the size of their team, or where they were located). The leadership criteria can be compared with a Service Level Agreement for Spotify managers.

Today, we recruit, train, evaluate, and sometimes redeploy managers using the agreed criteria. We have designed management and leadership development programmes where we carefully review what we expect from a manager at Spotify. We look at what effective leadership is from a strategic-philosophical perspective, what a growth mindset is, and how we can strengthen our employees' motivation through purpose-driven and passionate leadership.

Not much is mandatory at Spotify, but our manager and leadership development programmes are. It's a way of ensuring that our people managers, wherever they are in the world, work in line with our values. It's crucial to how we create a positive culture globally.

Challenges

Growing into a global culture, and then guiding, shaping and maintaining it, is a challenge. We need to constantly monitor whether we are truly living our values from a global perspective, while taking into account local cultural differences. The Spotify culture has Swedish roots, and striking a balance between our cultural heritage, our global culture and the local culture in each office has sometimes been challenging. This is why we have ensured that this work is not done in campaign or project form. It is imperative that those of us in HR truly understand what makes the Spotify organism live and thrive and progress, that we understand the core business inside out, and that we are *integrated into the business* rather than brushing the surface. It also makes our work more fun, more tactical, and more strategic.

We strive to be 'glocal' (think global, act local), and expect everyone in the HR team to have as much business acumen as HR knowledge. In the HR team, we have developed a great sensitivity to even small cultural differences, and are in a position to identify them. We give our employees and managers in the different markets the mandate to help drive our culture work and ask them to play a role in reminding us that we are a truly global company. Questions during recruitment and answers from employee surveys around the world have proved that most of our employees recognise that Spotify is a global company – and this is often one of the main reasons they joined the band.

Those of us leading HR at Spotify play a key role in showing our managers and employees what it means to work in a *truly* global culture. It also requires us as an HR team to be *truly* global.

PART 1

Part 1.
Attraction and Recruitment
– attracting and recruiting
the right people

Introduction by Dr Tomas Chamorro-Premuzic

HR professionals have been warning us about the increasing complexity and unpredictability of work, and its related talent market, for some time. In recent years, organisations have been forced to change and modernise in ways they couldn't have expected – it seems like the future is finally here, and there is no going back to rigid working, tech averseness and talent endlessness.

And yet, it would be counterproductive to forget that the critical questions around talent identification, at least on a broad and high level, have not changed that much. In fact, all organisations are still, in effect, concerned with the same old questions, namely: How do I find the right person for the right job?, How can I identify and develop future leaders?, and What is the best way to align my strategy, culture and talent?

If an alien arrived on planet Earth right now and they were only able to digest current thinking about talent, especially focused on new technologies and disruptive innovations, they would be missing out on a great opportunity: to learn from the past; not just understanding the present, but being able to use the past to predict and improve on the future. Indeed, for all the talk of unpredictability and all the unknowns, we should not forget that there is a well-established science to identify, understand, and improve human potential. Because of this science, there is really no structural impediment or constraint to organisations becoming more talent-centric and meritocratic – other than, of course, politics, overconfidence, incompetence, and an inability to learn from mistakes. Consider that human beings have not changed very much in 200,000 years of evolution, and that the fundamentals of human psychology – what makes people unique, how they are likely to behave and why, and what they are passionate about – change only in small increments. We still work to find a sense of purpose, to connect with others, and to achieve something that contributes to a wider cause. This is why understanding and betting on talent is advantageous for everyone: organisations win because people are key to advancing their strategies; and people win because in order to thrive, you need to find the right fit for your talents and be understood at work, which occupies a big chunk of our lives.

Still, there are also changes, cultural and societal, that need to be acknowledged. The new HR era is clearly focused on people-first and optimising not just for performance and productivity, but also wellbeing. Contrary to what people think, there is not a tension between the two. If you want people to give you their best and be productive, you need to look after them and help them look after themselves. Most of us spent the early days of the COVID-19 crisis on back-to-back video calls, without much time to eat, walk, breathe or dream. Then we remembered that this is our life – if we are going to live to work, we had better make work as rewarding as possible. And even if you love your job, there's a chance you'll burn out if you forget that there are other dimensions to life. Every new age brings new challenges, which are often best understood as polarities. Business leaders who are naive enough to believe that you can turn people into productive machines will not just fail their employees, but also lose the talent war. The best and most talented people in any industry want to feel loved before they unleash their full potential at work.

This is also the age of data-driven HR, which is bringing about a big change in real-world hiring practices. For every organisation that professes a strong intention to be evidence-based and science-driven in their talent identification approaches, there are nine that continue to base most hiring decisions on intuition, gut feeling, or 'social capital' (a euphemism for nepotism and political cachet). This is why so many companies love hiring for 'culture fit', why most managers think they 'know talent when they see it'. It's why it is rare for anyone to get a job unless they are evaluated more favourably than others in a job interview, despite overwhelming evidence that most interviews are biased, unreliable, and poor predictors of future performance (particularly if you need to look at candidates' potential for doing a job they have not done before). In a world where most organisations truly cared about accuracy, the Myers Briggs (MBTI)[1] would not be the most widely used personality test, and documentaries such as *Persona*, which portray psychometric assessments as inherently flawed, would not get the popular acclaim they do. Despite enormous advances in AI (Artificial Intelligence) and analytics, and the fact that science-based assessments can provide a much more accurate picture of a person's talent and potential than interviews or human intuition, we continue to favour our instincts over evidence, like the cab driver who ignores Google Maps or Waze in favour of their own experience. Except we don't even acknowledge when we get it wrong, because unlike cab drivers, in the world of talent, you can always pretend that you were right...

Still, there have been massive improvements in the world of hiring for those who want to opt in. It has never been easier to invite a wide and diverse range of candidates to interact with engaging and insightful tools; to learn about themselves, and their potential fit with a given role or culture. And there has never been a bigger appetite to hire for culture add-on rather than fit. The rise of diversity and inclusion (and belonging) is a true blessing for the world of talent, because it will do more to unlock the power of cognitive or psychological diversity, and leverage the distributed expertise of the knowledge economy, than any tool we had in the past. Equally, if there is one silver lining from this pandemic, it's the fact that people will take leadership more seriously: every human in the world has realised (sadly, the hard way) that it is generally advantageous to have leaders who are competent, smart, kind, honest and humble... as opposed to the opposite. This may reduce the historical tendency to promote overconfident narcissists to leadership roles, as well as the bad habit of making leadership a popularity contest where the most pathologically ambitious person (usually a white male) wins, to everyone's detriment.

With this in mind, you will appreciate this chapter on talent identification and recruitment, for it has managed the near impossible task of balancing the proven science of potential with the modern challenges of recruitment. Much like any other activity or enterprise at Spotify, the author's approach is optimised for rationality and balance, and manages to refresh established principles in order to boost their relevance and applicability to the modern world of work. The war for talent has been intensifying since McKinsey first coined the term nearly 25 years ago. It is safe to assume that in the near future, and particularly in the aftermath of this recent pandemic, the best employers and talent magnets will be able to leverage all available technologies to understand their people, help them be understood, and turn the unique perspective humans bring to the table into a true collaborative asset. People will want to join – and remain in – organisations that nurture and harness their potential, and that have the data-driven humility to challenge their own assumptions about how to unleash talent at work. This is not so much a talent philosophy as a cultural DNA. Importantly, one size does not fit all, but in reading the next pages you will appreciate the beauty of keeping things simple, and the elegant appeal of that undervalued strength called rationality.

Employer Branding
– our employee
value proposition

The official definition of the employer brand was formulated by Simon Barrow and Tim Ambler as "the package of functional, economic and psychological benefits provided by employment, and identified with the employing company".[2] It is the image and reputation of a company as an employer. Or, more simply: what employees say about their employer after two glasses of wine.

Regardless of how we define the phrase, employer branding efforts are most effective for organisations that are purpose-driven and values-driven, meaning all employees follow the same compass, understand the 'why' and want to contribute to the realisation of a common purpose or mission. When all employees unite behind this purpose and pull in the same direction, the sense of community is strengthened. Productivity increases. The external image of the organisation improves. This is extremely powerful for the business itself and also creates a unique and positive experience for employees.

It is our belief that all organisations are best served by having a clearly stated vision and/or mission and carefully communicated and supported goals and strategies, all of which are underpinned by shared values. In this sense, many organisations are quite similar. Yet the individuals working in a given organisation at a given time (in combination with the organisational design) – and their way of interacting, their drive and their genuine willingness to participate – can never be replicated.

Most products and services are best or biggest in their market only for a limited time. If they are good enough, and in sufficient demand, they will soon be copied, and possibly improved by others. A values-driven culture is different. It cannot be plagiarised. It is shaped by the employees who are right here, right now, signing an invisible contract to work together to: (1) create something bigger than its parts, (2) build an organisation that is stronger and more successful than the organisation they joined, (3) leave a mark for posterity, and (4) do something they can feel proud of (because those who feel proud will perform better).

Your employer branding strategy should unleash this power. It should permeate every decision and non-decision, even if it is invisible.

So how do you achieve this?

Never sell a fairy tale

Creating a good careers site or building contacts with students at the best universities and colleges is not enough to create a successful employer branding strategy. Nor should the task be delegated to the most junior HR staff. It is way too important!

To succeed in employer branding work, you first need to know your organisation – you need to know what is central and genuine for you and your employer brand. This is essential if you want to effectively communicate your employee value proposition (EVP). Packaging such an offer in a truly enticing and vibrant way is an art in itself. It can be disastrous if there is something in the promise that is not quite accurate, if you are pretending to be something you are not, or where your company values are not genuine, but just a veneer.

What you offer your employees in exchange for what they give you should always – always! – link back to your true culture and values and this link should always be made visible. Without that authenticity or honesty, you run the risk of people joining the organisation because you, your recruiters and hiring managers sold a 'fairy tale' during the recruitment process. If you sell candidates a story about who you are that is not true, then sooner rather than later, they will have a completely different experience. No one wants to be disappointed or discover that they need to adjust their expectations (not to mention the financial consequences of such a discovery). It's best to be genuine from the outset, reducing the risk of disappointment and giving new employees every opportunity to make a positive first impression. Every organisation has its unique characteristics and not all talented people are looking for the same thing – so never sell a fairy tale, a fantasy.

Authenticity is a value that helps you get the right people; people who want to work in your company for the right reasons, who understand the journey you've taken, know your shortcomings and want to be part of building something faster, stronger and better. As behavioural scientists, we know that people love freedom and flexibility (at least in moderation), yet still want to know what is expected of them, and preferably without surprises.

We can compare the recruitment process and the introduction of new employees to any other new relationship. A relationship that begins with dishonesty on one or both sides is unlikely to flourish or last very long. However, if both sides have a sober view of what they are getting into and with whom, most will be curious about where it will take them, what they will discover and how they will learn, develop and grow stronger together.

A CEO issue – where HR are the experts, but everyone jumps on the bandwagon

The design and development of the employer brand should be based on the organisation's core and business strategy. The brand should be visible at all stages of the employee lifecycle. Let's make no pretences here – embedding your brand this thoroughly is a lot of work – however, the sooner you start, the sooner you can reap the benefits.

It is not uncommon for one of the youngest and most junior HR staff members to be given the task of 'managing the employer brand'. You may be under the impression that employer branding predominantly centres around creating an online careers site and organising job fairs. For us at Spotify, and for everyone else who subscribes to the HR philosophy we believe in, the opposite is true. We believe that the ultimate responsibility lies with the CEO, but that strategy, philosophy and execution can be delegated to the CHRO. After all, it's all about attracting the right people to the organisation and then encouraging those individuals to grow and develop within it. Employer branding is about everything you do as an organisation, everything you don't do, and everything in between. If you get this right, are consistent and clearly demonstrate what makes you unique, your employer brand will be a competitive advantage.

As more organisations wake up to the importance of employer branding, interest in this area has increased. The more people in the organisation realise that employer branding (and HR work in general) is becoming increasingly strategic and less about 'support and transactional work', the more people will start to do parts of our work or move in to 'eat the candy', but not show as much interest in doing some of what comes with it – like brushing teeth and going to the dentist.

We have seen that there is sometimes a tug of war between departments when employer branding becomes a strategic issue, and this is something we in the HR team at Spotify have often been asked about. The marketing department is sometimes at the other end of the rope, pulling with all their might to 'win' the employer branding issue. The tech and communication side of the business has also started to show interest in the topic. Why is this? Don't get us wrong – of course collaboration between HR and marketing, communication and tech is essential for employer branding to be solid and successful. Of course the employer brand and the customer/product brand should be consistent. However, they have slightly different entry points (read: target groups). So, even though both are based on the knowledge of human behaviour, we expect slightly different outcomes. When well executed, it's intertwined with culture and personnel strategy; therefore, it should be managed by and belongs to HR.

Employer branding is very much about understanding your organisation in depth and then successfully communicating this to the outside world. Firstly, what is communicated to the outside world must be consistent with the employees' own experiences and perceptions of their employer. Secondly, employees must know what is happening in the organisation. A no-go situation is when an employee reads about their own organisation, and activities taking place there, from an external source. You also shouldn't have to hear from an outsider why you do what you do. Employees should understand the strategic play and why the team is set up as it is, and be able to easily communicate it to others themselves. If they are at a private dinner, an afterwork with friends, or simply get a question from anyone outside the organisation, they should be well equipped to explain these points. No one wants a stranger to tell them about what's happening in the company to which they dedicate 40 hours a week. They want to be in the know, to feel included and proud. And as we mentioned, proud people perform better, so this is in everyone's interest.

We aim to get all employees walking in step, towards the same goal and understanding: The Power of We. We want to ensure all employees know what is happening in the organisation before it is communicated to the outside world through external marketing or communication. This is what we in HR are trained and experienced in. Our focus is not on increasing sales, increasing the number of users or any other commercial goals. Of course, we want such goals to be achieved, but this is our indirect aim. We know that we can achieve those goals by finding the right talent at the right time, and then ensuring that this talent has the opportunity to develop continuously.

Those of us in HR and employer branding know how to attract the right people and how to retain them. We know how to be clear, consistent, compelling and therefore attractive in our employee value proposition (EVP), all whilst acknowledging that our offering will not appeal to everyone. Nor should it, which is also a point of effective employer branding

Storytelling

There is no one-size-fits-all guideline on exactly how to present your EVP, because every organisation has to do it in its own way. Your approach and how you tell your story should demonstrate who you are. Don't make the mistake of letting an agency do this job. Who knows you best – you or an outsider?

We are going to repeat this frequently: beware of looking at what others are doing and then trying to copy. This approach will not be credible to potential job seekers, nor (perhaps more importantly) to existing employees. In addition, a false promise, where new employees expect one thing from their new employer but then get something completely different, results in high attrition. Retention becomes difficult and recruitment and onboarding costs increase significantly.

Show who you really are and communicate it in a smart way. Say the right thing to the right people. Here you can use your employees as support. Treat them as the important and fantastic communicators and ambassadors they are, and they will share lots of good as well as true and relevant stories. They will show who they are and at the same time who you are and what you offer. Your employees are the real proof of your EVP, so identify your best ambassadors and set them free to spread your gospel. They have better judgement than you might think. Here, as in so many other contexts, trust is crucial – it's what the whole employer-employee relationship is based on. Moreover, if you don't tell your story yourself, someone else will, so better you do it than an outsider. Your ambassadors may not always say exactly the right thing, but it's also not just about *what* they say, but *how* they say it. Think about which audience will be exposed to which message, i.e. who will recognise the ambassador's story, identify with it and hopefully be attracted. You can train your ambassadors on what message(s) to convey, and then leave the storytelling to them.

Finding the right ambassadors, giving them direction and capturing their stories, is something that Spotify's Heart & Soul (Mental Health & Wellbeing) team are masters at. As part of the HR function, the team's core mission is to create a safe work environment where our band members feel valued for their unique perspectives and where they take care of themselves and each other. We will return to the work of the Heart & Soul team later in the book, in the chapter on diversity and inclusion, but here we note that the team's starting point is to create a safe environment, where employees' mental well-being is taken seriously. This can only be created from within, by the employees themselves (with the support of the team). It's a great example of why creating a strong ambassador team was a key starting place for the Heart & Soul strategy. We achieved this by building and communicating our central idea around mental health within the HR team and then offering guidance and a framework for our ambassadors to have the freedom to drive local initiatives that are relevant to their particular region, or work for their particular office and reality.

Of course, the best way to get good ambassadors is to encourage every individual to live the shared values and embody the brand. A really strong employer brand makes it easy for employees to be ambassadors. The key is not to try to squeeze out lots of initiatives and campaigns but rather to take advantage of all the ideas that contribute to creating a sustainable culture and community that employees enjoy and that they are happy – and proud – to tell others about.

Communication

As already noted, building a strong employer brand is very much about communication – both internal and external. When it comes to internal communication, we usually say that any organisation with more than two employees has difficulties communicating. Because it is that difficult. In order to succeed with employer branding, this aspect of internal communication must be the responsibility of HR.

You create trust by being clear, consistent and persuasive in your communication. No matter where you are in your employer branding journey, no matter the maturity of your organisation and no matter what your ambition is – *be authentic.* That's another message we will repeat many times. Future potential employees will perceive something as false if there is no consistency between what you say you are (your profile), what you actually are (your identity) and what others perceive you to be (your image). The importance of authenticity, sincerity and transparency cannot be overstated.

Once you have found your message, your appeal and your channels: say what you want to say, repeat it – and then do it again! You may find yourself feeling bored and therefore consider varying your message. Don't! Just repeat it. This is how you build a strong brand message through communication. Say it once, say it again – and then say it again: 'Hit, re-hit and remind!'

This does not mean that you should *never* adjust your message. Of course, sometimes you need to evaluate it, and your communication, and make changes. But this should be done as the whole brand evolves, not just because you feel like a broken record. The employer brand should change as the organisation changes. A message that was once genuine and an accurate reflection of who you are, but which is not updated as the organisation evolves, runs the risk of becoming just that: inauthentic and misleading. Then you end up promising your employees, existing and potential, something you can't deliver.

It may be time to update the message when new employees join the organisation. These employees need to have a chance to get a feel for the values. What do they think about the way you communicate who you are? What would they say or do differently? This doesn't mean that every new employee gets to rewrite everything on their first day, but you should definitely give your new hires time to let your vision, purpose and overall goals and strategies sink in. What they saw and read even before the first interview has to match both the picture painted during the recruitment process and the reality they will face on their first day at work (and beyond).

Make sure you spot any patterns in how new employees adopt the values, so you can catch when core values and behaviours are no longer fully aligned. Your culture and values are not just current guidelines, but should have the ability to be reshaped and adapted. The same goes for your employer brand and your EVP.

Measuring the results

It's no secret that measuring the impact of employer branding is difficult. However, a few metrics can give you an idea of whether your efforts are effective and how the strategy needs to evolve. Moreover, these metrics can often be used in communication with your employees, present and future, your stakeholders and partners, confirming that you are doing something that works.

We recommend that you measure your work in terms of Return on Investment (ROI), but also Return on Engagement (ROE). Try doing some due diligence on your own culture and then repeat the exercise, to get an idea of how your employer branding work has added value to the company. For example, if you remove the costs of offices, salaries, employees, management and other things that are easy to put a price tag on, what is the difference in company value? Doing this will probably mean that you get the true measure and value of your employer brand.

As always, you should link the metrics to your overall goal and that goal should be to become the employer of choice. Think about how you can determine whether you are, or are becoming, the employer of choice. One relevant metric is the number of applications you receive when you make an open call for a position. However, don't assume that a large number of applicants is always positive. If the wrong people apply for the position, it becomes a cost because each candidate should be given the same amount of time and the process becomes slower and more expensive. Receiving many applications from people who don't have the education, experience or skills you are looking for is a clear sign that your employer brand communication needs to be adjusted.

Therefore, we can say that attractiveness is a key element of measuring the success of your employer branding, but just as important is how many people choose to stay and how long they stay, as well as how many choose to leave.

Many companies focus on the Employee Net Promoter Score (eNPS), an adaptation of a metric from the marketing industry, to measure employee engagement and loyalty. It can be a good start, but don't forget that the results you get from the measurements you make must show what you need to develop to move forwards. Make sure that what you choose to measure gives you information that is detailed and nuanced enough for you to analyse it.

Last but not least, don't forget to celebrate your successes!

Living as you learn

So how do you ensure that all employees live your values and embody your brand? We have learned not to think too much about this question. It's often better to do something small and move forwards in small steps than to make branding too complex. Keep it simple – and put a lot of trust in your employees. Your culture is your people and your people are your culture. It's that simple.

A strong employer brand can therefore only be built on culture. Marketing your employer brand in a way that is not in sync with the culture will end badly. Imagine standing in front of a large shelf of magazines and choosing one that looks nice and interesting, but when you open it, you realise, to your disappointment, that the contents aren't what you were hoping for. You won't buy the magazine again, let alone start subscribing. When the cover matches the contents, the right readers will find the magazine and become loyal readers. That's the moment when they will start to talk about it and in the best-case scenario, they will feel that their own image and identity will be strengthened by it – and vice versa.

A strong employer brand has real business value and real value for employees. It is about attracting the 'right' people, who enrich the culture with new knowledge and perspectives and who also feel that their lives will be enriched by working in an organisation that wants to achieve something meaningful.

Finding such people in a competitive landscape should be a priority for the management of any global organisation. You therefore need to consider employer branding as a central part of your overall business strategy and find ways to unleash this power in your organisation. Treat this as the strategic work it really is!

CREATING AN EMPLOYER BRANDING STRATEGY

Since employer branding ties in with everything you do, it can be the most fun task on your plate, and also the scariest. Good advice is to start by drawing the 'boxes'.

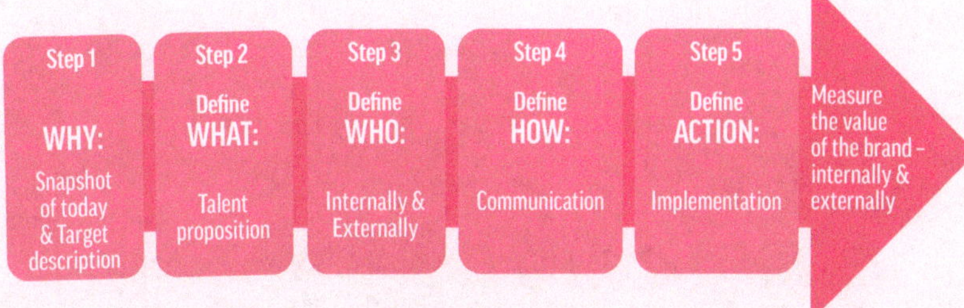

Start by making a mind map of what you want to achieve, how you will get started and the order in which the work will be undertaken. This will reduce the risk of spending time on the wrong things, avoid duplication of effort and avoid some headaches. Most of what you do on your culture and values journey goes hand in hand with your strategy and employer branding activities, so let your process (with boxes, circles or whatever you prefer) be detailed – but not too detailed. This leaves room for you to tie all the pieces of the strategy together, which helps both you and management to understand the initiative as a whole. You then all share the same truth, the same strategy and goals: your 'magic squares'.

As you start drawing your boxes, think about what will help make your organisation the best it can be. Think through all aspects – from mission to organisational design and employee experience. Consider how you will package these aspects in such a way that you live up to the employee value proposition. Take a holistic approach and start sketching out how your employer branding work will develop, including all the separate strategies and investments. Then – boom! Before you know it, your boxes act as a timeline and you're ready to decide how you will show who you are – your identity and appeal – and which channels you should use to communicate.

SIX QUESTIONS

There are some fairly simple questions that can serve as a guide in creating an employer branding strategy.

1. What do your employees think of you as an employer?
First, find out what your current employees think of you as an employer. Don't make assumptions here, do your homework. How are you perceived? Take advantage of workshops or any evaluation platforms, employee surveys or anything else. What's important is that you really *listen* to your employees, making sure that it's not just a small, homogenous group that gets to make its voice heard, but that the sample is representative. Identify the issues that resonate with many people. This is your employer identity.

2. Is the management team responsible for the employer brand in your organisation, and if so, what does that responsibility entail?
Those who understand the importance of the employer brand also realise that the responsibility for it cannot rest solely on the shoulders of HR. At Spotify, HR has designed the employer branding work, and it is HR that communicates the employee value proposition (EVP). However, we share the responsibility with senior management. Leaders automatically become spokespeople and should act as role models. It is important that they understand and live up to that responsibility in this context as well.

3. Who do you work with internally?

Employer branding should be driven by HR – there is no doubt about that. It's about your profile as an employer and the strategy you create to take care of your employees. It's not a solo show though. Employer branding should complement your customer marketing, your business strategy, your workplace strategy and all aspects of your internal communication. Conflicting messages do not help any strategy and coherent messages help all strategies. So start a professional love affair with the marketing department – right now! This will determine whether you will do an okay job, a really good job or a world-class job.

There are two other key stakeholders: the IT department (since everything is becoming more digital) and management. These teams need to understand the task, support it and, yes, be involved and sometimes help drive the strategy forwards.

4. Do you have an overall strategy for becoming a more attractive employer?

Start by defining your target audience: who are your current employees and who would you like to attract today and in the future? And why? All employer branding efforts are about how you communicate your workplace and culture to attract and retain people who are *right for you*. In other words, your target audience is not everyone in the world – it is potential employees, current employees and former employees. This simplifies things somewhat, but you don't always address everyone at the same time. You need to keep your clearly defined target audience in mind at all times. Once you know who this audience is, think about how you can engage them in a way that both strengthens your position and goes hand in hand with your culture.

There are many aspects of your HR work that you can discuss here: benefits and reward systems, job security, working conditions, development opportunities, sustainability, recognition/appreciation – the list goes on and on, and the majority can be achieved. Remember to think strategically. Don't start tinkering with the details until you have an idea of what you think will work best (in both the short and long term). You can't do everything straight away, so make a plan and stick to it – then fine-tune the plan as you go along.

5. Have you developed and communicated your employee value proposition (EVP)?
Once you have set an overall strategy for becoming a more attractive employer, you should focus on communication. You need to be strategic in telling your story. You need to send the right message to the right people at the right time. This is where your EVP comes in. Formulate a sentence about who you are and what you can offer your employees. Again, you should be mindful that you are not aiming to attract everyone. Start with your culture and values, look at keywords from workshops and employee surveys, and be genuine and straightforward – tell potential employees in a clear, consistent and compelling way what they can expect if they join you.

Spend some time thinking of creative ways to express who you are, both internally and externally. Build an employer brand identity by paying attention to the details, such as the visual impact you choose and the appeal of your communication.

6. Do you have a strategy for your social media presence?
Once you have your EVP and employer identity in place, think about your communication channels. Where can you reach your target audience and what kind of content do they tend to be interested in? How can you interact with them? Social media is a must. If you don't already have dedicated accounts and channels to showcase your employer brand, create them – now! Fill them with content that tells your story and provides an image of you as an employer. Be both soft and direct – mix 'behind the scenes' content with vacancy announcements. Make sure everything leads to the same place:

your careers site, where you clearly define yourself, and describe your EVP and your values. Don't forget to implement measurement points so you can see what's working best and what needs to be adjusted.

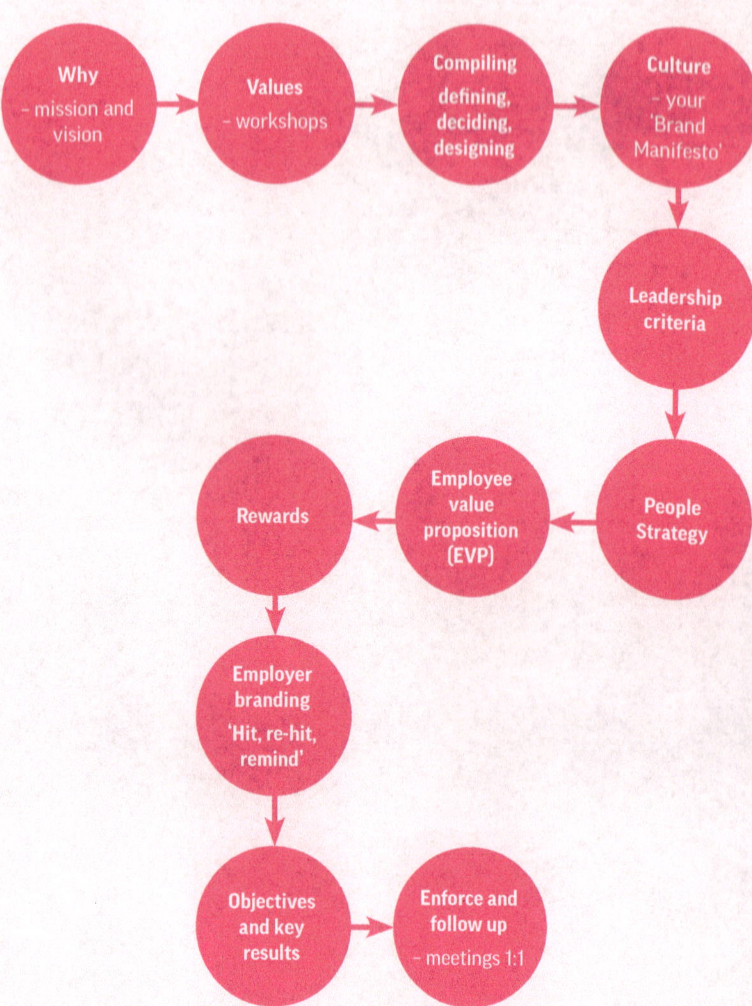

Why – mission and vision
Values – workshops
Compiling defining, deciding, designing
Culture – your 'Brand Manifesto'
Leadership criteria
People Strategy
Employee value proposition (EVP)
Rewards
Employer branding 'Hit, re-hit, remind'
Objectives and key results
Enforce and follow up – meetings 1:1

Talent Acquisition – recruitment

Nothing stays the same forever. Especially not what is known as the talent landscape. The world is changing and an organisation that wants to attract talented, skilled, creative, committed people with a strong desire to learn and develop – what we call 'talent' – must stay ahead of the curve.

So how do you build for what's to come? How do you shape the future of your business? With a robust but flexible recruitment strategy and a solid framework that makes you agile while reflecting your employer brand and culture. Simple, right?

It is actually quite simple, so long as you start from the needs of the business and don't compromise on the knowledge and/or experience of the candidates.

Framework and design of your recruitment teams

We believe that the new era of HR represents a paradigm shift, where people finally become the top priority, regardless of industry or sector. As we have said, you can have all the plans and strategies you want and a clear picture of how to implement them, but without the right people, you will fail.

Therefore, it is important, crucial even, that you build the function within your company that is responsible for identifying and attracting talent – your recruitment or talent acquisition function – in the right way. This raises a number of practical questions, such as where this function should be based geographically, whether or not it should be aligned with your business departments, where the people you want to attract are located, and the science, data and process on which you should base your design.

These are all valid questions, but the *most* important questions are: What will work best to support and drive the business forwards (in the long term)? How can you ensure that you are recruiting people who bring something to your culture, and who themselves feel the value that working for you will bring to their lives?

Your recruitment function should look and work in such a way that it provides maximum support to the organisation in identifying the right talent and connecting those talents to you. This approach requires a deep understanding of the business and a close relationship with the rest of the organisation – a partnership. You need to understand what the organisation's different departments and different managers are doing, what they are struggling with, what their needs are and what areas need to be developed. Having this understanding will increase your credibility and give you a firm place at the table as a strategic advisor. Don't get caught up in the idea of supporting individual departments – focus on how you can support the *business as a whole*. This broadens recruiters' horizons, getting them out of a geographical or local mindset.

The other major benefit of a holistic approach and close relationships with the organisation is flexibility. A recruitment team's ability to scale up with the business depends on how much room they have to accelerate and decelerate, i.e. to sometimes recruit faster, sometimes slower, sometimes somewhere in between.

This leads us to the next question: should you invest in a fully in-house team or should you outsource? When deciding whether to use external help or handle all recruitment internally, you must do what best supports your business most effectively. At Spotify, we do the majority of our recruitment work ourselves for a couple of reasons. Firstly, the company moves so quickly that it's difficult for an external recruiter to keep up to date. Secondly, we recruit a lot of new employees – and we have to get it right. We firmly believe that someone who is an employee and who knows our business and has a relationship with the candidates' managers and future colleagues is better placed to give candidates a true picture of what to expect and can more clearly communicate our EVP to a potential new employee.

However, we do use external support on occasion. The situation works much like a built-in rubber band that can be adjusted over time, when the need increases and decreases. It has been very important to have a good partner, with whom we work over a period of time, who knows our attitude to HR and knows our business. This allows us to move quickly and receive a better selection of candidates.

The flexible team

How should a team plan for (hyper) growth? How should they estimate how many people need to be recruited next quarter or next year? These are very relevant questions to consider. At certain points, growth will be higher, at other times lower. This must be taken into account when setting up your Talent Acquisition function.

Our best advice is to think about how big your recruitment team needs to be in different circumstances (scenario X, Y, Z...). Make sure you don't become *reactive* and instead prepare by getting better at strategic workforce planning (we'll come back to this in a later chapter). If you are successful at proactively planning your recruitment needs so that you can pull the right levers in order to scale the recruitment team up or down as needed, you won't be left with excess capacity when needs decrease. Managers can be supported as efficiently as possible when their needs increase.

The most common recruitment strategy is to either do everything in-house or to have a fully outsourced solution. Why not have the best of both worlds? Think about who should be at the core of your internal team. How many managers, recruiters, sourcers and coordinators do you need on a daily basis? Next, calculate what you might need when demand on recruitment increases. Once you have this figure, look for the optimal external partner(s) so that you are always ready and can adapt to current needs. The beauty of this solution is that you won't have excess staff, and you can stay ahead of business needs and fluctuations when they occur without panicking.

If you go down this path, make sure that the external recruitment partner you choose is an extension of your team, i.e. they really understand your business and your culture. They need to build a close proximity if the relationship is to be successful. Embed the partner into your business, so they can jump in seamlessly when needed.

Partnerships and cooperation

Most recruiters have a specific area of expertise. If they are required to recruit in that particular area, this expertise is an advantage. However, if they are required to support the recruitment in another area, this could be a disadvantage, at least if they are not able to adapt quickly. When putting together your recruitment team, look for recruiters who are multi-taskers, who can adapt and learn as required – 'on the job'. The ability and willingness to keep learning is important for any recruitment team that wants to bring something of value to the business. Having more multitaskers than specialists (some are always needed) in the team will make it extra strong and adaptable when it needs to be.

Another skill the team requires is the ability to collaborate and to understand the importance of relationships within the team, within HR and with other key people. *Partnerships* and *collaboration* must be a big part of the team's mantra. In particular, collaboration between hiring managers, the recruiter and the HRBP (HR Business Partner, as we call our senior HR leaders), is key! The relationships must be healthy: the team cannot function effectively if there are barriers between individuals within HR, or between the team and other parts of the organisation. The overall recruitment goals must be in line with the rest of the People Strategy and the business.

Particularly important is stakeholder management – both internal and external. The success or failure of the recruitment process depends on the ability to communicate effectively with both the hiring managers and candidates and to manage their expectations. You also need to act as an advisor. The destination matters but so does the journey – the way you make that journey will have an impact on the outcome. Of course, the end result is important, but the way you get there is just as important, since the approach in itself affects the outcome.

Our advice is: communicate a lot, and often! Both internal and external stakeholders need to know what to expect, what stage you are at in the process and what the next steps are. Effective communication is crucial. Damaging relationships along the way will have far-reaching consequences and will slow the process down. Creating a trusting and credible partnership is essential. Also, trust brings speed.

Relationships with candidates

At this point, we need to mention the employer brand again. As we noted in the last chapter, it is extremely important that you paint a true picture of your organisation. It's equally important that you treat each candidate with respect. Your recruitment team will often be the candidates' first contact with your organisation, and will therefore influence their perception.

Managers and recruiters alike often seem to forget that their task is not only to interview potential new employees, but also to attract them and keep that attraction alive. During the recruitment process, an organisation evaluates a candidate, but the candidate likewise evaluates the organisation. There is a degree of reciprocity taking place. Candidates will remember their recruitment journey. No matter how far they get in the process, they will carry their experience with them and they will almost certainly share it with friends, family and others. Their experience matters!

This relationship is very much about communication. Over-communicate throughout the process. Make sure your candidates know where they stand – be transparent at every step. In particular, candidates who have gone through an interview process several times in their career will see through a lack of authenticity and genuineness. Even if a process doesn't end up in favour of a particular candidate, how and what you communicate can still leave the candidate with a positive impression of you as an employer. Too many companies are excessively vague when communicating, if they communicate at all.

When it comes to attracting the right people, many HR professionals have spent a lot of time trying to figure out the best way to stand out and think outside the box. We believe it's more about *how* you do what you do: stand out by giving candidates a great experience, by communicating directly, clearly and frequently throughout the process.

Across the world, in every industry, recruitment teams are being heavily criticised – and rightly so. Candidates state that their recruitment experience was like falling into a black hole, or "felt impersonal". Why not address some of these common sources of dissatisfaction in your own recruitment process? Make sure you create a process where everyone who expresses interest in a position gets some kind of response. Communicate in a way that feels personal (and not like a robot is doing the talking). Communicating in an open and respectful way can go a long way to standing out!

Another way to stand out from the crowd is to link your product/service to the recruitment process. This is a simple but often appreciated approach. For example, if you (like Spotify) are in the audio business, tie audio to the experience. If you're in consumer products, tie those to the experience. This helps you to create an emotional bond between you and the candidates, which can have value not only during the recruitment process but at a later stage too. Existing employees may think back to this when considering other options, with the emotional connection reminding them of why they joined in the first place.

Basically, there is a simple truth here: You want to stand out? Stop misbehaving with your candidates!

Talent care

Talent care is not so different from customer care. If you fail, the 'customers' will talk about it more loudly than if you succeed. We have already mentioned the importance of communicating and staying in touch with the candidate during the recruitment process. There are other aspects that are just as important and, strangely enough, seem difficult to get right. Focusing closely on these aspects can greatly improve the candidate's experience.

Firstly, be honest with yourself about which school you belong to. Do you believe in keeping things secret from your candidates? Or are you transparent about what your company's strengths and weaknesses are? Are you transparent about your candidates' performance, what stage of the process you are at, and any concerns you may have? We belong to the latter group.

Secondly, never underestimate candidates' sensibilities. They pick up on every little detail and nuance – what you say, how your recruiters phrase their questions, what follow-up questions they ask and how they behave in general. For example, it's important for recruiters to be aware of their body language because it reveals a lot. Candidates are smart (that's why you're interested in hiring them), so treat them as the potential assets they are. If something is delaying the process or your mission is changing, tell them. If a candidate didn't do well in the interview, tell them. If another candidate is more suitable, tell them.

It is all about attitude. Is it you or the candidate who makes the final decision? According to the old school, and yesterday's truth, it is the employer who picks and chooses. However, the battle for talent has been raging for a while now and ultimately, it's employers who treat their employees – potential and existing – with respect who come out trumps.

Candidates choose you (at least) as much as you choose them. In order for them to choose you, you need to show your true colours. Candidates should be exposed to diverse existing employees with a range of backgrounds, gender, age, experience, etc. You should also be ready to provide as much information as they need in order to assess if your company is really the next step in their career development. In essence, are you the right employer for them?

References

For a while, it became unfashionable to seek references. It was considered obvious that candidates would only provide contact details for people who would give them good or even excellent references. This is not always the case. Much of what you want to capture before it's too late will actually come out, provided you ask the referees the right questions. Referees will also be aware – if they have any sense – that their personal brand is also at stake. Would they say that someone has a good work ethic, never misses a deadline, is eager to learn, is a good team player, and that they would gladly hire them again if it wasn't true? It could also be a good idea to talk with some people who are *not* on the candidate's list. Is that immoral? Or is it a case of simply doing your job properly?

Hiring the wrong person can cost up to a hundred thousand dollars (low estimate), so make the extra effort and contact people who have actually worked with the person you are considering hiring. Inexplicably, it is not uncommon to hear that someone we previously employed has been offered a new position without anyone contacting us at all. No one has asked about things that might be relevant to the next job, and no one has enquired as to why the person left. This is an odd phenomenon when you consider the effect that a new employee can have, not least in a small organisation. Especially when considering how expensive it is to get it wrong, whatever the size of the organisation. The relationship between employer and employee (or candidate) is similar to any other relationship. You discover each other, meet, hopefully like each other and want to spend more time together – and then grow together. Initially, most people expose only their best qualities, show off their best sides and want to listen to and learn more about the other person. Once the honeymoon is over, both of you will find the situation challenging if you pull back the curtain and things aren't as they seemed. A large organisation may be able to survive these sorts of situations and even continue to make the same mistakes over and over again. But this is not a smart or cost-efficient approach. For a small company, or an individual, it can be devastating.

Rest assured that today's job seekers use reverse reference checking: they will check up on you and they are right to do so. They do what all previous generations should have done – they compare their impressions and double-check everything you say. What will their journey with you be like? How will they be treated? Are you living up to your core values or not? How do you define 'learnability' and other concepts that are central to your culture? Is diversity and inclusion really part of your strategy? The list goes on. In short: they will analyse whether they will thrive, develop, feel at home and perform with you. If they like reference taking, so should you.

Psychometric assessments

What major life decisions, like buying a house or getting married, would you feel comfortable making without gathering as much information as possible when you have all the resources at your disposal? Not many, probably. Why should the decision on who will represent your company, be part of your team and drive your vision forwards be any different?

Yet, many companies around the world don't use any kind of psychometric assessments during the recruitment process. Sometimes, this is because they think it slows the process down, sometimes because they think it will be too expensive. But the consequences of getting recruitment wrong can be enormous – hiring the wrong person costs both time and money.

The only conclusion that can be drawn is that the reluctance to use psychometric assessments stems from a lack of knowledge about the benefits of these tests. Those who inform themselves with data are less likely to fail in their recruiting. We're going to spend the whole next chapter on psychometrics, so here we'll just note that no matter where your organisation is in the maturity process, assessments will benefit everyone involved (provided, of course, that the tests you select are reliable and appropriate for your selection process). They provide important information to hiring managers and reduce the risk of being blinded by your own prejudices or falling into various thought traps when assessing candidates. Psychometric assessments also serve as the first step in the development process for new employees, even before they have worked their first day.

Background checks

As a final step in the recruitment process, background checks are sometimes conducted. Depending on the role for which you are recruiting, and the sector in which you operate, such checks are not always standard – and sometimes not even legal. If you were to ask people working in HR why they use them, they would probably say that the checks aim to protect both the company and the employees, and are a reliable way to identify possible future problems.

Based on your business context, decide if and where (or within which departments) you will carry out background checks, taking into account local regulations. It may depend on the type of role a particular candidate would have, and how much information they would have access to – perhaps you should check everyone who will be working in finance, payment flows, legal or HR. Some companies do checks for all roles in order to minimise risks.

Once you've made your decision, focus on the candidate's experience of this step in the process. A background check can create stress and that stress can be exacerbated if you don't manage it well. When selecting a partner to conduct background checks, keep the candidate's experience in mind. Choose a partner that has high quality customer service, thinks logically, puts people first and communicates effectively.

Diverse hiring

We will devote an entire chapter to diversity, inclusion and belonging later in the book. Here, we'll simply note that the recruitment team drives the flow of talent into your organisation, which means they are at the forefront of your initiatives on these issues. Make sure the team – and the company as a whole – understands the importance of diversity and creating a culture of inclusion and belonging.

Things to keep in mind when developing diversity recruitment strategies:

- Visible support from your leadership team makes a huge difference, so business leaders who set the tone are essential.
- Expanding recruiting sources and external partnerships will boost your pipeline of diverse talent.
- Being intentional works – starting with a higher percentage of diverse candidates increases the probability of hiring top diverse talent.
- Continuing to share progress or regression is a good tactic to keep up momentum.
- Words matter – a lot. Always ensure job descriptions and candidate outreach drives are 100% inclusive.

To build inclusion into your Diversity, Inclusion & Belonging (DIB) strategy, you can't simply rely on your team's attitude towards it. Make sure you get input from people with different experiences, perspectives and backgrounds.

We cannot stress enough the importance of sharing your lessons learned in the field of diversity and inclusion and contributing to change, both inside and outside your organisation. We all need to do better in this field and we can all make a difference.

Fishing in new and bigger waters

The fact that we are all trawling the same waters (talent pool) for roughly the same skills and abilities means that there is a lot of competition for certain types of talent. As work becomes more digital and many workplaces become more global, new opportunities arise. We are gradually getting a more open and changing talent market. Our talent pool is simply getting much bigger.

What does this mean for your recruitment strategy? New opportunities! There are many cities in the world that have rather small and depleted talent pools, where some individuals are seen as outstanding simply due to the low volume of people with particular skills and experiences. Use your collected insights and mapping of competencies to identify the abilities and skills you are looking for, and implement strategies to attract and recruit people in cities and countries where you would never have thought to look before. Instead of looking in Silicon Valley, California, look in Phoenix, Arizona. Look in different European countries. We're not limited by geography in the way we work anymore, so why should we let geography limit us in our search for talent?

This is of strategic importance because the old approach is not sustainable anymore, especially for fast-growing (and global) companies. To be competitive, you need to fish in new and bigger waters.

Today there is huge competition for talent. To achieve your goals, you need to identify and attract the right people at the right time and then retain them. If you have a strong focus on rapid expansion and growth, or if you are experiencing changes in your business strategy that require you to find the right people faster, then you won't have the time to scale up slowly. Nor will you have the time to build a 'talent pipeline'.

Few business models are successful if they rely on being reactive. Your approach to recruitment, whether internal or external, is no exception. Your ability to adapt as your business grows, stabilise when needed, and sometimes slow down is critical if you want HR to be a strategic business partner to your business. Developing this ability allows you to be proactive, and that's how real business benefits are created. Then, you can still build a talent pipeline by honing your talent mapping skills, i.e. your ability to map the organisation's long-term skills needs. When done right, such mapping can take your business to a new level. In fact, mastering talent insights is a major competitive advantage because it acts as a compass for your skills mapping. Invest in people and technology to collect and organise 'skills clusters' – not just roles – that shape both your current and future business.

To be successful in this area, you need to move away from the idea of looking for individuals to fill specific roles and instead think about talent pools. Grouping individuals with similar abilities and skills, who are important for the business or for leading teams, but who don't need to be locked into a specific role, makes you more flexible when a role becomes vacant. More people can be considered; and vice versa – more roles can be considered for the same person. Thinking more broadly means an individual can be exposed to multiple opportunities.

So focus on finding clusters of skills, people with knowledge and abilities that are not only valuable to you today but can be transferred to other parts of your business in the future. Why? Because competencies can be developed, expanded and extended, while roles are specific to a certain person and a certain area of activity. That is the difference between hiring for a particular function and being *business-driven.* Synchronise your competency mapping with your overall approach to workforce planning, including your succession planning. Create partnerships within HR with key stakeholders, such as HRBP (senior HR managers), Learning & Development, and managers from within the business. This approach will ensure that the conversation is steered in the right direction and that everyone who is recruiting is thinking long-term.

In the same way that you prepare for forced, natural and unfortunate attrition, use data as an input to your competency mapping, succession planning and promotion. Not only will you be prepared, but this will also help you change the status quo and avoid struggling like crazy to find the right people outside the organisation in the same place everyone else is looking. Learn to trawl new waters!

Take advantage of technology!

In today's world, it should be obvious to use technology in the recruitment process. Technology will help you to know where talent is, both internally and externally. In particular, it can direct you to untapped talent pools, or highlight where the market is saturated. You will even be able to predict how likely someone is to leave their current position. If you haven't already, hire someone who knows how to use such data and turn it into insights that can influence business-critical decisions. This will help you find untapped talent where you least expect it.

When it comes to technology, the key is to identify the systems, platforms and other tools that best suit your needs. The foundation should be a system for managing applications, an Application

Tracking System (ATS), which can be scaled up as your organisation grows.

There are many such systems to choose from. When searching for the best option for your business, distinguish between what you *must* have and what you would *like to* have – no single system will ever be a one-stop shop. Make sure you involve the business in the selection process, as they will be using your ATS alongside your recruiters and HR team. Their input and opinions are valuable, and they need to be on board and buy into the tool(s). This will be especially key when you are well underway and need support with change management. You already have your allies aligned when you get to this point.

Once your ATS is in place, it should help you see who to recruit and where from. The technology should give the team space to focus on what is important and help both the hiring managers and candidates have a great experience. Technology will never replace recruiters – never. However, used correctly, it can improve your recruiters' efforts in multiple ways. For example, some of your other technology solutions should be able to connect to your ATS to automate things like interview coordination and candidate logistics because it will speed up the recruitment process.

You don't need fancy new technology to stand out from the crowd. Instead, think about how technology can help you hit the mark and communicate effectively. You don't need to incorporate every new technology and platform into your toolbox. Instead, select the tools that are most appropriate and work for you, so that you have a helping hand in improving the process and don't become impersonal in your approach to candidates.

The next step is to ensure that you are present and visible in the spaces that your candidates frequent. Put all forms of communication in place, including social media and appropriate platforms. Choose tools and channels that suit you and your target audience. Before you start searching or marketing on any social media channels, question whether you will find the specific candidates you are looking for there. Consider which social media platforms each type of candidate is on and seek them out there. Most people are likely to have their phone in their hand for most of the day, so use this fact to interact with them in a way that suits them best. Where can you find the people you are looking for? Where are they most likely to be searching for new opportunities? As always, it's important that the communication and actions you take reflect your values and that you repeat your employee value proposition (EVP) throughout the recruitment process, regardless of the technology support you have chosen.

Finally, it would be remiss not to mention Artificial Intelligence (AI) in a section about the opportunities technology opens up. The use and development of AI is completely transforming the recruitment process by allowing you to select candidates more efficiently, reducing the risk of being influenced by bias or falling into various mind traps, as well as improving the overall candidate experience. When this book hits the virtual bookshelves, we can be sure that the leaps and bounds AI will have made will surprise us more than we can ever imagine. Specifically, generative AI has taken the world by storm in the last year and transformed many aspects of how we do business, making processes quicker and more efficient. This is also true for recruitment processes and the trend will continue to develop – let's watch this space!

Implementation takes time

Finally, the core or purpose of any talent acquisition strategy should be to partner with and support the business operation. If you manage this successfully and ensure you build a natural, organic system of communication and feedback, the strategy will help drive the business forwards. Think holistically and take a holistic approach to *people* – to everything about the people who are already in the organisation and those who might join in the future.

SPOTIFY'S TALENT ACQUISITION APPROACH

At Spotify, we experienced hyper-growth for a number of years and this required everyone in the company, no matter what department they were in, to think about recruitment all the time. This situation forged a strong partnership between the business, the Talent Acquisition team and HR. The partnership is based on transparency and consistent communication, and on joint efforts. It's not acceptable for anyone to take the 'that's their job, isn't it?' attitude. Recruitment is everyone's job and responsibility.

THE TEAM STRUCTURE

The 'partnership approach' is reflected in the structure and working methods of the Talent Acquisition team. We have created recruitment teams that reflect each of our business areas and business functions. This approach allows us to embed talent acquisition resources into the business. We believe it is crucial for our recruiters to be close to and understand the business for which they are sourcing talent. The recruiters need to understand how candidates can thrive and grow and how employees impact the business today and in the future. It's not just about seeing what technical or business skills these talents should have.

We want people in the team who understand the skills and competencies required in our various units. It's important that we don't trip over each other when contacting candidates (i.e. the same person is contacted several times by different people). However, it's also important to look at the bigger picture, so that the business as a whole – not just certain parts of it – receives the skills it needs. For this reason, we have created the *Technical Domain Councils*, which meet regularly. These are groups of recruiters who support the same technical areas in different units. Based on our internal infrastructure and from their own ongoing discussions, they can identify challenges and opportunities, prioritise, share ideas – and candidates – and work together to position the business externally to find, interview and hire the right candidates.

ENCOURAGING THE RIGHT BEHAVIOURS

As already stated, you can stand out from the crowd by how you behave. At Spotify, we have recruiters who stand out by the way they think about their own development and learning. Unfortunately, not enough recruiters understand the intricacies of continuous learning. Many simply stick to what they know and use the same method they have always used, no matter what sector or company they work for. Some believe themselves to be experts and think that what got them where they are will continue to work in the future. This attitude is not sustainable in the new era. We believe that the key to success lies in constantly fine-tuning and adapting the recruitment process. Recruiters are the face of our business; they are the people that potential employees meet, regardless of the outcome. They have a significant and sometimes overwhelming task, especially in a growing organisation. In order to support the development of our recruiters, we send out feedback surveys to both hiring managers and candidates. We ask what we need to start doing, what we should stop doing, what we should keep doing, and what we should improve on.

Spotify's recruiters have a mantra of partnership, creativity and adaptability at their core. Without a strong partnership with the wider business, a constant and natural curiosity, and the ability to question and change processes and mindsets, we would not have achieved success. In order to best support the business, we have created and implemented a recruitment framework that:

- is fast, with regular feedback,
- is driven by the business/market,
- is based on a true partnership with the business. Partnership, partnership, partnership – this will always prevail!

OUR RECRUITERS' KEY SKILLS AND ABILITIES

There are a number of skills and abilities that are essential to the success of a recruiter at Spotify, regardless of the department they work in or the stage of their career. We should never overlook the need for excellent Project Management skills – the ability to plan time and prioritise. How a recruiter uses and plans their time and structures their days will (usually) predict the results of the task at hand. We can start by stating what does not work:

- Taking care of one task at a time.
- Sparse communication.
- Not delivering on what was promised (execution).
- Not following up.
- Not being able to focus on priorities.
- Resting on your laurels.

Recruitment is not a matter of life and death, but our recruiters need to be able to handle pressure, multitask and focus, even when there's a lot going on at once, just like a doctor in an emergency room.

We've already covered the second point on the list above – communication is the crux: invest in a *lot* of communication. Some struggle with communication, or don't understand its importance. A hiring manager who doesn't get any information about what's happening will start to use their imagination, and it's easy to imagine something negative rather than something positive. At Spotify, we counter this by over-communicating – making sure our internal customers get all the information they need and more.

We are fully aware that our hiring managers want us to meet their deadlines and to communicate with them regularly. In this process, we are careful not to 'forget' the candidates. We don't want any party to fall into that black hole. In far too many organisations, and all too often, candidates make contact or even come for an interview and then never receive any feedback. There's no excuse for such situations and that's not how we want to work at Spotify. We are fully aware that such behaviour does a lot of damage to the employer brand.

While the recruiters' main job is to help us identify the right people for Spotify – with diversity always at front of mind – we know that half the job is making sure our managers trust them and their work, regardless of the availability of candidates.

GETTING IN TOUCH

When approaching potential candidates, the timing and message are key. Some candidates may not currently be considering a career change and we can create a negative situation if we don't communicate and interact in a thoughtful way. Search recruitment is an art form in itself. The methods used to contact candidates and the type of information we provide need to be carefully considered. It's also important to keep in mind that the world is small and getting smaller, so never underestimate anyone's network.

INTERVIEWS

Behavioural interview questions are open-ended, designed for the candidate to give a more detailed answer rather than a yes or no, explaining how they would behave in a certain situation. Rather than asking whether the candidate is a good project manager, we might ask: "Give an example of a project you have run," and "Tell us how you went about planning and implementing it." With this interview technique, we get more detailed answers than with traditional interview questions and we can follow up with additional questions to help us paint a picture of how someone behaves, makes decisions and reasons. There are multiple advantages to this type of behavioural questioning:

- Increased predictability: we learn more about how candidates have behaved in similar situations in the past, so we can predict how they will behave and perform in the future.

- More accurate selection: according to a Harvard Business Review article, up to 80% of staff turnover is due to poor recruitment decisions.[3]

- Faster recruitments: the interview process becomes more efficient, resulting in faster decisions and recruitments.

When we switched to this interview method, we had to use a change management process to gain support from the recruiting managers. The results were well worth the effort. We now have a structured, predictive and reliable system in place that helps our managers make broader analyses and gain deeper insights into the candidates.

At Spotify, we also put a lot of emphasis on preparing the interviewer – helping them structure the interviews, for example – and on vividly and accurately describing what the role will entail and what opportunities it holds.

A BALANCE BETWEEN BROAD AND NICHE SEARCH PROCESSES

When it comes to volume recruitment (if we have several similar positions available in the same region, for example), it is important to build a *healthy funnel* – a smart, customised process. We map healthy pipelines populated with the right kind of candidates and these are often organised as talent for different regions and disciplines. These pipelines go to our recruiters, who sort and prioritise according to requirements.

For more niche search processes, involving senior and/or complex roles where the availability of candidates is sparse, the recruiters' approach is more strategic, focusing on specific qualities and experience needed in the role in question.

The key is to keep both these cycles going at the same time. One is not more important than the other. One does not exclude the other.

IDENTIFYING PEOPLE WHO
CONTRIBUTE TO OUR CULTURE

What we look for in our candidates, beyond the skills and abilities required for the role, never changes: we look for talented, curious and driven individuals who share our values and will bring value to our culture. As part of the recruitment process, we use the Spotify Assessment, a psychometric tool which increases the likelihood of matching the right talent with vacancies. The Spotify Assessment gives us an extra data point that is valuable for both us and the candidates. We can get to an in-depth interview faster and new band members can more quickly get a grasp of our 'game strategy' – this is our game philosophy. They will learn what it takes to help develop and change the rules of the game. We look for people who can bring not only new knowledge but also new perspectives and different experiences from those we already have in the organisation.

BACKGROUND CHECKS

Finally, background checks – yes, we use them for roles where it is logical, appropriate and legal to do so. For example, for leadership roles in finance and HR, and for people who will be handling credit card data. As mentioned, background checks are not done everywhere in the world, so it's important to be aware of the employment law in a given country. We do not do background checks for all roles or all over the world; instead, we have made conscious choices. However, we have not opted out of checks for fear of slowing down the hiring process or because we think we would lose potential candidates. It is our experience that candidates who are being considered for roles that require this extra assurance will be familiar with the process and will probably expect it.

At Spotify, we do challenge the norm with some aspects of talent acquisition. Other aspects are approached more traditionally and offer optimal solutions. The new school is quite often the old school, with some bold adjustments. The message is: don't be afraid of trying new methods. Some will work, some won't. Try to ensure it makes sense for your business, then give it a go. The status quo is not always best.

Psychometric Assessments – a complement to the recruitment process

Should you eat an apple or have a piece of cake? Should you drink tea or coffee? Should you go out or stay at home? Every day, we make thousands of decisions, both big and small. Some of them require more conscious thought than others (I allow myself to snack – but not cakes or sweets). We tend to automatically choose the mental shortcuts we have developed over the years.

Contemplating different options and ultimately choosing to act on one of them – or choosing to do nothing at all – is really a form of problem solving. It can be rational or irrational based on our knowledge, values and beliefs. To make good decisions, we need to balance emotion and reason – seemingly conflicting forces. In this balancing act, we try to predict the future, perceive the current situation as accurately as possible, and understand how others think and deal with the uncertainty that often exists. Most of us are unaware of the mental processes behind the decisions we make. Ignorance is bliss, as they say – what you don't know won't hurt you.

This attitude needs to be challenged if we are to understand the role of psychometrics in the recruitment decision-making process. Who to hire – and, perhaps more importantly, who not to hire – is one of the most important decisions an organisation makes. A lack of objectivity often exists in parts of the process. We are rarely fully rational in making these decisions, even if we want to believe otherwise. We base our opinions on our own beliefs and on the opinions and thoughts of people with whom we have close ties. These biases are usually unconscious. In practice, there are numerous sources of wrong decisions in a recruitment process: in addition to our own biases and preconceptions, we tend to fall into various unconscious thought traps. For example, we tend to make more positive assessments of people with whom we have something in common, who we think are good-looking or remind us of someone we like (or of ourselves). We may draw the erroneous conclusion that a person who is good at one thing is also good at a lot of other things (the halo effect). Indeed, the opposite can also be true (the horn effect). Our brains look for patterns, so we may see them – for example, in someone's behaviour – when they don't actually exist. We can also make different assessments of a person or a situation depending on whether our blood sugar levels are low (before lunch) or when we are full and satisfied (after lunch). The list goes on and on.

Simply put, the goal of recruitment is to hire the best available candidate, an individual who will add value to the organisation. How do we know whether we are hiring such a person? We can never really be sure. We can, however, ensure that the information on which we base our decision is of the highest possible quality, so that we can feel that we have done our best. This is where psychometrics comes in.

Psychometrics – what is it?

There are many misconceptions about what psychometrics really is – so let's start by clarifying what it is not. There is no crystal ball to tell us who the best candidate for a particular job is, no simple magic solution to this very complex issue. In the new era of HR, we need to use the tools available to get as accurate a picture as possible of a candidate's personality and problem-solving abilities, as well as a picture of how well they might fit the role and the organisation. Half the challenge of talking about psychometrics is actually the concept itself, which makes it seem so mysterious. Even to HR professionals, psychometrics can seem like some kind of magic that they will never really understand – but it sounds 'scientific', so it must work, right?

In short, psychometric assessments are used as an indicator of possible behaviours or of an individual's personality. They are useful because a candidate's personality and behavioural patterns can be much more difficult to assess during an interview than achievements such as education, measurable knowledge, and experience. Psychometrics is about gathering additional information in order to get a more nuanced picture of a candidate.

Psychometric assessments can be used to identify differences between candidates in areas such as motivation, values, priorities and opinions. They can give an indication of a candidate's preferred working style and how they interact with their environment and colleagues. The result is not a case of pass or fail; it provides a more objective view in the very subjective world of the recruitment process, showing how a candidate is likely to contribute to the business and react to the unique culture of the organisation. A more balanced image of a candidate can be achieved, revealing traits that may not be immediately obvious.

At Spotify, the psychometric tool – the Spotify Assessment – is an assessment of an individual's behaviour and reasoning skills. It is specifically tailored for Spotify and in line with our values and culture. Candidates take the assessment before having an interview.

It consists of two parts: one gives us a picture of the candidates' personality traits and the other of their ability to use their judgement and their reasoning ability. Combined, they indicate and measure traits and abilities related to the different competencies needed to succeed at Spotify.

The results are utilised in two ways. In most cases, there is a minimum threshold for how well a potential candidate needs to match our core values if we are to pursue them; we simply get an initial idea of whether the candidate has the qualities we particularly value. There are, of course, situations where we make exceptions. For example, a different aspect, such as extremely unusual abilities, could be more important than personality and analytical skills. The results are also used as a complementary tool. If a candidate has responded in a way that falls outside our framework (out-of-range scores), we can explore this further during the interview. Scoring too low or too high does not necessarily exclude someone from the application process. Rather, it gives the interviewer a chance to ask further questions. The aim is for both parties to go into the relationship with their eyes as wide open as possible, to hopefully ensure a long-lasting and fulfilling relationship.

Benefits of psychometrics

In addition to providing more objective information, there are other benefits to using this type of approach. This list is not exhaustive, but here are some examples:

1. STANDARDISATION

In a world as subjective as ours, a standardised recruitment framework, where all candidates go through the same process, can add a 'layer of objectivity' and fairness to the assessment. For example, CVs are carefully crafted documents that are often deceptively similar. During a job interview, not everyone may be given the opportunity to show who they are and what they can do. It's well known that some people (certain personality types) do better than others in an interview setting. Psychometric assessments can help give a more accurate picture and give you a chance to see introverted candidates in a new light, for example.

2. EFFICIENCY

Psychometric assessments help you compare candidates. You can study the results, set averages and distinguish between 'we'd like to know more' and 'thank you for your application'. It will not tell you which candidate is best suited for a position or who can enrich your organisation the most; rather, it supplements the information you already have.

As with standardisation, the goal is to improve the process. In this context, we want to reduce the number of 'maybes' to a shortlist of top candidates, so that recruiters' time is well invested and the overall hiring process is faster.

A recruitment process is effective if it is focused. You want to reduce the amount of time it takes recruiters to identify the best candidates for a position and increase the likelihood of your managers spending time with candidates who would work well as employees.

3. PREDICT WHO WILL SUCCEED

We have stated that psychometrics is not a magic bullet. However, if used consistently, psychometric assessments will give you a lot of valuable information over time, such as the correlation between how a candidate responded in the assessment and then performed in their job, which in turn can help determine whether certain traits are more important than others for success in your company. In the world of recruitment, it is important to constantly get a little bit better in relation to a clearly defined goal, just like an elite athlete.

Ultimately, recruitment is about finding people who help drive the organisation forwards and who thrive and develop in the process. If you manage to identify the qualities and abilities that are most important for someone to perform well and feel good in your company, you have also managed to identify qualities and abilities that are closely linked to the success of the organisation.

This becomes a self-reinforcing positive feedback loop. Someone who is good at maths as a child will think maths is fun. Someone who thinks maths is fun engages in more maths and then gets better at maths, and so on. The opposite is also true: those who don't enjoy maths do less of it, which means it takes longer for them to become proficient. Apply the same logic to psychometrics. If you can identify traits that work well for you, you can look specifically for those traits in your recruitment. If you adjust your recruitment processes to find more people with these traits, you'll get more high-performing employees. At the same time, if you make sure to recruit for diversity in other aspects (experience, perspective, needs, mindset, etc.), you are more likely to reach your goals as a company. Employees also benefit. Employees who are happy in their roles are more satisfied and engaged, have more influence and feel more involved in the success of the organisation. They have more fun, develop more and grow more as individuals – they also help the company to grow.

Things to keep in mind when selecting psychometrics tools

We have explained what psychometric assessments are and why they are valuable – but which tool should you choose?

1. HOLD ON TO WHO YOU ARE

The type of assessment(s) you choose must reflect your culture and values. You want to identify the characteristics that enable an individual to be successful in your company and contribute as much as possible to your business. Choose psychometric assessments that are in line with this.

2. RELIABILITY AND VALIDITY

When selecting an assessment, validity and reliability are important. The assessment(s) should consistently produce similar results and measure exactly what they intend to measure. You probably won't develop the tool yourself, but look for an external provider. The assessments should be validated by experts, which means they should be based on analysis by psychologists and other specialists and designed by experts in psychometric assessment design. Your assessment materials should be reviewed to ensure that they truly predict how candidates will perform in the job. Those who interpret the results should be adequately trained to do so. You also need to consider how the results will be used to provide feedback to candidates.

Ask potential partners about the scientific validity of their assessments and whether they keep up to date with current research and new findings. For example, you might want to ask how and when a study was conducted, who conducted it and what their qualifications were, how big the study was and in what demographic groups it was conducted.

3. UNDERSTANDABLE RESULTS

We have stressed the importance of reliability and validity, but you should never choose a particular psychometric assessment at the expense of its interpretability. No one – not you, not the candidate and not the hiring manager – wants to feel that they didn't understand the results or couldn't absorb the feedback.

The goal of psychometrics is to provide clarity and identify patterns, not to increase confusion. Don't get lost in the science. The results should be understandable and help you make the right decisions.

When using the assessments, don't forget:

1. FEEDBACK AND COMMUNICATION

Everyone taking a Spotify Assessment must receive professional and meaningful feedback afterwards, preferably orally. The certified assessment leader is responsible for communicating the results accurately and clearly. Be prepared and don't underestimate the importance of this step.

2. CONFIDENTIALITY AND DATA PROTECTION

Protecting candidates' privacy, and ensuring that results are kept confidential and secure, is a shared responsibility between you and the tool provider. Only certified users should be able to use the tool. They, and all others involved, must ensure that the results are treated confidentially.

3. THE QUALIFICATIONS AND TRAINING OF THE USERS

Certified users must act in an ethical and professional manner, ensure that they have sufficient and up-to-date knowledge to use the assessment at all times, and take full personal responsibility for their use. Recruiting managers should undergo basic training to better understand the assessments. This does not make them certified users, but helps them to understand the competency reports they receive about their candidates.

4. ENSURE THAT THE ASSESSMENTS ARE VALIDATED FOR YOUR MARKETS

Although the world is shrinking and global standards are becoming more common, behaviour still differs in different cultures and countries. Ensure that the assessments you choose are validated for the markets where they will be used and for the demographics that exist there. You need to ensure that they are certified according to the official standards of each market and you need to check the research – for example, by asking questions about the sample and control group. Your users will be compared to the control group, so it is very important that it is not just one demographic group but reflects the diversity of the talent pool from which your candidates come.

5. STOP GUESSING – START PREDICTING

Today we have greater access to data than ever before. The challenge is that the application of psychometrics can become an oversimplification of a complex decision-making process. We are emotional beings under the guise of rationality. Psychometrics cannot change this. Used properly, they can ensure that the recruitment process is not as arbitrary as it could be in the worst-case scenario.

In everyday life, we make snap decisions based on gut feelings, sometimes consciously but often unconsciously. We judge people we meet based on our first impression. Psychometric assessments can help us to challenge this first impression and gut feeling so that we can make the most informed decision possible in the recruitment process.

It is more important than ever that those of us working in HR understand what psychometrics is and why, and how it can improve our work. Time needs to be invested to get it right. With the right tools and if the results are used correctly, you are more likely to find those who can thrive in a specific role and in your culture.

IMPLEMENTATION OF PSYCHOMETRICS AT SPOTIFY

As Spotify started to grow faster and faster and we were assessing a great number of candidates every day, we realised that we needed to overhaul our recruitment process. We needed to make it more resilient to the increased pressure and also more dynamic for the fluctuations we wanted to be prepared for. Most organisations that grow from a startup to a scaleup and then mature will have to make these pivots numerous times during their development, just like we did.

We wanted to increase objectivity and ensure that we didn't rely solely on what the interviewers could observe. We were already working with competency-based interviews, where each person in the 'panel' of an interview group had a set of questions to focus on. We wanted our comparisons of candidates to be as objective as possible. At the same time, there is no escaping the unconscious bias that we all have. We don't ask questions in exactly the same way each time, nor do we interpret the answers in exactly the same way. Therefore, we decided to implement psychometric assessments. At the time, our team had a basic knowledge of the tools that were available. We enlisted the help of a psychometric expert and created a small working group with this expert and some of our internal recruiters to make sure we wouldn't fall out of one trap only to fall into another. What value do the assessments have for us? The first step for the working group was to determine the desired outcome – how would the assessments contribute to the recruitment process and what would be a valuable measure for us?

We tried a few assessments from different providers and we mutually focused on what we wanted to measure. This led us to choose a personality assessment based on the five-factor model[4] as well as a competency/ability test. The tool is based on research and has been thoroughly tested and the reports gave us results packaged in a way that allowed the personality assessment to be compared to our core values (and in the case of managers: our leadership criteria). As a values-driven organisation, this felt extremely important.

TIMING

Once we had defined more specifically what the assessments should measure, we also had a clearer picture of when in the recruitment process they should be conducted, who would have access to the results and how we would actually interpret and use this new data.

We decided that only the recruiter would have access to the results. The recruiter could choose between:

- conducting the assessments early in the process, when many qualified candidates exist, in order to help determine who should go forwards, or

- conducting the assessments later in the process – but as early as possible – before the final interviews in the office, in order to use the results as a basis for further discussions.

COMMUNICATION AND DEPLOYMENT

Since it was the recruiters who decided where and when in the process the assessments would be conducted, we organised training on how to interpret and use the results. To increase speed and flexibility, we intended to let the recruiters use the assessments and train our hiring managers along the way. However, we had a very small project team, led by an external expert, who did not communicate sufficiently, which meant that the dialogue with other HR and recruiting managers was quite limited. And when the resistance to the test became really noticeable, we were clearly heading for failure (it's easy to have hindsight!).

We received negative reactions from both managers and employees. We could immediately see what we had done wrong: we had not communicated the value of what we were doing to the organisation. We had not communicated our objectives and we had involved the recruiting managers after the decisions had already been made. In other words, we had skipped a crucial step in all change management: embedding.

The negative reactions were not in reference to the personality part of the assessments, as we had initially predicted. Both managers and employees reacted against the general competency/ability tests. A lot of research exists demonstrating that generic competency tests can predict performance, but many of our employees simply didn't believe the research. Perhaps we should have anticipated such a reaction. We humans are not particularly fond of change, especially if we have not been given sufficient information to help us understand the 'why', nor when we have had little time to think, ask questions and digest the practical impact. We react with scepticism, wondering, for example, how a general competency test can predict how a candidate will perform as a software developer.

We had also not made it clear that we were already using programming tests and case studies at other stages of the recruitment process. The general competency test was a complement, it gave us additional information beyond what we already had; we did not assess a candidate's abilities based on that test alone.

As a result, buy-in was very low at this stage. Since we hadn't been clear with our recruiting managers, and hadn't involved them, they couldn't help us explain the purpose, the method, the ethics or why we had chosen a particular test. As it turned out, they had not received the information they needed to handle feedback or answer questions.

In addition, the recruiters began to feel hesitant. We hadn't included them in the process either, so they were unsure of the approach and how they felt about the assessments they were going to implement.

There was nothing wrong with our intentions, but we did not take good enough care of our stakeholders. We simply had not communicated enough, or clearly, and did not anchor our initiative.

Those of us in HR at Spotify have definitely made our fair share of mistakes – but that's to be expected if you want to try new things and challenge the status quo. The important thing is not to be discouraged and paralysed by setbacks. We learned a lot from the failure of the first implementation and we are happy to share the lessons learned. If you want to attempt something similar in your organisation:

- Equip your recruiters properly. Don't take shortcuts in training, and hold many workshops so that everyone has the opportunity to learn, reflect and ask questions. Everyone should have all the knowledge they need to understand psychometric assessments, the science behind them, how to use and interpret them and how to manage the experiences of candidates and hiring managers.

- Communication is key! First, try communicating with a small team of managers and capture their questions. Then broaden the approach and make sure your HR people have the training they need to understand what (it's about), how (it's done) and why (you have chosen to use psychometrics as one of several tools) – as they will be your ambassadors.

- Once the hiring managers are on board and understand why this is being done, ask the recruiters (who are your local experts and ambassadors) to train the managers on how to use and interpret the assessment results.

- Make sure you have documentation in place that explains why you are using the assessments, what exactly you are testing, when in the process it is done and how you will use the results. Make the documentation simple and accessible to everyone. Transparency is important. And so is the candidate's integrity!

LET'S START OVER AGAIN

Even though the first roll-out was a failure, we still had a problem to solve, so we decided to make a fresh start. This time we took a broader approach. Alongside the recruitment team, we brought in learning and development experts, our people analytics experts, HRBPs and the team working on diversity, inclusion and belonging.

We started from what we already had: the assessment itself and the reason for using it. We created guidelines and designed training. We were almost ready to launch. However, once we had a working group of broader expertise and more eyes involved, we discovered that the 'norm' groups did not reflect the diversity of the society – representation from the USA was missing. The reason for implementing the assessment was to reduce bias, but the tests seemed to suffer from bias in their design. We therefore backtracked to rule out errors at the core. Based on this, we took the following steps:

- We put together a list of requirements and let the team discuss the requirements from different perspectives, always linking them to our core values (we want to bring in the 'right' people, who can add something to our culture and our company – culture add-on, not culture fit).

- We looked at and compared more suppliers to see what they could bring to our way of thinking and how they challenged our ideas.

We made sure that their assessments were based on research and relevant data and that the 'norm groups' included the diversity we needed.

- Together with our new supplier, we designed the performance reports in a way that made it clear how the results matched our core values, our culture, our leadership criteria and the required generic competency tests.

- We created a large working group and involved people from different parts of the organisation.

- We planned the communication, developed training and made a solid roll-out plan. We brought business representatives into the working group to help anticipate issues and get input on the communication and rollout plan from their perspective.

- We trained recruiters and HRBPs first, so that they understood the whole concept, the assessments, the underlying data – and how the concept would add value to the recruitment process. Then we trained all our recruiters.

- We rolled out the communication at the same time as the training, with a strong focus on internal communication, using a variety of communication channels, and held training and Q&A sessions.

- We increased communication with candidates, so that they would understand how we did the assessments and how we used the results, and so that they could understand the data and results themselves.

The most important lesson, and the advice we most want to share, is to anchor decisions within the organisation and to communicate, communicate, communicate. Don't forget what your goal and purpose is. Make sure the purpose remains consistent throughout the project. Remember that nobody is flawless. Failures – and the lessons we learn from them – are what allow us to improve. If you don't succeed the first time, take a step back, evaluate and decide whether or not you should try again. If you think you should, don't get discouraged, take advantage of what didn't go well and learn from it so you can succeed the second time around.

Talent Intelligence
– identifying future leaders

Talent intelligence is a forward-looking way to identify people who have great potential to become future leaders and specialists. The aim is to create a *substitute bench*, both internally and externally, and reach a point where you know, long before a business-critical position becomes vacant, who the three strongest potential replacements are.

When a key person tells you they are leaving, the organisation and the HR team should already have possible candidates in mind. This process often starts immediately after the person announces their decision and there's no shame in that. However, there are some important basic points to consider in this situation; if you bring in someone from *outside* of the company every time you have an interesting and important vacancy, it sends the message to existing employees that they have no chance of being promoted to new roles. The feeling could be that such roles always go to people who have not yet proven themselves and that external experience is almost always valued more highly. Moreover, such an approach is a sign that you are not working proactively, that you have no real sense of the people in your organisation and the skills they have or could develop. It signals that you have no desire to seek out existing employees in the organisation who may be doing great things.

Talent intelligence is about understanding your organisation's talent assets. Optimal talent intelligence will help avoid habitually spending time and resources looking outside the organisation with the help of headhunting agencies.

'Fika' as a tool

If you don't know what talents you have in your organisation, you can't know what you need to do to retain and develop them – nor what kind of skills you need to recruit to complement those you already have.

The bigger the organisation, the more difficult it is to keep track of all employees. In a modern, fast-moving matrix organisation – or any medium or large organisation – it's easier to focus on the task at hand than to plan ahead. Any manager who focuses exclusively on their employees in the here and now makes the organisation more vulnerable. Living in the moment – and at best being quick to plug the gap as soon as someone leaves – is not optimal. There are several risks involved. The most obvious is that a hiring manager fills a vacancy with exactly what is needed right now. It's far from certain that it will be a good fit in six months or a year, and you'll fall off track and lose your ability to deliver and focus. You may cause increased staff turnover because you're constantly crossing the river to fetch water – you're repeatedly disappointing talented employees by recruiting from outside rather than promoting and investing in your internal talents (who will eventually get tired and leave).

We recommend using what we at Spotify call '*coffee scouting and assessing*' – using fikas (informal coffee meetings) as a tool to scout and assess talent internally. This is a simple way to reduce the risk of the organisation falling into a 'stop and start' pattern every time someone in a key role leaves.

Talent intelligence is an ongoing process, a scouting function that lives by the motto *'no scouting, no idea'.* This function can be part of the Executive Search team's work and it also interfaces with the Talent Growth team that is tasked with finding successors for key positions and complements other processes related to recruitment, skills development, performance development, succession planning and promotion. Either way, you need to make sure this runs smoothly and goes hand in hand with everything else you are working on.

Choose an approach

Effective and proactive talent intelligence requires careful coordination of recruitment, development, assessment and reward of the talent pool. All HR sub-teams (if you are large enough to have them) must work together for this to be successful. If cooperation is unclear, employees in the different sub-teams will swim in each other's lanes and get in each other's way instead of working together.

Traditionally, senior HR leaders (HRBPs) are responsible for finding successors, in cooperation with the managers who need their help. HRBPs have a good grasp of the part of the organisation they support, and if they are proactive and understand their role, they are already working to develop and retain the talent available to them. However, in order to take a holistic approach, it's a good idea to have a central Talent Intelligence function – albeit a small one. It becomes the internal equivalent of a headhunting consultant and does exactly the same thing: looks for future leaders, both outside and inside the organisation. Instead of external executive search, you create an internal 'talent matching intelligence'.

If you split the work between the HRBP and a central Talent Intelligence function, the latter must also have the trust of the organisation and colleagues, otherwise this approach is doomed to fail. Everyone involved must understand and respect what is and is not part of their role. Talent intelligence is an internal skills mapping exercise. And it's a constant work in progress, because new talent is constantly entering, developing and leaving – especially if you are in a phase of rapid growth. Therefore, this group needs to be really good at managing expectations, so that both managers and HRBPs are engaged in a constant and dynamic dialogue. There should be a structure for regular meetings that specifically focus on finding the right successor.

Between meetings, you should have a structured method to get to know internal candidates more closely and find out how they view their development and future through interview-style conversations. This is where 'fika as a tool' comes in. Through such ongoing mapping, you can quickly fill senior positions even outside the talent's existing departments, with people who are already part of the organisation. The river is thus moved closer and no manager, HRBP or recruiter has to cross it to find what they are looking for.

The gardener's philosophy

At Spotify, our attitude is that an employee 'belongs' to the entire company and never to a specific manager or department. Each individual should have the opportunity to grow elsewhere in the organisation – under a different manager, in a different team, in a different department, in a different office – if it suits both the individual and the organisation best. We sometimes talk about our 'gardener philosophy'. Anyone who spots a shoot that has potential to be a strong cutting should be able to take that cutting and replant it elsewhere in the garden (provided the cutting and the garden will thrive from the move).

Talent intelligence is about finding the 'right' individuals, no matter where they are in the organisation. The mapping is therefore based on the entire organisation. It will also give you a better idea of which individuals are ready for new challenges. The search for potential successors will be more comprehensive and employees will have better chances to develop. We also get a natural transfer of knowledge between departments, which builds bridges and contributes to a holistic perspective within the organisation.

Managers who have embraced the gardener philosophy understand that they should support employees in their development and always be open to letting them change their soil so that they can continue to grow. If you have managers in your organisation who hold on to 'their' employees, it will affect your staff turnover. Good employees who are ready for different and new tasks and challenges will go elsewhere. Why should your brightest individuals have to leave the company for new, challenging tasks, if they could access them internally and stay in the organisation?

Saving time and money

There are many benefits to this way of working but it can come at a price. If the collaboration in HR isn't tight and well-functioning, it won't work. When it runs smoothly, you save time. A lot of time – and a lot of money. When a key person in the organisation, perhaps a senior executive, has decided to leave or move to a new position internally, it can be costly to start looking for a successor. We don't need to tell you what a benefit it is if, in such a situation, you already have two or even three internal candidates and as many external ones in the pipeline. Everyone knows that it is extremely important to keep up the pace. Every vacancy slows you down. So keep the searchlight on at all times.

When it comes to money, the maths is simple – if a single person dedicated to talent intelligence can add maybe six key positions internally each year, you've already saved money. Not to mention motivation that can't be measured in money. Hiring and introducing someone new from outside not only takes time, it's costly. If it goes wrong... well, let's not even start doing the maths in that case. Should you fill more roles, you actually start saving money. You'll also reduce the risk of your existing employees feeling frustrated and disappointed that they're not seen and valued, resulting in lower staff turnover. Don't forget to take really good care of your existing employees and provide them with opportunities to develop. Besides lowering attrition and increasing performance, this will help you in your relationship with the union. You can also never know for sure if the people you bring in from outside will really bring something to your culture and enjoy the way you work, nor how they will deliver and contribute.

Attrition

It costs more to acquire new customers than to retain existing ones. The same goes for employees. Let's take this opportunity to give some simple, practical advice on how you can work in a deliberate and structured way to retain, develop and promote talented employees throughout the employee lifecycle – into the organisation, within the organisation and out of the organisation.

- Visualise the recruitment process with all the aspects that aim to reduce the risk of something falling through the cracks. This joint view also reduces the risk of making the process unnecessarily complicated or missing a certain group of employees who are ready for new roles.
- Artificial intelligence (AI), tests/assessments and in-depth interviews can help you speed up the process of matching a potential candidate to a particular role. However, the difference between an internal and an external candidate is that the internal candidate already knows the organisation and has had the opportunity to prove their abilities.
- It is important to define what's what – the words and concepts you choose are important. For example, you need to know what you mean by 'talent' and 'top talent' and what you are actually looking for.
- There are so many data points. Try to collect and use these wisely, it will help you create a process that helps you retain and develop your talent.
- Consider how you will deal with succession planning and talent mapping – do you tell the employees on the map or not? There are pros and cons to being transparent.
- Make sure you are communicating about employees who are changing jobs internally, or who choose to leave for a new external opportunity, with just as much care as you are vocal about new hires. It is important to have a well thought-out plan and a clear approach to these processes as well.

- Being proactive about all vacant roles is preferable, of course, and it is equally important to question whether a vacant role should remain the same when it comes to skills and experience needed.

From defence to offence

Finding the right people, at the right time and for the right roles is crucial for any highly competitive business. If you want to secure a healthy pipeline of candidates (internal and external), you should have a clear strategy and tactics for implementation. Here it is often true that attack is the best defence. Make an effort to go from defence play (backfilling positions) to a more offence play (be on constant lookout – internally and externally – for future needs and roles). Through a more proactive approach, you will reach conclusions faster and be more accurate in your approach.

Succession planning 2.0

What if you take succession planning one step further? If you cleverly combine your internal talent market with an external one? If you 'weave' your planning to include not only the talent you already have but also a pool of external talent?

When you don't see a potential successor either inside or outside your department, you should proactively identify external candidates. Especially if it is a key role, where the current incumbent is likely to leave (or is not performing at their best).

If you can combine an internal talent market with an external one and manage to start thinking beyond the departmental boundaries of the organisation, then you are approaching what we can call Succession Planning 2.0. If you also find a way to increase diversity not only via external recruitment but also through internal promotion, you will be really making a meaningful impact. You are using a strategic muscle and you are also making sure that it becomes part of the muscle memory of everyone in your HR team and of your managers – the gardeners.

The process – a well-oiled machine

So how do you go about collecting the information we are discussing? Firstly – involve managers in the process. Then map out the following:

- Business critical roles – your key roles.
- Flight risks – employees in these key roles who may leave, given what you know about them and/or the business they work in, especially where normal operations are threatened if they leave.
- Existing gaps – gaps in the availability of skills that prevent your company from being as good as you could be.
- Future gaps – skills and abilities that you do not need today but that you foresee you will need in the future.
- Internal top talent – existing employees who you think you can develop to fill identified gaps, now or in the future.

Once you have collected this information, decide how it can be organised and where it will be stored. Ensure that your solution (whether it's a worksheet or an electronic database) keeps the data secure and confidential. Recruiters and HRBPs can then use the information to develop a comprehensive plan.

Business plans don't just involve business strategies and expected outcomes – to implement the strategies and achieve the outcomes, every successful organisation must have the right people in the right place. By taking these steps, you are investing not only in the future but also in the present.

SUCCESSION PLANNING THE SPOTIFY WAY

To show what this looks like in practice, let's take a concrete example from Spotify. It started with an HRBP identifying a 'flight risk' – a manager who was likely to leave. For that particular role, we hadn't identified a potential successor within the department in question, at least not one that we felt was ready to take over there and then. Nor had we found a potential successor elsewhere in the organisation. Thanks to the proactive and good collaboration between HRBP and the Talent Intelligence team, we were able to start looking for external candidates even before the need actually arose. Four months later, the manager resigned and on the same day we had four finalists knocking on the door. We hired one of them.

It is not unusual to do something like this, with long-term networking – building relationships with senior candidates who might be interesting hires, either now or in the future. However, it is not common to work on this in a systematic way. Doing so can reduce uncertainty in the organisation and of course – as in the example above – avoid long recruitment processes and vacancies in key roles.

At Spotify, we made a conscious choice to keep succession planning fairly informal. During our startup years and even during the scale-up period, our more casual approach worked well, with tools like *Talent Snapshot* (which we'll describe in more detail later). Then, as we continued to grow, from a more stable base and as a more mature organisation, we began to feel the need for a different, more long-term approach. With an overview of existing and future top talent and business-critical positions, we could more easily identify gaps and minimise risks. It would create more reflection in the planning of external talent pipelines, contributing to the continuity and stability of the business and clearly exposing which competences were missing and when and where we should make 'tent-pole recruitments' (i.e. recruit a person who is able to carry, and thus accelerate, the development of an entire team).

At this stage of Spotify's journey, the goal was to have more continuity and a clearer picture of what talent is needed where and when, so that we could be more effective in both identifying and retaining people with the leadership qualities we are looking for. We needed an approach that worked for small teams, larger teams and entire departments. It needed to include assessment criteria for succession planning and to demonstrate how the business would use these criteria. This was required without unnecessary administration or time-consuming coordination needs (of course!).

The really tricky thing at a stage like this is to make sure that succession planning does not become 1) a tick box task/paper product, 2) an informal promise of future promotion, 3) a disappointment, or 4) the solution when people say they want to develop their career but are in fact mostly interested in a new title and higher salary.

We wanted to play offence instead of defence or, in other words, create succession plans that are invaluable to the business. Our goal was to have good succession planning that was proactive rather than reactive and that allowed for more relevant and honest performance reviews.

PLANNING FOR BUSINESS CONTINUITY

It is said that "talentism is the new capitalism".[5] Talent has replaced capital as the most crucial factor for success. Maintaining an updated view of our top talents and key roles, both now and in the future, helps us to develop both them and our business. By regularly discussing key roles, flight risks, gaps, top talent and potential successors, we can also anticipate the need for new talent. We are able to detect signals that some kind of change may be coming, whatever the reason. For example, if we develop a new activity within the company, which requires senior leadership or narrow knowledge of some aspect of our business, it should not be too difficult for us to fill the role. We've already identified potential replacements on our substitute bench – we know who's there, we know their strengths and weaknesses, and we know where they have scope for development.

THE GARDENER'S PHILOSOPHY

This 'gardener's philosophy' may sound simple but in reality it is a challenge. Most managers hold on to their employees, especially the good ones. Anyone who has nurtured a seedling, watched it grow and develop naturally, doesn't want to see it uprooted and transferred to another manager. Besides, the better you are at growing, the more cuttings get taken from your 'plants' to find homes elsewhere in the garden. We want our managers to see their employees as Spotify's rather than their own. A good gardener works with the best interests of the *whole* garden in mind.

Those who are able to understand the gardener's philosophy will nurture employees who do not ask for the traditional career ladder. They will trust their managers and the process because they will know that the organisation is investing in them. Attrition will be less of a problem and employees will stay longer as they are offered new and exciting opportunities.

A PIPELINE OF EXTERNAL TALENT

By identifying the business-critical positions of the future and the people within the organisation who would fit them, we make it easier for our Talent Acquisition team to proactively build a pipeline of external talent. This allows us to quickly scale up and quickly fill gaps. In the best-case scenario, we can build a database of names, so that hiring decisions can be taken immediately when key roles become vacant. This approach also reduces the risk of getting it wrong when selecting a candidate. It also helps us to compare external talent with internal talent in real time.

What principles do we follow for this new, more rigorous succession planning? We map roles and employees in four areas:

- Business-critical roles of today – if these become vacant, there will be a significant impact on business continuity.

- Business critical roles of the future – roles that will differentiate us from our competitors in the future.

- Employees who are ready now – individuals who go the extra mile, who act as role models and who already have a measurable impact on Spotify.

- Future-ready employees – individuals who are adapting to the Spotify of the future and are developing new capabilities and gaining both broader and deeper skills.

An important part of the process is to take what you know about these people and use that knowledge wisely. For example, you need to distinguish between important roles and business-critical roles. You need to distinguish between an employee who plays an important role, one who performs well, one who performs at the top and one who performs eight times better than their colleagues. This doesn't mean the rest are unimportant or don't have important roles, but such mapping is crucial for more rigorous succession planning.

Finding a framework for succession planning is not really that difficult. The tricky part is making the best use of your valuable data from analysis and discussions.

At Spotify, we started by having the most senior HRBPs sit down with their respective most senior managers to define how they wanted to do succession planning and identify what problem we are trying to solve. These discussions helped us to define the four mapping areas above.

We then held a meeting with all senior HRBPs in order to ensure we were all approaching the task in the same way, as well as to give each other input on succession planning in different departments. A lively discussion ensued and led to several additions and changes to the data we would use.

Before the roll-out, HR discussed and anchored the initiative with the management team to ensure that everyone was on board. Ever since, both management and HRBPs have continued these discussions and regularly check our succession planning to make sure we are being consistent. In addition, HRBPs continue to flag current vacancies at senior level to each other, as well as to potential internal candidates.

For the whole process to work, those involved in the conversations need to be open to 'losing' key employees to other positions within the company – they need to be good gardeners. In our view, this is more important than writing a development plan that no one ever looks at again. This can't be something you do once a year but must be done on an ongoing basis, based on data, and through continuous dialogue with the appropriate stakeholders, the management team and the HRBP.

AN EFFECTIVE TOOL

How many times have you worked on succession planning or other related issues and had all your data, your plans and all other information in spreadsheets or some other rigid template? Far too many, probably!

We have had enough of spreadsheets. This work is far too important to end up in a tool owned by someone else. Therefore, we built Scout.

Scout is the first of its kind. It's a new type of talent intelligence platform. It's our way of leveraging our employee data to consolidate all of the relevant information; taking inspiration from the world of sports, it proactively scouts our business to identify our current top talent and our future rockstars. All of this is packaged into a unique user interface that allows our HR teams to explore everything they could wish to track around talent. Whether that's career history, roles that they are considering successors for, or an employee's development history. Scout allows all of this to be accessible at the click of a button.

The ability to proactively scout the business for talent is what really makes Scout stand out.

We are very much driven by the philosophy of being data-informed at Spotify. Scout is a perfect example of this. There's an art to identifying and making judgement calls on talent. Judgement calls are often made on the unquantifiable – experience or observation. What Scout does is provide us with the ability to identify talent at scale; it casts a net that isn't siloed in individual business areas. It also allows us to include a whole population of individuals who aren't always visible. When an organisation reaches a certain size, it's impossible for an HRBP to know each and every individual. It's likely they will focus on talent at the top end of the organisation and miss out on a whole host of talent further down in the organisation. Scout allows such individuals to be seen. Not only does this have an impact on how we think about planning, but it also enables us to be even more deliberate, equitable, and make inclusive decisions on nurturing talent. These could be project opportunities, internal mobility or other development opportunities.

PART 2

Part 2.
Culture & Retention
– the employee's journey
and development

Introduction by Alexander Westerdahl and Johanna Bolin Tingvall

You've found the right person for the right role, but the job isn't over – now phase two gets underway! There is a direct correlation between how the onboarding of a new employee is handled and how long they stay with the company. We know that there are things we can do to strengthen the individual's motivation and that motivation is directly linked to the ability to develop and learn.

Once the right person has been recruited, how can we in HR create the best possible conditions for the employee to perform at their best during their time with us? How do we create an environment where every employee feels motivated, feels that they can contribute to the culture and to the success of the company? In other words: How do we create the optimal employee experience?

To make an analogy, when you plan for a journey, a holiday for example, you have to consider all aspects of the experience – who you're going with, where you're going, what you're going to do when you get there, and so on. It's not as simple as going from A to B, rather about the overall experience you will have. The more the trip matches your expectations, the happier and more satisfied you are.

The same applies to the employees' journey within your company. You need to think through every step of this journey, making sure the culture is reflected throughout, minimising disruption and ensuring that employees can focus on performing at their best. Give them a compass. That way, you can help them navigate the unknown and likewise strengthen their loyalty and prolong their tenure.

If you're going to approach the employee experience as if you were planning a real journey, attempt not to design the different parts in isolation from each other, even if each individual initiative is a stand-alone concept. If there is no common thread, the result will be shaky. Lack of coherence between the different parts of the journey creates friction and confusion and ultimately slows progress.

We cannot emphasise enough the importance of creating a consistent employee experience from a design and culture perspective. Culture is shaped by your business and your employees and must be reflected in all phases of the employee journey, in all aspects of the employee's experience of their time with you. Your role as an HR professional is to combine your knowledge of the business with your knowledge of people to ensure that everyone is moving in the same direction.

Hence, embed culture in all your work – let it guide you when it comes to what you look for when recruiting, which behaviours you accept and which you do not within your culture, who you highlight as role models internally and who acts as ambassadors in your external storytelling. For example, do you reward the employee who always achieves their business goals, even if they do so in ways that are not in line with your values? Where are your boundaries? These questions are much easier to answer if you have connected all the different initiatives related to the employee journey and if all employees know what is expected of them and what is and isn't acceptable in your company. This will simplify your relationship with your employees and, just as importantly, allow you to focus on equipping and empowering your employees throughout their journey so that they are not only employable now, but will remain so.

In this second part of the book, we will describe our view of the employee experience in more detail and show you how you can create a 'culture thread' that will tie everything together in order to create a great journey.

Onboarding
– taking care
of new employees

If you successfully onboard your new colleagues, they will feel welcome, positive, included and safe – and therefore be more productive sooner. The link between onboarding and employee retention is not always visible in plain sight and it is easy to miss that there is a direct correlation to attrition. Likewise, neglecting this important step is neither considerate, nor is it good for the business or productivity.

It's easy to understand why some HR professionals shy away from tackling the challenges of onboarding in a structured way. It's not uncommon to sit back and think that if a contract is signed, the recruitment process is over and essentially, the job is complete. There are so many ways that onboarding can be implemented and its purpose can be unclear. In addition, in many organisations, the pace is fast and you may be working in a hyper-growth or global business where there is a lot of uncertainty. A good starting point is to define your goals (for your employees and your business), as onboarding can cover so many things, and a large time span.

Helping new hires become independent

As human beings, we have a need to feel included and connected and we want to feel that we are contributing. Those who are new to the job don't want to stand by and be an observer for longer than necessary, feeling like an inconvenience. In addition, ensuring that new employees become productive quickly is central to the business. With this in mind, onboarding can be defined as the process of making new employees feel like they are in the right place and are able and willing to add value.

Our overall advice here is to focus on autonomy with accountability – on helping new hires become independent. They should receive the tools, knowledge and contacts they need in order to perform. This creates a win-win for everyone and neither the HR team nor the new hire needs to be overwhelmed.

Properly managed, onboarding is a stepping stone that strengthens a new employee's drive and creates a bond with the organisation. In fact, it is one of the most significant steps in the employee journey, affecting both the success of the organisation and the individual. In short, in the new era of HR, ensuring that the onboarding process works really well should be a given.

The onboarding journey

The fact that it can at times be difficult to identify what should and should not be included in onboarding, and where it begins and ends, is due to the fact that it is so closely linked to other important HR activities (employer branding, recruitment, etc.). Managing this overlap will make the process smoother for the new team member. Everything rests on the culture, which is constantly evolving. You could argue that the process has begun even before the person attends their first job interview, i.e. even before a candidate applies for their prospective position. If there is a sober understanding that culture is something that is constantly changing organically, the onboarding process can technically be considered endless. Perhaps that's taking things a bit too far.

This lack of a clear start and end point can make it difficult to implement scalable (global) solutions. The result can be that HR focuses on the simple, visible parts of onboarding that are not always relevant to either the individual or the organisation.

To keep the HR team focused, at Spotify we have set the starting point of the onboarding journey to the moment when an individual accepts a job offer. Everything from that point onwards will undoubtedly affect the person's sense of belonging and increase the likelihood that they will thrive and be able and willing to do their best.

At Spotify, the onboarding journey has its most obvious end point during our introduction days – Intro Days – a community-focused event where new employees, 'band members', learn about the company's history and culture in a deliberate, transparent and playful way. It culminates in a 'big bang' experience that aims to solidify a sense of belonging and ensure that all key aspects of Spotify's identity and culture have been introduced. Setting a start and end point of the journey allows you to plan the framework and experience along the way, ensuring that learning and engagement are present at each stage. Regardless of where the journey begins and ends and regardless of what it covers, we can agree that a successful onboarding experience causes the new employees to:

- Feel welcome (even before they start).
- Receive a relevant introduction to the organisation and colleagues.

- Get a compass to help them navigate the immediate work environment with confidence (from finding their way around the office to internal structures and tools).
- Receive 'keys' to understand and embrace the values and culture.
- Be reassured that productivity is not expected from day one.
- Feel that they can contribute and influence as quickly as possible.

If we constantly compare our planned efforts to the desired end result, it will help us in designing a good onboarding experience.

Who is responsible?

To determine what the journey should include, you need to identify all the levels at which onboarding takes place. HR plays only one role in the overall experience. Other departments and the new employees' teams, managers and buddies also contribute.

To boost both employees and the business, a framework designed by HR, with modules created by other departments, can be a sustainable approach. What should be included in this framework?

The different stages of onboarding

To reduce the risk of a new hire unnecessarily feeling like the only one who doesn't get it, put extra effort into communication. Start communicating and create a dialogue as soon as the contract is signed and the candidate becomes one of the team. The following list mainly deals with the stages where HR has the ultimate responsibility to keep the ball rolling. In addition, there is local and departmental and/or role-specific onboarding for each employee.

1. PRE-BOARDING

Those who have direct contact with new employees obviously have a big impact on their experience. Don't let that distract you from the importance of a more centralised introduction to the company culture. In other words, managers and new colleagues will naturally reach out to new hires, yet an additional welcome from HR, that reflects the culture, will create positive feelings and expectations. It will lead to new employee awareness of the support they can receive from the HR team as they try to understand their new employer and workplace.

2. HR-ORIENTATION

Provide new employees with an initial introduction to the company: who you are and what you want, your structure (units, functions, departments, teams), practical information (getting started with the phone, computer and your systems) and how compensation and benefits work. Ensure this is done very early on (ideally on day one), as it will be a starting point and a survival kit for the first few days. Remember the first days in a new job, when simple things like booking a meeting room or accessing the intranet, calendars or contact details suddenly became insurmountable obstacles?

3. LEARNING PORTAL

Culture is central to creating a sense of community among employees. Autonomy with accountability, a Growth Mindset, the individual's ability and drive to learn are key in the new era of HR. Therefore, there needs to be a place where new employees can easily access information about how things work at your company and where they can continue to drive their own personal development with ease. Creating engaging and informative onboarding content and making sure it is available online also reduces geographical barriers and makes it easier to have a workforce where many people work from home (or from any location other than the office).

4. MANAGER ORIENTATION

A managerial role brings additional responsibilities and expectations; therefore, new managers with human resources responsibilities (people managers) need an extended programme. In turn, they need to understand how to onboard new employees. It is likely that they will require extra guidance, training and information to help their new employees crack the code and feel a sense of community, contribution and influence. Managers are crucial for quick and painless onboarding, but if they are not adequately prepared and supported they can also confuse and create unnecessary anxiety during what is for most people a stressful adjustment period.

5. INTRO DAYS

Coming to a new workplace, especially one that is growing and changing rapidly, can be a bit like jumping into a tumble dryer. You go round and round, and then realise, somewhat dizzy and rather sore, that the stop button is on the outside while you are stuck inside. A few months into a new team member's employment, it's important to help them establish a clearer overview and get to the point where the pieces are starting to fall into place. Our Intro Days tie up the loose ends and aim to provide a good vibe, a sense of clarity and a sense of connectedness and belonging.

In larger organisations, such an event is also a great opportunity for leaders to add some personal spice to the company's history and culture. If several new hires share the same experience, they will form bonds that are valuable to both them and the company throughout their tenure.

Team onboarding

A new employee also needs a more tailored onboarding to their specific team, department or function. They will need help to understand relevant structures or learn skills that are particularly important in the new role. It makes sense for such 'add-on' programmes to be created by people with expert knowledge, in the relevant team or department. However, it is good for HR to act as a support and sounding board in the design of the more tailored part of the introduction (we will describe this approach in more detail at the end of the chapter), to ensure that the programme is truly complementary to the interventions offered to all new employees.

Implementation

How should onboarding activities be implemented? What content/material should a new employee have access to? Whether text, videos or audio, be mindful that it is easy to fit into the individual's schedule.

When planning activities like introduction days, consider whether new employees should participate physically or virtually. Most events and training can work equally well both ways, so make sure you know why you are choosing one over the other. If the decision is not tied to a budget, consider what aspects can work optimally in each scenario. If you are going to meet physically, in which moments will the investment yield the most return?

At physical gatherings, in a short period of time, employees can build deep, strong networks, get their 'culture, values and organisation inoculation', and gain a better understanding of other teams and build trust. In a virtual environment, it will take longer to achieve these aspects. If you choose to hold a virtual event, make sure to put a lot of energy into creating a safe space for interaction and networking, to build a sense of trust and community.

Reduce the feeling of being overwhelmed

The onboarding journey can be incredibly demanding – for HR, for hiring managers, for colleagues and for new hires. Break the experience down and define the stages (including the start and end). As a result, the steps that need to be planned, designed and implemented will be clearer and can be better tailored to both the individual and the organisation. If you know what you want to achieve and what the desired outcome is, HR can focus on the big picture, infusing the plan with their insights from behavioural science so that the needs of both the individual and the group are met.

It can be tempting to constantly expand the onboarding process and it's easy to get caught up in back and forth discussions about what should be included and what role HR should actually play. This has a negative impact on the end result. It is optimal to define a goal and a framework – and then ensure there's built-in flexibility to collaborate with relevant departments, add and subtract, and evolve the experience over time.

We've said it before, but it's critical that new hires understand the common 'culture thread' will run through the entire onboarding journey. Design the onboarding experience with this in mind and reinforce the new hire's sense of autonomy, which will allow you to tap into their natural curiosity (they've come to a new workplace after all). Then you can create an effective, impactful onboarding programme that isn't just a bunch of organisational charts piled on top of each other but covers – and delivers – much more.

As already mentioned, strive for a flexible approach to the onboarding process, ask new employees about their experience, look at the results and adapt if you want and need to. This could be as simple as using a survey to ask new employees the impressions of their first day, whether they feel they have started their work satisfactorily, and whether they feel included and productive. Once you have the data, be prepared to make some adjustments to develop and improve your onboarding.

That feeling of being in a tumble dryer is not uncommonly experienced by new employees and can also be experienced by those responsible for reviewing, designing and implementing the introduction of new employees. So aim to minimise this feeling – for the comfort of everyone involved!

ONBOARDING AT SPOTIFY

– One example

The early versions of the onboarding process for Spotify's new hires in the area we now call R&D (Research & Development, encompassing Engineering, Data Analytics, Product, Design), called boot camps, were two-week camps where new employees worked on real Spotify projects and thereby learned about our systems, our 'studio model' (small product development teams with members from multiple departments) and our way of working in the engineering department.

It was an excellent model in many ways. It allowed new hires to learn by doing – and the projects they worked on often came from the R&D to-do list, so the new hires created real business value right from day one, which they found particularly positive.

However, the programme was not so easy to scale up. As Spotify's growth rate increased, there weren't enough resources to organise such boot camps, not least because of the new and diverse roles that were being added to the already long list of different profiles and professional roles the programme had to adapt to. It was time to rethink. We needed a model that was scalable and worked for all teams.

A NEW ITERATION

We wanted the new onboarding programme for R&D employees to be more consistent and modular, so that it could be more easily adapted. Of course, we also wanted new employees to feel both included and inspired and to return to their teams with a deeper understanding of who we are and how we work.

The programme was therefore designed to:

- Create an extra layer of information, in line with the culture, adding further depth to help new employees navigate the structure and understand the procedures and ways of working that are unique primarily to engineers.

- Communicate overall approaches and beliefs regarding products and technologies.

- Allow new employees to meet and build relationships with colleagues, even outside their specific area of expertise or team.

- Provide (continued) opportunities for practical learning and demonstrate concrete applications.

- Take place over three days and include a number of modules in the field of R&D, based on the three Cs: Context, Culture and Connections.

CONTEXT, CULTURE, CONNECTIONS

Context: An introduction to who we are as a company, where we come from and where we're going – our strategy – as well as what the organisation looks like (especially in R&D).

Culture: In this onboarding programme, culture can be defined as 'how we do things'. It is explained through workshops on our core values and design thinking, with participants from R&D departments sharing their personal experiences. We also talk about how we build and deploy code.

Connections: During the three days we use a structured approach for relationship building, combined with less structured methods for participants to socialise and network.

The modular solution has allowed us to fine-tune the programme as needed and experiment with when and where we run the modules. We can run them entirely in classrooms, entirely virtually, or use a mixture of both. We can also split the programme into several sessions or run it in a more concentrated way.

As the organisation grows and changes, we will need to review the introduction programme – we evaluate continuously to ensure we are hitting the mark.

When correctly implemented, onboarding is a good investment that pays off in both the short and long term. It becomes a gift that keeps on giving. If it is carried out in a clumsy way, or not carried out at all, you miss the opportunity to give your most expensive and important investment a really good, fun, pleasant, inspiring and effective start.

Total Compensation
– on pay, remuneration
and benefits

Almost all compensation and benefits strategies have the same goals: to attract and retain good people, reward performance and recognise individual achievements. We all use the same data for comparison and hire the same consultants. As a result, our unique 'compensation package' is likely to be quite similar to everyone else's.

In the new era, we cannot attract and retain employees by giving them everything they want. We should not fall into the trap of only offering 'sugar kicks'. *We shouldn't just pay for the candy – but also for the dentist visit.* Now, don't get us wrong, we're not saying that you shouldn't pay your employees well enough or not provide any kind of rewards – but giving them everything they ask for (especially when they're screaming loudly):

- is neither a strategy nor a philosophy,
- won't drive or increase engagement,
- won't make you stand out,
- will dilute your culture and ownership capital, and
- is crazy expensive.

We believe that a compensation strategy is most effective when it is designed to reflect your culture and your 'game plan' – the kind of company you want to be and the people you want to attract, develop and retain. You need to know the business and adopt a holistic approach. Employees should be rewarded fairly and in line with what you're trying to achieve. This will reinforce employees' loyalty to their job, their team and the organisation as a whole.

Create incentives for your employees to behave in a way that matches your values, reinforces your culture and helps them focus on what matters, so you can achieve your (business) goals. Weave the compensation strategy into your employer branding strategy and your talent attraction strategy. Think about how your rewards can be aligned with your skills development plan and how you evaluate performance.

Start with the basics. Don't be fooled – the basics are not simple. Benchmarking, job levelling, promotion guidelines and all the other elements that are at the heart of compensation work are complex areas that require specialist knowledge and an awareness that compensation varies between different groups of employees. Industry, length of service, laws, rules and practices in different countries and regions, as well as many other factors, have an impact. While these aspects are important and complex, they are not the real 'jewels in the crown'. Once the basics are in place, it's time to let go of the benchmarking for a while.

If you know your employees, you know what is 'non-negotiable' when it comes to compensation and benefits. This allows you to question elements that employees expect but may not need. If many or all companies in the industry are offering their employees something specific, such as a particular benefit, that doesn't fit with your culture and what you stand for and believe in – have a discussion about it. Replace industry standards and expected processes with your company culture and let it be your guide in this process.

Let's say that comparisons show that you should (but not must) have a bonus scheme. Bonuses are incentives for short-term behaviour and can often be at odds with long-term business strategy. Instead, set up a programme that aligns with your culture and a business strategy that creates longer-term incentives. By all means keep an eye on aspects like attrition among those who have been given this model, to see if you've found the right reward structure. Don't get caught up in any particular trend, and dare to let your culture and values take centre stage. Be brave and pave your own way. *Be BOLD!*

Many HR professionals can feel trapped by the conventional view of pay and benefits, as well as burdened by the long list of 'must haves' or 'offerings'. Especially since management and supervisors can have quite strong views on these issues. Don't give in to the pressure. You are the experts in the field and you are not helping your company or your employees if you choose solutions for the sake of simplicity and pay to avoid discomfort. Instead, remember that there are many variables to play with – there are endless ways to provide benefits and compensate employees. Make sure you have a healthy, sustainable, different and relevant method of rewarding your employees so that you attract and retain the *right people.*

Spotify has deviated from the norm with a few different approaches over the years, such as the global parental leave policy, the flexible holiday policy and the incentive mix (we describe these in more detail later in the book). More and more companies are following in the same footsteps, which is how an industry standard develops. By the time you read this, things like flexible leave and benefit programmes where employees can choose their own benefits may well have become the norm. Challenging the norm should not be done for the sake of it. Do it if it's right for your organisation and your employees.

If you are not sure when to be innovative and when to stick to the basics, try to use the following principles as a guide when creating your strategy.

Principle 1: Differentiate

What is considered an excellent benefit in one country may be seen as trivial and obvious in another. What is a good incentive for Generation X may need to be reconsidered for Generation Y. To address this challenge, you need several different jewels in that crown. Even if you find one that everyone likes (which is highly unlikely), over time it will lose its lustre. It will either become standard or stop adding value. Then you have to find a new one.

Principle 2: The 90/10 principle

Sometimes, an external consultant or employee with no HR experience identifies logical gaps or unwanted side effects of an incentive programme or benefit. It's easy to get distracted and spend time trying to solve the issue. The problem is that a new solution often creates new gaps. Everything you do involves compromise – and if at least 90% of employees are happy and the compromises are manageable, then you're on the right track. You will never get 100% satisfaction.

If you have the luxury of participating in policy decisions, you have probably worked hard and made some bold moves to reach that position. We have to remember that today's solutions can often become tomorrow's problems – and your job is to solve problems, including problems you created (even if they were created for the right reasons at the time).

This mantra doesn't only apply to compensation philosophy but to almost all decisions. Decisions must always be evaluated in the context in which they were made. Don't be alarmed if they create problems in *another* context. You just have to solve them. You didn't expect life lessons in a chapter on compensation in a book on HR, did you?

Principle 3: Think long-term

Try to strike a balance between giving your employees what they want and creating a more long-term, strategic benefits package. After all, it's easy to find benefits and solutions that your employees want. Do you want lunch? We're hiring an office chef! Don't have a place to live? We build homes and let our employees use them! Do you have children? We will arrange a nursery for you! Your partner's unemployed? We'll employ them! You want to take more time off? Don't worry, we'll give you more vacation days! Doesn't that sound like the best employer in the world? What does it sound like to the person working on the compensation strategy? Like a total nightmare! You're digging a hole for yourself that will be so deep, you'll never get out of it. You don't want to end up just reacting and spending your time putting out fires. You want to adopt and build out those really attractive initiatives, the ones that have real impact.

Moreover, if you don't think beyond meeting the needs and demands of your employees, your packages will be tailored to the employees you currently have, making it difficult to use compensation and benefits to increase the diversity of your organisation. In short, reacting is extremely costly for the organisation, both financially and in terms of the 'diversity debt'. By providing benefits that attract talent in the short term, you are actually creating a headache in the long term. Avoid this trap at all costs.

Principle 4: The right people

A person who is the best in their field may not necessarily be right for your organisation. To understand when this is the case, you need to have a clear idea of the direction you want to grow in and how. Then remind yourself of your priorities and values at every stage of the hiring process. As your organisation evolves and changes, you will experience what can be described as a 'natural' turnover of staff. How and if this will affect your compensation strategy is something you should consider. It is important to focus on creating incentives for development and rewarding your existing employees with thoughtfulness and longevity rather than having an anxious reaction every time someone chooses to leave.

Of course, salaries and rewards should be as fair as possible. While this has a big impact on whether your employees feel fairly treated, satisfied and motivated, it is far from being the only motivating factor – perhaps not even the main one.

At Spotify, we want our employees to be 'missionaries, not mercenaries'. We are looking for people who want to be part of our development journey and who believe in our purpose, not for people who are here primarily for compensation. If all they are looking for is compensation, then they can take up employment anywhere and at any time.

We don't believe in paying extra for people to want to be part of our journey. We also don't want to pay more to keep them, if for some reason they say they are leaving. This would only be a temporary solution and it's rarely long before the employee says they're unhappy again. Such an approach would be like using a life-support machine and will cause managers, colleagues and HR to lose focus. Essentially, it means you're keeping the negotiation window open all year round, which creates uncertainty for everyone else who becomes aware of this strategy. Instead, make sure your compensation strategy goes hand in hand with your People Strategy, your culture and values, and your approach to performance and competence development (which we will look at in the next chapter).

Principle 5: Focus on the right type of package

Focus on what is *really* important – "wildly important", as we sometimes say – to keep your employees motivated. Your game strategy, your culture, vision and mission, your People Strategy and your goals should be reflected in your total compensation (salary, remuneration and benefits) strategy. The offer must be competitive in relation to your peers. Taking performance into account – the employee's skills, contributions and behaviour – should be central to your strategy. This way, compensation is linked to performance and therefore keeps your teams motivated and eager to innovate.

Offering co-ownership is another possibility. It is an approach that takes into account both the business and the employees: all employees can become shareholders and are jointly invested in the future success of the company. This can be a good way to share both successes and setbacks. Your benefits programme can then be adapted to be competitive in each local market and extended to all employees, regardless of seniority.

Principle 6: Allow for freedom of choice

Many employers have already realised that they will not be successful in the long run if they give in to all the wishes of their employees (or potential employees). However, giving employees the opportunity to choose between different paths and options can be beneficial. Provide support, offer choices and make sure they have the information they need to make the choices that best suit them. *Flexibility*, especially in a long-term incentive plan, can be a very shiny jewel in the crown (we describe our incentive mix at the end of the chapter).

However, this should be in line with the rest of your company's approach – for example, how you work with learning and development. Allowing this flexibility works well when other factors related to development support the initiative and when – as in Spotify's case – everything is underpinned by a growth mindset.

Principle 7: There will be outliers

Yes, there will be *outliers* – exceptions to the rule – in the sense of employees who have knowledge and/or experience that is very unique and where you need to go outside the boundaries of the regular compensation and benefits strategy. These are people whose skills and expertise are in demand right now, who can solve some of your most pressing challenges, who lead by example and inspire and support others to perform at their best.

Outliers should not be ignored, but focus on the majority and the big bets when creating your pay and performance strategy. Remember, it is unlikely that all your employees will be happy all the time so don't let your outliers disrupt your strategy as long as they are in the minority. Don't exclude them either. People in HR, especially those in compensation, often spend far too much time discussing what would happen if everyone was an outlier and got a bespoke compensation offering (undermining the strategy). We think it's best to put that question aside, at least until the day when your outliers are too numerous to be called outliers.

Instead, focus on the behaviours that are important to the business and on what makes the people you really want to work for you engaged and motivated. Knowing both your business and your people, and creating harmony between them, is key. The key to harmony, especially in this new era, is to be open to the fact that some things may need to be restructured. Since this approach to compensation and benefits is focused on employee *development*, there are other teams whose strategies will play a role in the compensation and benefits strategy.

A benefits package

Traditionally, many pay and reward teams also deal with *fringe* benefits (benefits beyond compensation). It's also not uncommon for them to be responsible for the broad concept of employee experience. Let's say you want salary and benefits to contribute to increased diversity in your organisation. In such a circumstance, start thinking about how to choose a structure that fits your way of working, with the best interests of the organisation in mind and where all aspects are integrated. Silo thinking won't check the box here.

Anyone creating a package of 'freebies' needs to make sure they choose things that are attractive at a local level (taking into account what works in each country), but still fit with the company culture, employee promise and employer brand.

Working with compensation and benefits is exciting, creative and – when you find the right balance that suits your business and your employees – has a big impact. That's when a compensation strategy can be a really powerful HR tool. It will allow you not only to attract great people but will also shape their development during their time with you.

SPOTIFY'S INCENTIVE MIX

Long-term incentive programmes have always been a focus at Spotify. We want every Spotifier to have a chance to own a piece of the company, so employee stock options (ESOP) are part of the mix for everyone. It's a strategy built around our culture.

Another aspect of our culture is that we believe in autonomy with accountability, in letting our people decide for themselves what they want, as far as possible. We want to give our people direction, offer them choices and make sure they have all the information they need. We expect each employee to have ownership of their *growth plan*, meaning they take responsibility for their own personal and professional development – with our support. Therefore, when we updated our long-term incentive programme a few years ago, we focused on maximum flexibility and let each individual choose their own incentive mix.

There has been a lot of research into which incentive programmes work best. Numerous surveys have been sent out asking employees what they want, in the search for the perfect programme – but people want different things depending on their life situation. Some are young, others older. Some have children, or plan to have children, others do not. Some want to buy a house, others want to live in an RV and surf a new continent every four months. People value capital and money differently. Each individual therefore has a unique answer to the question: What is your ultimate incentive programme? We aim to attract and retain all kinds of talented employees.

Our solution was to stop trying to create a perfect programme and instead let everyone choose their own mix. That way, each employee can choose the programme that suits them personally, and we get a better return on our incentive investment in the form of happier employees.

We started testing the new model on a small scale in 2017, when we introduced a limited choice model for existing employees. They were given a new opportunity to participate in an option scheme, choosing between warrants and cash. This worked well, and in 2019 we expanded it to all employees participating in the stock option scheme (both new hires and existing employees) and offered more options. Before the allocation of actual shares in the stock option plan, the employee is told how much value they have been allocated – an 'incentive sum'. The employee can then mix *At The Money Employee Stock Options* (ATM) or *Out of The Money Employee Stock Options* (OTM), *Restricted Stock Units* (RSU) and *Cash*. All options have similar life expectancy, vesting period and conditions.

At The Money (ATM) is the most common way to structure personal options today. Out of The Money (OTM) means that the options have no value when you receive them or, in other words, they are worthless until the stock reaches the predetermined exercise price. The compromise for the company is to give the employee more options because they are taking a greater risk. Restricted Stock Units (RSUs) mean that the employee will receive shares in the company in the future.

Most conversations with employees and potential employees revolve around the concepts of risk and reward. All people try to maximise reward and minimise risk simultaneously. Maximising a potential reward always means greater risk.

A large part of our work involves educating employees so that they make their choices with their eyes open and the range of both risks and rewards is wide. Most employees should be able to find a mix that motivates them and suits their finances. We have created some rules, mainly to make the choice easier and also to avoid administrative chaos. At the time of writing, we allow 22 different incentive mixes. The process looks like this: the HR system we use (we will return to this system in the third part of the book, in the chapter on HR technology) creates a choice module. Through this system, the employee receives an invitation to make their choices, and then has a week to pick and choose, make a decision and agree to the terms in the system. We then transfer the data to the system that manages all the different accounts and implements the employee's choices. In essence, each employee gets a certain amount of money and can choose how to distribute it across different types of stock options, conditional shares and cash, with the same vesting periods.

We can't give advice on what to choose, but we provide information, brochures, examples and calculation software so that employees can make the most informed choice possible based on their preferences, how long they intend to work with us and how they think our share price will develop. For those who don't want to make their own choice, we have a standard package.

The programme has been well received by both new employees and employees who have been with us for a while. They appear to prefer the freedom of choice to a standardised programme. A somewhat unexpected bonus effect is that we receive far fewer questions and support cases for the programme now than we did for the old programme. In retrospect, we can see that the concerns we had going into the launch – that we were offering employees too many choices and an overly complex programme – were unfounded. When the Talent Acquisition team can casually talk dollars and cents with prospective employees, we have initial proof that most people will understand what it's all about – and employees can focus on the options offered. This solution has been built on the basis of our business, our people and our culture. That's how we know it's the right approach for us right now.

Learning
– creating a learning culture

Today, when rapid change is perpetual, companies in turn need to constantly evolve and adapt to new conditions. Employees also need to continuously develop their skills and how they use them. The old status quo is redundant, where the starting point was typically a university degree, followed by a few decades of climbing the career ladder and finally, retirement. Today, many skills have a much shorter lifespan, which creates a need for continuous learning – for upskilling and reskilling. If employees learn more and develop their skills during their tenure at your organisation, this is positive for both the individual and the company. It is a fundamental part of the new era of HR.

A shift in thinking

We are in the midst of a shift, if not globally, then at least in Western society, where views on careers and working life are changing rapidly. There are many reasons for this, but perhaps the most obvious is the rapid development of technology and how it affects our jobs. Fewer people are dedicating their entire lives to the same profession; instead, they may have shorter career stints with blocks of training and learning in between. Each individual must take responsibility for maintaining their relevance in the labour market

– i.e. take control of their own development. Simultaneously, there is an expectation that employers should support their employees in their learning.

Companies that are breaking new ground in any field may find that the competences or skills they are looking for are not yet offered by universities. This is another reason why continuous development and learning needs to be encouraged and enabled internally. This approach enables the individual employee and the entire organisation to stay relevant and it drives innovation. If employees are afraid of stagnating with you, you will never be regarded as an attractive employer.

In addition, there is great joy in learning. Learning creates motivation and a sense of purpose and community. We need to change our approach to learning. It allows us to stop focusing on running faster and faster and start thinking about how we can do new things differently. Learning brings about the realisation that we are running a marathon rather than a sprint. Even if we need to run fast, it is also important to pace ourselves and occasionally stop, rehydrate and consider whether we are running in the right direction and at the right pace. Time for reflection, contemplation and training/development should not be considered a cost, but rather an investment.

Continuous learning

There have been quite a few studies conducted on how much time an employee nowadays has for learning. It is limited. There is a logical fallacy here, where learning is interpreted as something you do 'on the side': taking a course, participating in a programme or reading a book. When the need for learning is paramount, we need to rethink what learning means. The workplace of the future is here, and work and learning cannot be separated. We need to find a way to do both at the same time. Learning is work and work is learning.

The value of continuous learning during working hours and through work tasks becomes apparent. Under such conditions, learning – and therefore development – can take place everywhere, all the time and perhaps predominantly through daily work. Undertaking a new task or a new challenge is when learning takes place. Experiment and try something new and when you see the results, reflect on and learn from them.

More and more organisations are realising that they need to find methods to access and benefit from daily learning in a systematic way. This requires creating an environment of deliberate learning. Learning and development must be an important part of the culture for this to happen. By strengthening the culture, the HR department can help employees learn more and faster. Learning itself becomes a raison d'être and crucial to business success.

Creating a learning culture

How do you create an environment and culture where learning, development and growth are central? We believe that some pieces of the puzzle are particularly important in order to achieve this – as follows, in no particular order.

1. VISION AND PURPOSE

First of all, a learning culture is based on a strong vision and a clear purpose. It is important for employees to be able to link the purpose of the organisation to what they can contribute. The feeling of doing something meaningful and contributing to something bigger than yourself is a strong motivating factor for everyone, regardless of gender, age, background, etc. It also drives learning.

2. AUTONOMY AND COMPETENCE

In order to create an environment where learning really takes place – because employees want to learn, not because they are forced to – each individual needs to have some freedom to control their own work and development. We have talked about the importance of autonomy at several points in this book already. Research shows that autonomy is crucial for motivation. Perhaps we should be talking about trust-based leadership rather than autonomy, because it's not about everyone being able to do exactly what they want, but rather about treating employees as adults rather than micromanaging and controlling them.

Make it easy for your employees to learn. Make learning attractive. The learning opportunities need to be exciting and interesting and there need to be many different ways to learn – this is an effective approach to increase the speed and level of learning. Give employees the support, tools and conditions they need to take responsibility for their own development.

Alongside the need for autonomy, there's also a human drive to build mastery – to learn, to improve, to grow and share our learnings. The need to build competence is two-fold; as an individual need and as a need for all employees to grow and develop at a company level. Empower your employees to assume the accountability to grow, develop and essentially get better.

3. FAILURES AND LESSONS LEARNED

Consider this thought: if your people always play it safe, they will never fail – and they will also never innovate. If they try new things, if they experiment, then sometimes things go wrong. That's part of the package. In order for there to be any point in failing, they have to learn from their mistakes, even if it's not always easy in those first moments of pain when something (or perhaps everything!) has gone wrong.

For employees to be able to experiment in this way and then share what they experienced – so that everyone can learn something – the workplace or team needs what is called *psychological safety*. Employees need to feel that it's okay to fail. Here, managers need to act as role models and share their own failures and lessons learned to help create a trust-based and safe environment for their teams. If we want to create safety, it is counterproductive to punish failures and the courage to own them. Rather, it should be encouraged with the reasoning that failures should be highlighted as good examples to learn from.

To learn from our failures, we need to think of learning as a cyclical process. You need to pause and record your outcomes. The next step is to reflect on the facts, draw conclusions about what you could have done differently or what assumptions should be adjusted – and next, adjust your plans and try again.

4. CONTROLLED CHAOS

Breaking routines and old ways of thinking is the basis for all innovation. Allowing a little chaos and unpredictability lays the foundation for new unexpected connections and ideas. Avoiding cumbersome processes, or guidelines for everything, creates space for such chaos and encourages learning and exploration.

The challenge is to create an environment where employees are ready to take on the unexpected and are comfortable with a degree of disorder. While some assume that great leaders create stability, our experience tells us that a healthy dose of the discomfort that uncertainty creates can make us more resilient, robust, innovative and determined. The individual and the organisation that learns to deal with this uncertainty is also better equipped for what may come, whether that's paradigm shifts, new recessions, revolutionary technologies, new pandemics... the list goes on. In this sense, controlled chaos and continuous learning also become a form of resilience training and a key to success in a world that increasingly demands flexibility and resilience.

5. INTERACTION AND COLLABORATION

There are many great inventors and scientists that society has put on a pedestal. People generally assume that these seemingly exceptionally talented and creative individuals succeeded solely because of their brilliance. However, if you put their successes under a microscope, you see that they often achieved what they did by interacting with others. For example, we know that Darwin wrote about 15,000 letters during his career and received at least as many in return. Through this correspondence, he naturally gained new ideas and thoughts that contributed to his work.

Development is rarely the result of the hard work of a single individual but of the collaboration of people with different experiences and ideas. This also means that cognitive diversity is essential if we aim to challenge old patterns of thinking. We need to share ideas with others, exchange thoughts and be inspired by each other's opinions. We can achieve deeper and faster learning by embracing and expressing our differences. Being challenged to rethink by someone who is completely different to us gives us more to contemplate. We will come back to the issue of diversity later in the book and for now want to emphasise: *encourage and enable such collaboration, and you will get learning in return.*

6. PERFORMANCE AND DEVELOPMENT

If learning is as important as we claim, then performance evaluation should be linked to development. When assessing your employees' performance, consider their development to be as important as their ability to deliver. *Don't be blinded by short-term goal achievement!* Managers should be encouraged to take into account the employee's willingness to take on new challenges and learn along the way. They should consider how the employee grows in their professional role. When development is valued, assessed and recognised, it contributes to a learning culture. We will talk more about this in the next chapter on performance development.

7. GROWTH MINDSET AND LEARNABILITY

In order to create a flow of learning in your company, embrace and encourage a growth mindset. Leaders who adopt a growth mindset themselves, and show their teams that anyone can grow, will come to understand that intelligence and talent are not static. Understanding that dedication and hard work are the path to learning and success makes us more resilient and gives us the courage to take on new challenges.

With this mindset, we will enjoy learning, even the learning that happens when things go wrong. This is important – a failure that you don't learn from is a mistake. We need to assume that we all always have the potential to be better, because then failure becomes an opportunity to learn. No one can think this way all the time, and failure hurts, but with practice and a supportive culture, this mind-set can increase your employees' ability and willingness to learn.

8. THE APPROACH TO CAREERS AND LEARNING

Finally, in this new era, companies and employees alike need to rethink, innovate and develop new skills at an accelerating pace. We need to redefine – or at least broaden the definition of – career and learning and support this transformation in a variety of ways. Also, it enables us to actively create a learning culture.

A career is not synonymous with slowly advancing in the same field, or staying in the same profession for a lifetime. It should perhaps rather be a portfolio of different experiences. Such a portfolio can demonstrate gathering skills and experiences from careers in different fields, during shorter periods of time. Growth becomes the central aspect of a career rather than an exercise in collecting titles and positions. Learning does not become synonymous with attending a course and can, for example, be achieved through new work assignments or shadowing and mentoring. This is a form of learning that can and should take place constantly in everyday life, a form of learning that will act as 'insurance' to help an individual stay relevant throughout their professional life. To support such a change, offer employees some kind of platform or structure for on-the-job learning. Identify vacancies, projects/gigs, mentors, and also offer new tasks and mentoring. This type of platform or structure can then act as a marketplace for skills, increasing the flow of knowledge, experience, skills, ideas and perspectives between people and departments.

Never stop learning!

Larger companies often have a central Learning & Development department that provides development opportunities for employees. Whether you have a dedicated learning and development team or not, try to create your own 'learning realm'. Create an environment, a culture and a structure (or non-structure) that encourages, facilitates and enables employees to learn and relearn. Learning should be part of your employee value proposition, which in turn strengthens your employer brand, makes your employees more engaged and drives innovation. Whatever you do, never let your employees or your organisation stop learning.

SPOTIFY'S INTERNAL TALENT MARKETPLACE

Internally at Spotify, we talk a lot about the paradigm shift we are in the middle of, where the old career model no longer works. As an employer, we have a responsibility to make it easier for our employees to drive their own development so that they can stay relevant in the labour market.

Even though new opportunities for development are constantly appearing in a fast-growing business, it can be difficult for all employees to see them. Some individuals have a high self-awareness and know what to look for, but not everyone's the same. As employers, we can't expect everyone to be constantly on the lookout for new jobs and internal opportunities. We need to ensure the opportunities can be accessed by everyone.

We decided to create an internal talent marketplace so that employees had greater visibility on what positions are available internally, as well as projects and other ad hoc opportunities. We toyed with the idea that the opportunity to grow and learn would 'echo through the walls' at Spotify. That's why we call our internal talent marketplace *Echo* and we aim to *let opportunities echo*.

INCLUSION

Offering an internal talent marketplace is one way to make more development opportunities available and more varied development opportunities visible to everyone. Of course, this can only happen if the marketplace is designed in such a way that everyone feels welcome. Technology can be used to achieve this and it was crucial to our approach. We wanted a system that would be inclusive and based on matching talent based on skills, experience and ambitions, rather than background or ethnicity.

Hence we use artificial intelligence (AI) to support our employees' learning and growth. Internal jobs, projects, gigs and various kinds of mentorships are matched with the individuals' skills and experience with the help of AI. The AI technology helps us visualise and match new opportunities for development to Spotifiers, without managers or unconscious bias getting in the way of a fair matching.

THINK BROADER

Echo allows us to exceed the traditional paths for development opportunities. This doesn't have to be a new position alone, a full-time project or mentorship, but can also offer the opportunity to *shadow* someone for a period of time, or to be an *embed*, i.e. stepping into another team for a short period of time as a team member. We had seen this work with our engineers and we wanted more people to try it. We simply wanted to create a platform where opportunities for short-term projects and other time-limited initiatives could exist and be visible company-wide, regardless of the department or profession.

The technology behind Echo enables automated matching based on skills, experience and development goals. This allows our managers and project owners to access a longer and more diverse list of internal candidates because we look beyond the usual selection criteria, such as background and education. Here are some typical examples of what Echo is used for:

- A junior employee finds a mentor through Echo and can accelerate their learning about the organisation and the world of work.

- Someone from the marketing department in one of our regional offices will find projects in another department and may eventually move into a new role in product development.

- An engineer identifies a skills gap in their team and uses Echo to find a hands-on project where they can get the necessary skills and then returns to their own team to fill the gap.

- A manager has an ambitious and high-performing team that needs more challenges. In Echo, they find a major project that involves collaboration between several different parts of the organisation. The person who launched the project solves their needs faster than expected.

- A recruiter with a bunch of positions to fill uses Echo with hiring managers to view and find internal candidates.

- A senior manager wants to contribute their knowledge to more junior employees. The manager becomes a mentor through Echo and finds more meaning in everyday life and gets to know a colleague in another part of the organisation.

LAUNCH AND LESSONS LEARNED

Bringing a new tool like Echo into the organisation required a lot of preparation and change management. We relied on a network of employees from different departments and locations (our Echo Ambassadors) to help us evaluate and test Echo before the launch. We also had sponsorship from senior management, since we knew this would be crucial for a successful implementation.

Once we launched Echo on a wider scale, we had time to make several adjustments based on the feedback from our ambassadors and senior management testers, which made the launch much smoother than it would have been otherwise. The initial small mistakes didn't have to become big mistakes and instead could be learnings that helped us to tweak and iterate into the best product possible.

In the first month following the wider launch, we saw an interest in participating; our employees were enthusiastic, they registered in the system so as to receive and share information and to seek development opportunities. More and more mentoring relationships were created, confirming that the demand was indeed high. We could also see that there was a lot of interest in projects, and nowadays it is not uncommon for employees to 'guest star' in other departments. Links are being created across departmental, competence and national borders!

Today, Echo is an integral part of the Spotify learning and development ecosystem, we learn from the data we get from the system, and we continue to broaden our approach to creating and highlighting development opportunities. Although the interest is great, we have seen that we must always work proactively with Echo to keep it relevant, to constantly inform and educate managers and employees on how to get the most out of it. It's also apparent that the more data we can collect and analyse, the more evidence we have to show the benefits and contribute to business planning. If our employees are the obvious resource, we need to ensure they have the skills we need and build them internally!

Regardless of the industry, we in HR need to understand that continuous learning is absolutely necessary for employees to thrive, feel engaged and experience growth and development at work. That it is essential to keep the right talent with the right skills on board.

Performance Development
– how performance and development go hand in hand

Everything we do at Spotify involves people: artists and creators, customers and our audience – and, not least, our band members (our employees) who create the Spotify experience! Ensuring we retain the right people and making sure they have what they need to perform (we'll come back to our definition of performance), so that they can reshape, preserve, improve and enhance the creation that is Spotify, is the core task of the HR team. With that in mind, let's take a look at one of the tools we use to enable our people to perform at their best in the long run: performance development.

Performance Management

For most companies, *Performance Management* (PM) is one of the key HR processes. According to Wikipedia, PM is "the process of ensuring that a set of activities and outputs meets an organisation's goals in an effective and efficient manner". It is a rather good definition. Note, however, that the focus is on the *process* and on *managing* production resources. This reveals a rather outdated and angular view of employees.

Many companies that use traditional PM processes do so because there is already an architecture in place, not because they have made a conscious choice about what the processes should look like and then implemented a system that supports it. There is a system that they have invested in, where they set goals: activities to be performed during the year, linked to the goals adopted at management level. Then there is the annual performance review process, where an employees' performance is assessed by their managers. Often, the employee will also conduct a self-evaluation. The outcome is linked to the compensation review process – the salary discussion, with a possible salary increase linked to the assessment – all in the same system. It seems fair and objective. After all, the aim is to effectively check that employees are contributing to the company's goals.

The problem is that very few people seem to like this system. Employees feel disengaged rather than inspired and motivated, and for managers, the system entails a lot of administrative and time-consuming work at the end of the year. Very few people like to sit in an inflexible meeting that should have taken place much earlier and hear what they did and didn't do, what they should have done and how they can improve: an assessment of their performance over the past year. It's actually not surprising that if they receive feedback that's long overdue, or after an event has taken place, with no option to amend it in real time, they view it as a 'verdict'.

Many people believe that as long as there is a system, a process and a template in place that everyone can follow, this system is fair. We don't agree.

Why doesn't performance management work?

1. WE IMAGINE THAT THE SYSTEM IS OBJECTIVE

Many believe that using a performance management system, where everyone follows the same steps and goes through the same process, makes the process more objective and fair. Can a system be objective in itself, or does it depend on what you put into it? Whether you use a standardised system or not, there is always a manager doing the evaluation and assessment, so the system itself does not guarantee objectivity or fairness. It can also be easier for a manager to 'hide' behind a system and process than to take responsibility for having a regular, constructive dialogue with their team members.

That said, there is nothing wrong with using a system per se. We need to be aware of why we are using them, and where they help, or perhaps hinder. Any discussion on technology and systems you might consider should be undertaken with eyes wide open.

Challenge your truths about what constitutes objectivity or fairness. As humans, we all inherently have lots of biases and no matter whether there's a system or not, we constantly need to remind ourselves of the plethora of biases. They are lurking in our brains and we must do the best we can by questioning our decisions systematically to uncover both implicit and explicit bias.

2. IT KILLS MOTIVATION

Many companies have built their PM process on the belief that employee performance can be managed and improved through rewards and punishments of various kinds. Of course, we can behave in a certain way if someone gives us a reason to do so, if we get something we want or if we don't get something we don't want. However, thanks to research on motivation, we now know that external incentives do not make us more motivated and can even worsen our performance. If you add the slightest complexity (which is the case in most professional roles today), the carrot-and-stick philosophy will not work.

Money (the most obvious form of extrinsic incentive) is important because we all need it to live. Research demonstrates that it is basically a hygiene factor – you will simply be very dissatisfied if you are not fairly compensated for the work you do. If you are already being paid a fair wage, you will rarely see any reason to do a better job just because you are paid more – on the contrary, you may lose motivation!

It's more human to be motivated by things like feeling a sense of belonging and community with others and by achieving something meaningful, where a higher purpose can be identified. This kind of motivation can be blocked by the classic PM processes, which focus on goals that are simply about increasing shareholder value. Few people find quarterly reports particularly exciting. Of course, the business results are important, but to motivate employees to perform at their best, the business results need to be combined with your 'why' – the company's true purpose.

As already noted, another important motivational factor is the feeling of autonomy or self-determination, of being (somewhat) free to control one's own life. In order not to miss out on this motivational factor, you need leaders that show that they trust the employees to do their job. Set a direction and let employees plan the journey. Don't set too granular goals for each individual or team.

It's also human nature to be driven by curiosity; we have an inherent desire to learn, develop and grow. This curiosity helps us build the skills we need to do our jobs and take on new challenges. It's the cornerstone of Innovation.

3. IT ENCOURAGES A STATIC MINDSET

PM processes based on performance ratings are not the best solution to increase performance. Studies show that such ratings reduce motivation, and research in neuroscience shows that ratings activate part of the brain's alarm system – the fight or flight system. Who wants to be put into such a state of mind? Does this mental state aid creativity or induce eagerness to come up with new and exciting ideas? No, absolutely not.

A positive rating may make someone feel good and smart. They will be motivated to do more of the same, of what they are good at, which reduces their desire to think differently, try something new and take risks. Studies have shown that employees who are told they are considered great performers and are labelled 'high potentials' or 'top performers' will be less innovative and will invest more time in maintaining their status. On the other hand, if someone gets a low performance score, they are likely to feel unsuccessful, lose motivation, and may even be afraid to try something new, as they will be predominantly focused on proving themselves by playing it safe. In both cases, ratings encourage a static or fixed mindset – the opposite of the dynamic, growth mindset that we want to see more of – and neither encourage risk-taking or curiosity. As a result, the company loses much potential for innovation. We need to create an environment where every employee believes that they can improve at everything, if they practise and dare to try. Those who fail can learn from their mistakes and move on. We want to encourage everyone to identify opportunities and embrace challenges.

Just imagine what so-called 'forced ranking' can do. It was popular in performance management in the 1980s, when General Electric CEO Jack Welch introduced a system of comparing employees to *each other* rather than to an objective set of performance measures. This meant that some employees always ended up at the bottom of the performance scale and others at the top, regardless of how they actually performed. Today, we know that such a model encourages internal competition rather than collaboration and does not lead to healthy teamwork. Fortunately, fewer and fewer companies are using this model today. Few businesses can survive in the current complex business landscape if they promote internal competition. A one-man band is rarely the path that leads to success. When it does happen, it is usually short-lived and only in a limited part of the organisation. Collaboration is the sustainable way forwards.

4. A FALSE SENSE OF CONTROL

With an effective PM process supported by a PM tool (software product), you can access a lot of data. You know who is following the process, who performed well and who didn't cut the mark given the standardised and graded assessments that have been made. The assessments are also aggregated, so they can be linked to other data within the company, which the People Analytics team appreciates.

The system can easily provide a sense of control. But will it show us what we really want to know? Will documented measurement and grading of goal achievement and performance appraisals really give us more motivated employees and make them perform better? Probably not. Don't assume that control brings efficiency. Don't use data to gain control. Instead, reframe data as a way to help you to find connections that make you a more professional HR department that makes better decisions and provides better business advice. This is how you can work more proactively, with the long term perspective front of mind. It is this approach that works in the new era.

5. SLOW AND REACTIVE

The typical PM process is based on annual target planning. Goals are set at the company level and propagated down the hierarchy through the PM tool. Even though goals are followed up on, for example, every quarter, it is what happens at the beginning of the year that sets the goals for both teams and individuals. Often, the team and individual goals feel rather watered down and not relevant when they reach the individual level, especially when the initiatives come only from the top. This is why it's good to also involve the employees themselves when setting goals and initiatives.

If you work in a fast-moving, changing environment – as most of us do today – you will need to review and sometimes adjust your objectives throughout the year as the context and conditions change. In addition, if you only properly monitor staff performance against targets once a year, providing thorough feedback annually, it will be too late. The typical top-down process, where it takes a long time for any changes to reach all employees, becomes unsustainable. This approach is far too reactive to be suited to the new era.

It is extremely important to make this process more dynamic and to check in several times throughout the year. Make sure that there is an ongoing dialogue regarding delivery and performance instead of staring blindly at the results when it is too late to remedy them.

6. THE ADMINISTRATIVE BURDEN

The number of hours managers and employees spend on the typical annual end-of-year PM process is daunting. When you try to cram all the feedback and assessment into a single session, it becomes a cumbersome process. Moreover, if this is done at the end of the year, it comes at a time when many are struggling to tie up all the loose ends. The administrative burden of the traditional process – with detailed evaluations, ratings, assessments and boxes to check – is huge. Is it worth the effort? No!

7. THE DEFINITION OF PERFORMANCE

Finally, let's look again at the definition of performance. Many PM processes are based on assessing performance using the definition: *achieving a goal.* This goal could be related to revenue, number of active monthly users or other business-related metrics. This metric becomes what teams and individuals are evaluated by and recognised for. None of this encourages employee innovation or continuous improvement, or creates the conditions for a healthy culture. It does not reward curiosity, collaboration, development and learning, or behaviours that are in line with a culture where these are core values.

Performance Development

We believe in a broader definition of performance, where the focus is on both corporate and individual development. Performance and development go hand in hand, hence the name *Performance Development.* Instead of simply looking at what someone has achieved in the past, help your managers and their team members to think ahead, to see potential in the long term. To achieve this, you need to develop the right mindset within the organisation.

We believe that a growth mindset benefits both the individual and the company. We also believe that in the long run, intrinsic motivation is better than carrot and stick. With this foundation, you can challenge the old truths of traditional performance management and focus your time and energy on performance *and* development. In reality, they can't be separated.

When considering how to address this challenge, remember that the process must be designed so that it links to your culture and People Strategy. The underlying principles it is based on must be anchored with senior management: if they don't believe in them, they won't act on them and employees will pick up on this. All decisions should be based on your core values and then your beliefs must be defined (what is important to your company). This will provide a basis upon which to start creating a process that suits your organisation and your people.

Thus, traditional performance management was never an option at Spotify. Our 'game strategy' (the kind of company we want to be and the kind of players we want to have) is based on a values-driven and trust-based leadership. Real-time performance development, with weekly check-ins between managers and employees, is our motto. Looking in the rearview mirror once or twice a year doesn't make anyone happy, nor can you do much with a landscape you've already passed. It's much better to talk about where we are right now, what challenges we see ahead, how we will get to the next point, what is needed from all parties to get there, and what and how we will learn along the way. Constantly developing and taking advantage of one's curiosity, asking for help and getting help, allowing oneself to be challenged, daring to question – these are the key components of our performance development approach.

HOW WE STARTED WORKING WITH PERFORMANCE DEVELOPMENT

At Spotify, we call our overall development philosophy *Drive Your Development*. This is about empowering each individual to take control of their own development. No one should have to wait for their manager to initiate a development conversation or set a standard for their development. We believe that employees want to be empowered to take this responsibility and you don't get to where you want to be as an individual by putting the responsibility for your development in someone else's hands. However, it is important to point out that the manager has a great responsibility to support the employee's development – but the manager does not own it.

So we begin by asking – what does the employee need to grow and develop at Spotify? Next, we make sure that there is plenty of support in the form of learning opportunities, training and tools, and that the leaders support the process. Employees can schedule a development talk with their manager, choose what support they want and need, and decide which tools to use. We have a specific training package for employees to master this process, including what a growth mindset means, how to practise such a mindset, self-leadership, and our overall framework for how to drive their development at Spotify.

The four pillars of Spotify's Performance Development approach

1. CONTINUOUS PLANNING AND ONE-ON-ONE MEETINGS (1:1)

This is the first and most important pillar of performance development: everything is based on conducting meaningful conversations throughout the year. It is most relevant to talk about challenges, successes, needs for support, direction and so on in everyday life. Our internal data shows that 1:1 meetings increase overall engagement. There is no one standard template or agenda for these meetings but we support managers through training on how to hold a good 1:1, including checklists with examples of topics for discussion. The main focus is on nurturing high quality dialogue that is meaningful and helpful to both parties. We then encourage employees and managers to agree on the frequency, and the look and feel of their meetings.

2. DEVELOPMENT TALKS

Even if there is a continuous dialogue throughout the year, we recommend two development talks per year for a longer and more in-depth discussion. The purpose of these discussions is to match the company's needs with the employee's long-term development goals. The employee can schedule the meetings and likewise collect feedback from their colleagues. During the conversation, we take a look at the past, but focus mainly on the future and the potential.

When talking about performance and development, three areas are considered. The three criteria for success are called CAB: *Competence* (knowledge, skills and learning, building mastery), *Achievement* (whether you have reached your targets) and *Behaviour* (how you have reached your goals and lived our values). In our view, performance is not only about reaching goals, but also about how you achieved them: the professional growth journey and becoming a role model for others.

3. TALENT SNAPSHOT

The *Talent Snapshot* is a tool/model that helps our managers (zoom in and) map where individual team members are on their performance and development journey. It provides a (zoomed-out) snapshot of the team's overall strengths and weaknesses. It's not so much about exactly where each individual team member lands in the model, but rather about facilitating discussions and planning for development.

This 'snapshot' of a team when it comes to performance and development is then discussed in a workshop within the lead teams of the various units. The main purpose of the workshop is to obtain a clearer picture of the actions required to develop the individual, the team, the unit and the company as a whole. It also acts as a method to identify both obvious and hidden talents within the company and provides managers with a chance to share their experiences with each other.

4. COMPENSATION REVIEW

The compensation review process is a separate story, but since we pay for performance (competence, achievement and behaviour), it is linked to our performance development approach. When it's time for a compensation review, nothing should come as a surprise – employees should already know where they stand in terms of performance because they have regular weekly 1:1s with their manager and development talks twice a year!

Performance Development system support

As you have probably now understood, we do not use a Performance Management system. We are averse to using systems to check boxes, or to prove that performance goals have been set, approved and evaluated. Instead, we have a framework of principles and tools that aim to empower each individual employee to drive their own development. We focus on creating the conditions for good conversations and continuous follow-up and feedback.

As a result, our managers need to be adept at supporting both teams and individuals in their development. It's not HR's job to keep track of how many conversations are held and collect evidence that they've taken place. We focus on providing managers with the tools and knowledge they need to talk to employees in a way that really helps them develop.

We have a system to support note-taking and feedback gathering. Each team can use that system in whatever way they see fit. We try to make it easy and not an administrative burden or obligation to check off a list. We adapt and evolve our whole approach based on the feedback we get – staying true to our philosophy and to what is in line with our values and culture.

Growth is our mantra

Why do we work this way? Because we believe that a growth mindset, where learning and development are in focus, is really the best for our people. We are convinced that it is the right way to create high performing teams and individuals. This mindset, which we are now all gradually practising, is a true competitive advantage.

Spotify has a strong brand and a strong employer brand and many people want to work with us. Our substitute bench is full. At the time of writing, we have over 100,000 applicants every month. Once the candidate has signed the contract and become part of the band, we want them to sustainably perform at their best. That's why it's more important to us that we continually equip our people (we sometimes talk about 'dressing' them) so they're ready for any kind of weather. When they feel good, the organisation feels good. When they develop themselves, the company develops. This belief shapes our core: how we organise ourselves to achieve our goals, how we view leadership, how we define our values together and how we live, behave and make decisions in line with those values.

Diversity, Inclusion & Belonging – the journey to driving change and creating equity

Welcome to the chapter on one of the younger, albeit most complex and central, areas of HR today. We will start by contradicting ourselves. In the preface to the book, we wrote that the new era of HR is not about questioning everything you already know and can do. Now comes the metaphorical slap in the face: you will never be able to lead a fearless and forward-looking HR department or People Strategy if you don't get on board with Diversity, Inclusion, [Equity], Belonging (DIB). This topic means questioning everything we in HR do and know. The old playbook has to be torn up and thrown out to make room for new learning. The traditional way of working with diversity, inclusion and community needs to evolve – it can never again be an 'add-on' – it needs to be embedded in every part of HR and the business as a whole.

Anyone who wants to run a successful business today needs to understand that a DIB strategy is a business imperative. This is important to all companies and of utmost importance for global companies. DIB is the engine for making other HR measures work effectively. What's more, if you don't know what's trending in this area, that ignorance – and the reactivity that follows – can bring the whole business down. Frankly, if you don't get this part right, you can forget about modernising your HR approach.

Why work with DIB?

A company filled with a diversity of experiences – and the different perspectives that come with it – leads to a better environment for everyone, a place where everyone can feel included. No matter what kind of company you run, where you are in the world, or who your customers are, diversity is good for business and good for people. It drives innovation, makes you smarter, helps you understand your customers better and helps create real change in the world. Plus, it's hugely positive for the employer brand.

In a multinational company, many different understandings may exist of what diversity and inclusion are, as they are complex concepts. Diversity is the unique set of experiences, backgrounds and other human characteristics that exist within a group. When we talk about diversity, we also tend to focus primarily on individuals whose experiences have historically been underrepresented in a particular place. Therefore, we need to think about diversity from a 'local' perspective, in the sense of taking into account how geography, culture, religion – and also, for example, language and nationality – can affect someone's experience. For example, not all women have identical experiences. Intersectionality is still something that we do not take into account sufficiently in diversity work. There is much to learn and much we can improve on.

Differences between individuals in terms of, for example, gender, ethnicity, nationality, age or sexual orientation can contribute to increased diversity in a workplace or team. The extent to which this happens depends very much on the cultural norms of the country in question. There is no certainty that the diversity of a group is really expressed just because it exists. For this reason, we also work on inclusion and belonging – not just on diversity. Diversity is actually the easier part of this trinity.

All three parts or 'pillars' are necessary and you have to find the right balance between them. It is counterproductive if you only take care of one pillar. If you are aiming for greater diversity, you need to have systems and processes to manage effectively. In practice, it doesn't matter how much you increase diversity if you don't have a culture where employees feel understood, heard and seen – where they feel they belong. Without inclusion and belonging, diversity can exist only superficially.[6] Therefore, strive to find the right balance of focus and energy between these three pillars.

If the issue was easy, everyone would have solved it. It takes a lot more than what we do today to make the diversity mix work. The greater the differences in perspective and experience in your organisation, the more effort you need to put into ensuring that each individual's unique identity is valued and that everyone has the opportunity to perform at their best, together.

It is of course easier to be inclusive when everyone is more or less 'like everyone else'. Research shows that we are most comfortable with people who are similar to ourselves. Identifying and making room for differences is challenging and requires hard work. The effort that is required will make a difference to your people, your culture and your business as a whole.

The DIB journey

For anyone involved in HR, as well as for many leaders, diversity work has been a journey. It still is – the journey is ongoing and capricious. In many companies, the perception not too long ago was that diversity was something you should strive for, mainly to avoid negative perceptions. It would be ticked off the list and was mainly about being politically correct: a 'look-at-how-good-we-are' tool. Many also believed that just by dipping their toes in the diversity pond and by being careful not to make any ripples, their employer brand would be strengthened and they would attract the 'right' people, or at least not get any negative attention.

Looking back on this, we see the naivety of this attitude. Of course, this attitude can't be bestowed on everyone – even when the topic first took off. However, this is most probably how the journey started for most organisations. The subject was mostly about equality and equity and less about diversity. Even today, many companies only talk about gender equality – about men and women – and don't touch on all the other perspectives and aspects of diversity. Fortunately, attitudes have changed, and continue to change over time. We need the talents of underrepresented groups. A one-size-fits-all approach to attracting, recruiting and retaining employees no longer fits the bill. People are different and therefore, we need to be able to work in different ways to meet their different needs.

Working with diversity is central to attracting talent and therefore affects how we at Spotify work with all aspects from recruiting and hiring, compensation and benefits to development and advancement opportunities. Yes, it even affects how we design our offices. None of this is about complying with laws and regulations. Rather, it's common business sense in this new era. We are at a point where senior management should not only 'allow' the HR department to develop new DIB strategies but also actively encourage, welcome and proactively take part in this sphere.

The issue of diversity, inclusion and belonging can be overwhelming. In order to simplify, we will stick to describing three phases.

Phase 1: Laying the foundations

The first phase involves getting a number of key building blocks in place:

PURPOSE

Why are different perspectives important and why should we subject ourselves (the organisation) to a topic that could slow us down? This is a question that you should aim to answer for yourself, your people and your organisation, in order to form your first building block.

CHALLENGES

People with different backgrounds, experiences and needs, different ways of communicating and approaching things, can be like a speed bump that's slightly too high. It's frustrating, slows the organisation or team down and can initially feel unnecessary. Openly discuss the topic. Recognise that in the short term, diversity comes with resistance – and not just from those who think diversity is unnecessary, or an issue that you care about just because it's currently trending. Also discuss the long term, where diversity can be crucial to the innovative power of the group or the entire company and to the profitability of the business.

AWARENESS AND KNOWLEDGE

Ignorance, fear and unfamiliarity are often the main reasons why people avoid rethinking and re-learning. Invest time in informing, communicating and discussing your DIB strategy – and explain why you spend so much time and other resources on these topics. Clarity will help bring about understanding.

TARGETS AND MEASUREMENT

Set targets, measure, monitor and be open about how your DIB work is developing and what is being measured and implemented. Communication – let both those who think the diversity initiative is a good idea and those who think it is a bad idea have their say. Communicate, communicate, communicate: why, what, how, when. This is necessary both when you reach your goals and when you miss them.

EDUCATE

With education and knowledge building as the foundation of the work, change can happen faster than if there was no education. However, there are differences of opinion on whether 'bias training' works, i.e. whether it is really possible to learn to be less prejudiced and to fall into fewer thought traps, or whether perhaps such training has the opposite effect. Our experience is that if you don't do anything beyond educating, the awareness of prejudices increases, but no real change will ensue. By placing education at the foundation, change can be facilitated faster.

The building blocks – and possibly more on top – need to form the basis of your diversity efforts. You need to keep your business and profitability in mind at all times. Building that foundation is a multi-faceted effort and whilst you can begin from a variety of starting points, two areas are most common: demographic data and diversity in recruitment.

An organisation without a well thought-out DIB strategy or DIB ambitions often gets stuck in Phase 1 when analysing demographic data (e.g. focusing on gender and age). This is because they are simply responding to reporting regulations and the initial focus is on the numbers, where a clear picture of an 'appropriate' level of diversity in the workforce is painted. Be aware that whilst such an approach can create a foundation that can eventually make room for inclusive actions and helps leaders, employees, partners and customers understand their importance to the company, it will not create the inclusiveness and community that allows the culture to flourish.

Another aspect of building the foundation is to consider the way of thinking and working that characterises your organisational culture. Since you need to get the majority of employees on board in order to create any meaningful impact, you need to challenge those who are currently privileged. Often they will be unaware of their privilege. Again, a growth mindset is helpful: an underlying belief that an individual's abilities can be developed and improved. If you hire based on potential and competence rather than merit, you will inevitably have a greater representation of different back-grounds and therefore more perspectives among your employees. As Dr Carol Dweck explained in an interview, "The more a company embraces a growth mindset, the more welcome women and mi-norities will feel there."[7]

When adopting such a mindset, you need to align your recruit-ment process with your employee value proposition and other aspects of employer branding. A growth mindset should support hiring managers in making recruitment decisions. Every step of the process should be seen from a 'learn-grow-develop' perspective and with the aim of implementing best practices in DIB. Organisations that have a static or fixed mindset very rarely recruit from within, because they find it difficult to see that a person currently doing X could be taught or trained to do Y. They only accept candidates with a certain grade point average, from certain selected companies or from certain selected universities. They reject candidates for unsubstantiated reasons such as "I don't think that university has a good programme" or "they are not technical enough". The result is the creation of homogeneous teams that are unable to question and challenge each other from different perspectives. They miss out on qualified and motivated candidates who do not meet all their (unfounded) requirements in terms of education and experience.

A well-thought-out recruitment process starts by embedding a growth mindset in job ads. Although we adopted a growth mindset approach at Spotify, when we evaluated our recruitment process more rigorously, we still had plenty of work to do when it came to weeding out the more rigid language used in job ads. For example, a description could say "good knowledge of Excel", "expert" or "excellent communication skills". We had to be honest with ourselves and realise that we didn't always get it right, even though we knew that mindset had to be part of the process right from the start. Sometimes we were working under time pressure, which resulted in not ensuring that the mindset was visible in the ads. Here's a fact for you: one of the main reasons that underrepresented candidates don't apply for certain positions is because they don't consider their abilities in a field if they don't have the right qualifications on paper. Reports show that this behaviour is more common among women than men and that those who are well-represented (the majority) take a different approach when applying for jobs.[8] Those who are well-represented are more likely to see themselves as experts – perhaps because they have already been called so a number of times and have had this image confirmed. Studies show that a small change in language can result in twice as many women applying for a position and recruiters being able to fill a position eleven times faster (by having a better pool of candidates overall)! It is good to be aware that how you communicate about – let's say, qualifications – has consequences. Gender-neutral and inclusive language can make a big impact.

Other things to consider when making recruitment decisions are whether the candidate in question has unique qualities that are lacking in a team and could therefore increase the range of perspectives in the group. Or they may possess experiences and skills that can be applied to the job in a unique way, or demonstrate a growth mindset when examples from previous jobs/assignments are looked at.

If you haven't already done so, talk to management about the risks and opportunities of hiring outside the box, as well as the importance of a growth mindset. You can lay this foundation by finding a way to access and report data, adopting a dynamic mindset and developing your recruitment methods. Once these parts of the puzzle are in place, you can progress further. Phase 2 is about receiving support from senior leaders, and understanding the importance of creating role models.

An important final remark on Phase 1: When you want to move forwards, there is a great risk that you will choose to do what other companies have done before and try to keep the pace high in order to reap benefits as quickly as possible. We share a word of caution here: the process is not quick, because it involves a radical change in the behaviour not only of individuals but of the whole organisation, society and the world. It's likely that once you move past Phase 1, you realise the extent of the work that needs to be done. If you try to skip a step, you will not succeed in engaging everyone, nor will you take into account the uniqueness of your company. So take the time to identify what that uniqueness is. Building a strategy that is tailored to your organisation and your people is extremely powerful, but it takes time – not least because some of the decisions that need to be made will not be appreciated by everyone. However, with a multi-faceted, authentic approach and a strong commitment from senior management, anything is possible and you can go far.

Phase 2: Inclusion and belonging through role models

Good 'diversity statistics' have never been the ultimate goal for us at Spotify – it's easy to focus on the numbers, which only provide half the picture. Representation is certainly important – meaning that people from different backgrounds are included in decision-making groups, lead important initiatives, have a seat at every table (figuratively speaking) and are present at all levels of the company. However, imagine you get a 50/50 split in the management team, half men and half women, but the group listens more to the men than to the women. This can't be the end point of your work on representation. Companies that are good at DIB work are aware of this.

At Spotify, we believe who is visible in leadership roles matters. This affects the next generation of leaders – you can't be what you can't see. Role models are important. Make it a habit to ask yourselves: Who is not at the table? What perspectives are we missing when making business-critical decisions? This can cause frustration in the short term, as old structures may have to be redrawn and people may have to relinquish power.

Change comes at a price – but it is worth it. As a business, you simply can't keep up the pace of innovation required to survive without a true diversity of perspectives. These are organisation-wide goals and so company leaders need to support them – they need to adapt business processes and act as role models. They need to be the change.

Persuading management to understand this should be easy – at least in theory. We know today that organisations that take the issue of diversity and inclusion seriously are more financially successful. A report by McKinsey[9] shows a clear correlation between gender and ethnic diversity on the one hand, and profitability and value creation on the other. Studies have shown time and again that different experiences, cognitive diversity and constructive debate lead to more innovative products, systems and environments. However, many organisations are still struggling with the issue of diversity and have failed to clarify and make a business case. If you are one of these organisations, address the challenge or you will not make any real progress. This is the second phase of the journey.

Those of us in HR, with our knowledge of behavioural science, have a very important role here. We can help our organisations understand the importance of employees from different backgrounds who feel that their unique identities are welcomed and even sought after in the workplace. We know that engagement decreases when employees feel they have to adapt to fit in, and this in turn leads to lower performance.

More specifically, management needs to really understand how important employees' emotional well-being and their sense of belonging are to their everyday behaviour at work and their performance. For some employees, work is mostly something they do to get paid; for others, it's an identity. Either way, we will help them create space for themselves and a career that does not interfere with what is important to them on a personal level. Whether an employee sees you as a long-term or short-term career choice, make sure that during their time with you they feel valued, seen and understood. There is tremendous power in that. It also reduces the risk of 'imposter syndrome', i.e. employees who walk around feeling like an intruder or a fraud who could be 'exposed' at any time. It also reduces the risk of 'code switching', where employees adapt their way of talking and behaving to fit in. There is a big difference between the feeling of belonging and being part of the community and the feeling of being a visitor who might be asked to leave at any time. When your employees feel seen, valued and heard, it increases psychological safety in the workplace, which in turn creates better conditions for further work.

We are also aware that in our connected world it is increasingly important to find a balance between work and other parts of life. Stress is detrimental to performance in the long run. Even at Spotify, employees sometimes suffer from mental health issues or symptoms of exhaustion, or they are affected by major life changes. Therefore, we strive for a culture where people are encouraged and helped to take care of themselves and where there is an acceptance and openness to deal with such challenges honestly. We have a lot of work to do in this area, but we firmly believe that the mental health of employees is key. When they are well, they can do great things and be great colleagues and friends. In fact, this issue is so important to us that we built a separate pillar of our strategy around it. Our commitment to and focus on a 'stigma-free workplace' for mental health is an important part of our DIB work.

In order for management to act as role models, they must understand the importance of inclusion, of inclusive communication and behaviour that creates a sense of belonging. When people who have typically been underrepresented in the company feel like they belong, everyone wins. A strong and inclusive culture leads to greater job satisfaction, longer tenure, healthier employees and better performance.

We know that for a majority of people, a sense of belonging in the workplace is when their own values are aligned with the organisation's purpose, goals and core values and when they are valued for their individual contribution. A genuine sense of community and a sense of belonging is an effective way to reduce unwanted attrition.

Globalisation and modern communication technologies are creating conditions for greater cultural integration. The world is getting smaller and to some extent, cultural and social norms are being 'standardised'. The employees of a global company like Spotify, wherever they are in the world, should experience the same overall company culture, live by the same values and – above all – treat each other with respect.

Maintaining a vision at the global level and implementing it at the local level complicates the design and implementation of the DIB strategy. Different markets have different characteristics and unless you understand all the nuances of each market, it can be difficult to understand the role your brand and company plays in different countries/markets. Diversity and inclusion also mean different things in different parts of the world. Awareness of local cultures, experiences and communities is crucial to success.

One way of addressing global challenges related to, for example, gender, ethnicity, sexual orientation and disability is to provide employees with a mandate to contribute to diversity and inclusion in the way that is relevant to them. We have learned that each country makes its own unique DIB journey. That said, remember that we humans share more similarities than differences after all, so don't forget to recall and build on what you already do well, what is in place and working, and what unites you.

Phase 3: Leading the change

For a leader, the goal is to make employees feel wanted, valued, heard and seen. Feeling wanted is linked to diversity and inclusion.

Early on, we borrowed a quote from Vernā Myers: "*Diversity is being asked to the party, Inclusion is being asked to dance.*" We added our own: "*Belonging is when they play your song.*"

So far in this chapter, we have described a kind of *followership* rather than leadership. We have talked about a journey and stages, in order to demonstrate that it is impossible to just jump in and reach the destination. The whole approach must be rooted in the organisation and have the support of a majority of employees. There is no shame in followership – in not having made the entire DIB journey. Diversity, inclusion and belonging are moving targets and, as mentioned, an aspect we haven't worked actively with for very long. There are many new concepts, new knowledge is constantly emerging and some issues are trending because of activism. In practice, relatively few people are trained in this area, or have much experience of running a DIB policy in large organisations. However, these are issues that can attract very high levels of engagement, although being a minority yourself is not enough to master this complex and rapidly evolving field.

There are not many organisations – perhaps none at all – that have managed to show true leadership in this area. That is to say: anticipating challenges, driving diversity, equality, inclusion and belonging, and fundamentally changing the system. If it was easy to crack this 'everybody wants to join' code, most would have already done so.

We humans are good at taking mental shortcuts. Our ability to draw quick conclusions and see connections and patterns allows us to navigate the world quickly and with ease. When we only rely on our own past experiences or gut feelings when it comes to judging people, we get into trouble. This can cause us to draw hasty conclusions and see connections and patterns where none exist. Leaders in particular have to work hard not to fall into such traps or be influenced by their own unconscious biases. In fact, this is perhaps what separates good leadership from great leadership – especially when it comes to leading a team where not everyone thinks, feels and behaves in the same way.

Education and training to raise awareness and promote diversity and belonging can encourage a more open way of thinking and working where a commitment to inclusion, equality and diverse representation is a given. It is important that the programmes designed and offered are based on research on inclusive leadership. Four key aspects of inclusion to be considered and often referred to are: voice, objectivity, growth and belonging.

In order to lead the change, we firstly need to ensure that not just a small homogeneous group is invited to the party. Next, just as importantly, we need to affirm that everyone who has been invited feels welcome. The leader has a key role here. A candidate/employee feels wanted when they know that all aspects of their identity – what makes them unique and special – are valued, respected and wanted by the company. There is something special about feeling valued: it creates an experience and a bond like no other!

The manager must also ensure that the candidate/employee feels 'heard'. This feeling of being heard is largely linked to inclusion. However, those who want to feel heard must first identify their own voice. This requires a degree of personal commitment and self-confidence and needs to be achieved individually. This can be a bit of a Catch-22, because there is no real equality here – not everyone starts at the same starting line nor has the same conditions.

The organisation must also identify its own voice. You need to be clear and consistent in the way you talk to your employees, as well as in the way you communicate externally. There should be a personal approach that is in line with the culture that employees recognise and understand. A 'voice' is of course more than just words. It is actions, behaviours, activities, decisions. The voice of the organisation is also the voice of its people, so there must be room for them to be heard.

For the individual employee, 'finding their voice' is about identifying what makes them unique, and only the employee can know what that is. For the organisation, 'finding your voice' is less about words and more about creating a culture where all voices are heard. Those who express themselves need to feel safe and part of the ecosystem (as long as they express themselves in a respectful way).

Finally, the leader should strive to make every employee feel 'seen'. It is in this aspect that the wonderful feeling of belonging is located. Making someone feel seen is difficult, as it requires both employees and managers to show vulnerability. HR professionals must help enable a sense of belonging and the culture that makes it easy to show such courage.

There is tremendous power in an authentic DIB approach. The better you embed these three components – valued, heard and seen – in your People Strategy, the further you will be on your journey towards a more evolved culture. This is what Phase 3 – 'leading the change' – entails.

Organisations and leaders who want to be part of fundamental system change need to recognise that it will take time – a long time – to unravel hundreds of years of inequality. We can and should accelerate in some areas, but our approach needs to be holistic and ongoing. The vision needs to be shared by the majority and there needs to be a determination to keep working despite the discomfort and even resistance that change always brings.

At the time of writing this book, few – if any – organisations are in Phase 3 of this journey. However, more and more people are realising that DIB is an obvious way to work, rather than a trend or 'something we should look at more'. At Spotify, we are far from having cracked the code and we haven't always taken the right steps in our own DIB journey. We do truly believe that we are now creating change – in different industries, in different places and through technology – which creates new opportunities. We have always wanted to break systemic inequalities and find ways to unleash human creativity. We are convinced that we can challenge old truths and structures in more areas. Leading meaningful change of this kind requires bold, conscious action. It's about creating the culture we want through what we say and do, through our behaviour and through what we co-create. It's about leading the way and not waiting for others.

Spotify has the unique opportunity to do this through audio – after all, music and stories connect people and provide new insights. We believe that each organisation, by making its people feel valued, heard and seen, can lead the change in its own field and space.

SPOTIFY'S DIB JOURNEY

A number of years ago, during a town hall meeting which involved the entire company, we saw an excellent example of what happens when you are not fully equipped to discuss issues of diversity, inclusion and belonging in the workplace. At a point when a sensitive issue was raised (it was a name on a playlist that could be perceived as inappropriate and hurtful), due to technical problems, the question could not be heard clearly and there was an audio delay between New York and Stockholm, which created both uncertainty and thus nervous smiles. There was a fear of saying the wrong things or using the wrong words. The executive team therefore appeared to the audience to be slightly disrespectful and perhaps even a little nonchalant and did not seem to take the issue nearly as seriously as they should (and do). At that moment, it was bad, but in essence good, as the situation triggered much needed efforts. After this incident, the executive team spent almost a week discussing both the issue at hand and why it happened, and what could be done to ensure that something similar would not happen again. Through their behaviour and communication, they had managed to unintentionally hurt and provoke. We realised that we would need to acquire more knowledge so that we could feel more confident about these issues – not only for our own sake, but for the sake of all employees and the future success of the company.

As HR professionals, we decided to focus even more on diversity and make inclusion the most important parameter in our DIB work. It was important to get the numbers right, set targets and measure (diversity), but it was even more important to make it clear that our 'nirvana' was inclusion.

Correctly or incorrectly, during the first year we focused on raising awareness and knowledge. We chose to focus on two areas of improvement in the first step of our DIB journey: gender and age. We wanted to be able to measure, report, engage, debate and then showcase examples of what statisticians say is almost impossible to achieve: hiring at a high rate while making significant positive changes to under-represented groups. Our hope and ambition was then to apply the lessons learned to the next area of improvement in diversity: ethnicity.

We have learned a lot along the way. For example, DIB work must be embedded in everything the organisation does, not just in what HR does. Also, that change comes at a price – and that this is something that needs to be openly discussed. We're not talking about financial costs, but rather the fact that recruiting in uncharted waters makes processes slower. It is also harder to onboard people with different backgrounds, experiences and opinions than to bring in 'more of the same'.

If you make the same journey, you will probably feel that resistance too. For every person who takes a seat at the table, someone else has to vacate their seat. Why would someone with privilege and power want to give it up? Most people agree that diversity and inclusion are important – until it comes at a cost to them personally. Under such circumstances, it is easier to demand that your organisation or DIB/HR manager should fix the situation, whilst maintaining what was nice, warm and comfortable. This isn't possible. So again – be open that DIB has its price, but show that the price will be even higher in the long run if these issues are not addressed seriously.

SOME EXAMPLES OF THINGS WE HAVE LEARNED:

- Women generally perform worse than men when they are asked to stand up and solve an R&D problem on a whiteboard and they perform significantly better than most men if they sit down and solve the same task on paper.

- Creating a small DIB team and simultaneously stating that everyone in the HR team is responsible for this area can be confusing, even for the HR department. However, we believe that this is the best solution if the DIB work is to be something that really concerns everyone and is deeply embedded in the organisation as a whole. Be prepared that it will be difficult to understand your strategy in the beginning, even if you communicate it repeatedly.

- Spotify is fundamentally a Swedish company and it seems natural for us to believe that a sense of autonomy, mastery, relatedness and benevolence is motivating for all people, no matter where they are in the world. During the implementation of our Drive Your Development approach, we revealed unexpected cultural differences. Our design for Performance Development at Spotify is based on self-leadership and on dialogue, openness and transparency, as well as on the fact that most of our employees are highly motivated. Several of our underrepresented groups made it clear to us that we are not all equal in this (even though the philosophy behind our approach says otherwise), so we had to make adjustments. The playing field is not the same for everyone and everywhere. We have different backgrounds and baggage. A naive approach to this issue and an idea of equality can in practice stand in the way of diversity, inclusion and belonging – because we have built programmes and mechanisms based on the idea that everyone is equal.

- Since we believe in 'home-grown' talent and like to hire internally, we needed to take a closer look at how we had been promoting people. We saw that while we were getting better at hiring diversity, we also needed to get better at promoting diversity.

- Not daring to talk about ethnicity, skin colour and prejudice is not good. Only when we work on all aspects of diversity and inclusion can we work towards equity and create an inclusive culture, where all employees feel a real sense of belonging.

OUR JOURNEY IN THE FIELD OF MENTAL HEALTH

We are particularly proud of the work we have done to promote the mental health of our employees. As mentioned earlier, employees' emotional well-being and the relationships they have with colleagues, managers and others around them have a huge impact on their performance – how they prioritise, what risks they take, whether they ask for help, whether they support their colleagues, how creative they are able to be, and so on. This is something that we in HR have been thinking about for a long time. When we made the decision that mental health would be one of the pillars of the DIB strategy, surprisingly, the DIB specialists were very hesitant about the idea.

This was several years ago and at the time, the topic was somewhat of a blank slate. We knew that we wanted to work to remove the stigma associated with mental illness and support our employees in a variety of ways when it came to their mental health and wellbeing. How we would tackle this was not defined. However, we realised early on that it would not be possible to live up to our ambitions if someone were to run this work 'alongside' other tasks – as an additional project. We therefore created a role entirely focused on global mental health at Spotify and called it Heart & Soul.

It was not necessarily obvious that this role would be part of the DIB team. However, we felt that mental health is an important part of creating a sense of belonging in the workplace. We realised that it was important to create a culture where 'everyone's brain could fit' and where different needs and different ways of feeling could contribute to diversity. We also realised early on that this could not purely be an HR initiative. We wanted people to understand and be able to relate to the work being undertaken and therefore, it had to be driven by employees.

The vision, strategy and framework came from HR, but in order to ensure real change, we realised that the actual work, and the will to change, needed to be largely driven by employees. Huge local differences also exist when it comes to mental health, especially in terms of how taboo the subject is. We realised that we needed to involve committed employees locally in every office in the world in order to achieve success. We needed help from people who could talk about mental health in a way that was in line with our strategy and approach but who also worked in their particular part of the world (with the necessary training, if required, of course). Local connections and courageous, generous staff and leaders who share their stories and experiences have been extremely important. For these reasons, we decided from the start that the Heart & Soul strategy would be set by the HR department and driven by a team of ambassadors supported by a dedicated resource with responsibility for Heart & Soul. Employees could apply to join the team and soon we had a group of fifteen people from different parts of the world.

In order to understand what kind of mental health initiatives employees wanted to see, we held eight focus group meetings, in different locations around the world, including a total of 800 participants. This gave us a wealth of insights. The data we collected, combined with external data on mental health trends and insights from our health insurance plans, helped us set a vision and strategy: our goal is to create a safe, stigma-free environment where there is acceptance, support and knowledge of mental health and illness. We want to create a culture where we take care of ourselves and each other and a place where employees can be themselves and where they feel like they belong, no matter what they're going through and what's going on inside.

Our mental health strategy is based on the following three elements:

1. Raising awareness and building knowledge.
2. Making it easier for employees to take care of themselves and to get professional support.
3. Normalising conversations about mental health to reduce stigma.

We believe that all these elements must be prioritised in order for the whole picture to be effective.

Among the first initiatives we launched was Spotify's self-care platform, our Self-Care Hub, which included free access to a meditation app. To coincide with the launch, we held a week of internal seminars on topics such as depression, addiction and how to take care of your emotional well-being. In the first year, our focus was on raising awareness of the work of the Heart & Soul Ambassadors and increasing staff knowledge of mental health and illness. We wanted to raise the general level of knowledge in the organisation as a whole.

The team of ambassadors grew from 15 to 50 people from 20 different offices – all with the mandate and budget to run their own initiatives that suited their local conditions. These ambassadors have played a very important role in helping us to understand the local reality and in driving the Heart & Soul work locally. They embraced the concepts and ran them so well that they have created something truly amazing.

Since our ambassadors play such an important role, we train them in Mental Health First Aid (MHFA), enabling them to provide a form of 'first aid' to employees who are unwell. We ensure they have enough knowledge to support those who reach out and ask for help. They also have enough knowledge to decide when they need to hand over to external expertise. The ambassadors are in a vulnerable position, so we make sure they have the tools they need if a conversation becomes difficult and offer them unlimited free psychological counselling.

We take the opportunity to anchor initiatives on the annual international World Mental Health Day on 10th October each year. By picking this date, we get more attention and shine an even brighter light on mental health issues. Most activities on this day are local and organised by our Heart & Soul Ambassadors. So far, meditation sessions and inspirational talks and workshops (from artists who have shown their work and also talked about their own difficulties, for example) have taken place. We also share our own stories with each other, in panel discussions, at breakfast meetings or anonymously.

These initiatives confirm our belief that just by talking more about mental health and illness, we can go a long way. We also want to make information and resources available so that everyone can take better care of themselves and others. This involves both resources for self-care and access to professional help.

Choosing different themes each year has allowed us to delve deeper into a particular issue. For example, the theme 'Every Day is a Mental Health Day' helped raise awareness that mental health is something you need to work on every day. There are lots of different ways to enable support of mental wellbeing. The aim here was to show our employees that it is okay to feel how they feel. Taking a day off from time to time to take care of yourself and your mental health (the concept of 'taking a mental health day') is a positive thing.

SUPPORT – ANYWHERE, ANYTIME AND FOR ANYONE

When COVID-19 hit, from a mental health perspective, we were ready to provide support. Since mental health had already been a focus at Spotify for over a year before the pandemic started, the ambassadors were able to quickly mobilise resources to support employees when working from home. They also focused on how leaders could support and check in with their teams when everyone was working from home. The ambassador team transitioned their solutions to virtual offerings and created opportunities for employees to interact with each other through Heart & Soul Connect, which aimed to help employees connect with their colleagues on issues that could increase their wellbeing and resilience.

We believe in creating an environment where our feelings are validated, where it's acceptable to feel vulnerable and overwhelmed at times and where it's okay to think life is tough. This environment helps us all deal with anxiety. We can talk more openly about stress and worry and about common symptoms. It also makes it easier to recognise our own triggers and those of others. It allows us to be proactive and act before things get worse.

The world has changed dramatically and our collective attention has been fragmented – we are thrown from one disaster or nightmare situation to the next. As a consequence, according to data from around the world, we have seen a significant increase in anxiety and depression. There are also concerns about a pending mental health pandemic, with an exponential increase in addiction and suicide.

At any moment, we all can experience crises, like the loss of a loved one, or other forms of grief. Circumstances in life can lead us to feel overwhelmed or guilty (which most parents or team leaders will recognise). Individuals may find themselves falling back into mental illness, often combined with a sense of loneliness and isolation. Someone else may see, or experience, the injustice faced by so many historically marginalised or underrepresented members in society (or in the workforce), which increases their risk of mental illness and causes deep wounds. There are lots and lots of reasons why we believe the investment in Heart & Soul is worth every cent – and why we see it as a natural part of DIB's work, not just for those directly affected by mental illness. It is important that mental health is on the strategic HR agenda in these uncertain times (read: always). We believe in our global approach: more knowledge, more support and more conversations.

EQUALITY AND MENTAL HEALTH

There is no universal solution when it comes to mental health. Circumstances such as the country we are born in and where we grew up and live can affect our mental health status. In short, not everyone is equally likely to suffer from mental health problems. Underrepresented groups are more likely to suffer due to issues such as racism, homophobia, transphobia, sexism and hatred, which can leave permanent emotional scars. When designing the Heart & Soul programmes, we made sure to take such experiences into account. We have developed special programmes for the historically marginalised or underrepresented band members and for employees who are transgender or non-binary, to name just a few groups.

COURAGE AND VULNERABILITY

The Heart & Soul team works to encourage more people to show their vulnerability. We believe that openness is healing – it's important to talk about how we feel for real, not just in a general and superficial way. We know that many people suffer in silence and feel ashamed. Through being open about our experiences, we realise that we are not alone, that help is available and that even if we live with a mental illness, we can still live a good life.

We believe that in order to balance the stress of modern society and the modern workplace, each individual needs to take care of their mental health. We also believe that this balance can look different for different individuals.

SHARING IS CARING

We are happy to tell you about our DIB work – and not only about what worked well, but also about internal resistance, painful mistakes and other difficulties. We do this because we believe that other organisations, other HR teams and other leaders can learn from our journey and do better and move forwards faster than we could. For example, in our eagerness to involve employees, fearing that those who wanted to contribute could feel excluded, we spent some time spinning in circles, rather than taking real steps forwards in our DIB work. This led to starting several different initiatives in different parts of the organisation at the same time as larger comprehensive and strategic initiatives, which in effect resulted in no direct forwards movement. When we decided to make fewer, targeted and limited efforts, we achieved measurable results.

Leadership
– shaping great leadership at Spotify

Everything you've read in this book so far involves some aspects of leadership. Both informal and formal leadership is a part of everything we do and experience in our daily work lives. Leadership touches pretty much all levels and aspects of work in an organisation and that's why we believe that it's one of the most impactful levers we can pull when building a great business. Great leadership means leaders and managers who dare to lead and push boundaries, who lead with trust and whose mindset and behaviours will support the employee value proposition. They will encourage continuous learning and understand the value of a culture where the employees feel that they can contribute, influence, belong and ultimately be their best selves, in order to do their best work.

In this era, leaders need to manage a high pace of change and adapt their leadership to the current needs of the business and individuals without losing the visionary, long-term perspective. It's not an easy task and copy-and-paste solutions that fit every context don't exist. The first and most important prerequisite for great leadership is self-awareness. Know thyself first! Leaders who are aware of their own motivational factors, communication style, strengths, weaknesses and triggers will have a better understanding of how to manage themselves and better understand how their actions affect others. This will help them to make the right decisions in order to deliver value to the business, individual employees and teams.

In many ways, leadership is a balancing act. Employees and their aspirations, motivations, skills and abilities are on one side of the scales and the business opportunities, goals and purpose of the organisation on the other. A leader's task is to find the balance between the two sides. Too much emphasis on one will tip the scales, creating instability and upsetting the balance. Leadership in the 21st century is about supporting *and* pushing, it's about care *and* accountability. It's never one or the other, it's not either or. It's *both and.*

For leaders to be able to develop and focus on *both and*, they need to utilise their HR team's expertise in behavioural science and organisational theory and practice. This will set them up to ensure healthy growth for both the organisation and the people in it.

Droves of books have been written on leadership and management and there are many enlightening and interesting theories and methods on the subject. Allegedly, Kurt Lewin, the German-American psychologist, said "Nothing is as practical as a good theory" and at Spotify we share this sentiment. However, our ambition with this book is not to create another theory or model around leadership, but rather to share our experiences and give our point of view on what great leadership can be.

Manager *and* Leader

Sometimes, a distinction is made between being a *manager* or a *leader*, where being called a leader is more desirable. To us, this is a misplaced and unnecessary distinction and discussion, since we believe that the two ideas go hand in hand. A manager has a formal mandate and decision making power and is expected to *manage* a group of employees. A leader, on the other hand, inspires and *leads* through vision and direction. People will follow a leader because they *want to*, not because they have to.

To lead a team or a company, you need to both manage and lead. These two roles are not at odds with each other, but rather two sides of the same coin. The required balance of leader and manager qualities varies depending on the situation, the role, where the team or individual is within their development journey, and much more. To separate being a leader and a manager is the equivalent of separating the body and soul – we can't live our lives without having both. In a complex environment, a leader must understand all the intricacies of today's world of work, and business and work holistically. This means they must have the broad business acumen to be able to navigate the stormy waters of an organisation in controlled chaos, to guide their team and make the right decisions.

Leading a company and managing people is about organising work efficiently, inspiring and leading the way. Hence, at Spotify, we look for strong managerial qualities in our leaders, in addition to the ability and willingness to lead and inspire. When we talk about managers and leaders, we use the words interchangeably, knowing that the need for one will be greater than the other in specific situations.

Leadership in a distributed and global organisation

Having a distributed team has a significant impact on leadership. It's one thing to have all your team members in the same office, leading them in person. It's a different ballgame entirely when the members of one team are distributed over many locations in different time zones and most likely with different cultures too.

Many organisations have employees who are somewhat dispersed, it may be in different offices, in multiple cities, or countries. Nowadays, as we see many companies offering hybrid working arrangements or even fully remote options, where employees can work from home part of the week or full-time, it's important to consider how this affects leadership. Many researchers, HR practitioners and leaders are debating the topic. We believe that each organisation must decide on what's right given their specific business context, culture, and ability to attract employees and/or find the right competencies.

It doesn't matter whether the members of a team are in the same office, spread across several continents, in different local offices, home offices, or co-working spaces – the foundations and goals of great leadership are the same. Clarity on goals and priorities and on what kind of leadership the organisation expects will help to guide leaders, whatever their particular circumstances are. However, it should be noted that managing a distributed team is likely to require a greater emphasis on some areas, especially when time zone differences and physical distance are at play.

From our experience, these are some of the most important considerations in need of extra attention when leading distributed teams, the 7 C's:

1. CLARITY AND COMMUNICATION

A leader who doesn't meet their team members in person during the work week will find it harder to know what they do. This situation requires a shift from valuing *tasks* to looking at *results*. It may be more difficult, but – from our point of view – it's a healthy move away from valuing the fact that you can see that a team member is busy, to valuing the outcomes and results that they are producing – which is really what we are after! Setting a clear direction, clear goals and expectations becomes very important in leading distributed teams and achieving the outcomes we expect. The leader should consider how to communicate clearly, including what and how much information they should share and what communication channels they should use. This is especially important when the information can't be shared simultaneously due to different time zones and varying working hours.

2. COMMUNITY AND CONNECTION

Belonging and a feeling of inclusion may be hindered when working in hybrid or fully distributed teams. Leaders therefore have a greater responsibility to support their team by creating a sense of community. They need to make a concerted effort to help their team members connect with one another and support them in building deeper levels of trust and stronger relationships. Leaders do well to remember that bonds are not created by discussing the details of a project, but rather by finding personal connections that demonstrate care and empathy, and essentially creating moments where bonding can take place. These moments help make up for the clues and cues that are easily missed when the team doesn't meet in-person. Deliberately creating spaces and places to meet and connect is really important.

3. COLLABORATION AND COMPASSION

One of the biggest challenges faced when working with distributed teams is collaboration. When managing a distributed team, leaders need to be more intentional when it comes to enabling teamwork and understanding what forms of collaboration work best for the team. They should be clear on what specific pieces of work need to be done synchronously (in the room, or online) and what types of work can be done asynchronously. For team members who are not used to collaborating in a distributed manner and who might prefer group work done in-person, it's of extra importance for the leader to enable and support the shift thoughtfully.

Another important aspect to make collaboration in distributed teams work well is to cultivate a sense of compassion. Compassion is the ability to understand the emotional state of another person (and of oneself). Compassion enables connection. To be compassionate is to show respect, to care and to encourage. If leaders can build this into their teams, collaboration and trust will flourish.

4. CREATIVITY

When there's a strong sense of belonging based on sincere communication, collaboration and trust within a team, creativity can bloom. At Spotify, we rely on innovation to stay ahead of the curve – it's critical to our survival – so we're committed to creating opportunities for our people to be creative. When everyone is in the same place, it's easier to soundboard and build on each other's ideas, whether that's in front of a whiteboard, at the coffee machine, at the water cooler, or on the way to or from the office. The planned and the unstructured ideation that comes from serendipitous encounters is equally as important to creativity. However, when everyone, or the majority, are working in different places and at different times of the day, ideation sessions can naturally become more difficult.

As HR professionals at Spotify, we've made a conscious effort to create a culture where the spark of creativity can be found even when employees are not in the same place. Our advice is to give leaders the necessary tools to support creativity and reflection, whether it's a virtual office space where employees can meet their colleagues, or digital whiteboards for brainstorming, methods for brainwriting, or other collaborative spaces and tools designed for co-creation. That said, there are times when it is better to meet – for example, when working as a team on planning, strategy and innovation. During these occasions, a physical office space plays an important role.

5. CULTURE

Saying that culture plays an important role in creating an environment where our employees feel included and invested is like kicking at an open door. Nonetheless, it is true – and even more so in a global and distributed setting. We have seen that it helps immensely to offer clear guidance in company culture and values so that everyone has the same sense of direction regarding how to treat one another and what the expectations are in terms of ways of working.

Since culture is so important to the sense of community and connection, which in turn builds engagement and retention, every leader should consider how to highlight and make the culture more tangible to their team and how to make the desired culture something that is present in everyday work life. One way to do this as leaders is by being clear and reminding everyone of the company's vision, mission and goals. Weaving this into team meetings, planning meetings and other forums is a tactic to help these values resonate. Another powerful (and the most important) tool a leader should use is to be a role model – to act in line with company values and highlight the organisation's cultural assets.

In reality, leaders should do all this and much more in order to make the culture visible and tangible. A thriving culture is essential for the well-being of individual employees and the wider teams. It will help them understand not just their job, but the context they are in, to be able to influence, develop and perform at their best.

In the next chapter, we'll look more closely at how you work strategically with your company culture to strengthen the sense of community and belonging.

What should great leadership look like in your context?

Given your unique blend of industry, type of business, product/service, labour market condition, employees, etc., the recipe for great leadership will differ in parts from that of other companies. To create a recipe, start by making a list of the most important components of leadership at your organisation. Make sure to base the list on your values and your context. Involve relevant people from the organisation in order to get diverse perspectives and a better outcome.

Once you have collected all the components of great leadership and worked them through to cover what is essential for leaders in your organisation, you will have a draft of your principles for great leadership. Communicate these principles to leaders, giving them the opportunity to digest them well – explain what they mean, train leaders on how to live by them and make the basic expectations regarding these principles clear. Embed the principles in your processes; specifically, in how you hire, assess, compensate and promote leaders. Then, support each leader on their personal and professional leadership growth journey. This way, both the individual and the organisation will continue to develop.

Only you can decide what kind of leadership is needed to create a successful organisation where all your employees can do their best, learn, develop and thrive. There is an abundance of research on the characteristics of great leadership; however, leadership must still be adapted to the culture of each organisation.

When talking about great leadership at Spotify, we always come back to our list of guiding principles, which we have distilled into what we call the *Manager Manifesto*.

FROM THE LEADERSHIP CRITERIA TO THE MANAGER MANIFESTO

– A continuous journey

THE LEADERSHIP CRITERIA

When we could still count our bandmates in hundreds and not thousands, we saw a need to create our own leadership principles. We already had clear values and a vivid culture to guide us along the way, yet we hadn't defined what a great leader at Spotify should be and do. We did, however, have a need to ingrain a common leadership approach in several processes from hiring and training, to assessing performance, compensating and promoting.

As we set out to create our leadership principles, it was important that we didn't only rely on knowledge about great leadership in general and we wanted to ask our leaders and employees what they had observed in great leaders at Spotify in practice.

First off, during one of our manager strategy gatherings, which was attended by sixty of our most senior managers, we collected stories about what a great leader at Spotify does, how they act and what the results of their behaviours are.

The next step was to gather stories, experiences and opinions from our band members on what constitutes great leadership in our context. We asked them to provide examples of Spotify leaders at their best through a global survey and local focus group discussions. We made sure to collect input from all parts of the organisation.

We considered both the past and the future as we were keen to build on what we were already doing well and think about what it would take for us to be successful in the long term. The result was the *Spotify Leadership*

Criteria. Initially, we had five criteria. After a few years, as the company grew, so did the Leadership Criteria, and we created a second iteration. Our *Leadership Criteria* expanded into seven criteria with a long list of behaviours and skills connected to each criterion.

MAKING OF THE MANAGER MANIFESTO

Change is a normal state for us and we continuously adjust and adapt our ways of working to reflect this. Therefore, after we'd had our second iteration of the Leadership Criteria in place for a few years, we decided to revisit and simplify them. This list that was supposed to be used as a guide had become too wordy and complicated and was difficult for managers to remember, so we asked ourselves how we could simplify things without losing the essence. Here's what we learned and did.

First, *less is more* – keep it simple. In a fast-growing organisation, during continuous change, managers have a lot on their plate running a business, delivering results and leading employees. Most often, they need to move quickly from theoretical knowledge to practical action in all aspects of their leadership.

Hence, we decided to create vital and simple leadership criteria. The goal was to stick to around three or four criteria, which would make them easy to remember and act on, resulting in greater impact.

We also concluded that we should use a storytelling approach to provide more context, rather than listing competencies and behaviours. Again, we wanted our managers to carry the criteria with them in their leadership on a day-to-day basis, and stories are more engaging and easier to remember and act on.

There was also a need to link our new leadership criteria to our *Band Manifesto*. The Band Manifesto is our mission statement of the *Spotify Way* – a way to give a clear and common understanding of our culture, our values, and essentially defining what it means to be a Spotifier.

When making a new version of our leadership criteria, we vetted them internally with a selection of internal stakeholders.

Finally, we turned our new leadership criteria into a *Manager Manifesto*, which kept the same underlying values as before. The Manager Manifesto sets expectations on what we think is the dynamo of the vehicle named Spotify. By being clear on what we expect, how we recruit, develop, evaluate and sometimes even deploy managers at Spotify, we hope that all those who sign up for a managerial role know that this is not a title or a privilege – it is a profession in itself.

Here it is – the Manager Manifesto – the four beliefs of great leadership at Spotify and the stories that make them come alive:

THE SPOTIFY MANAGER MANIFESTO

We believe:

- In purpose-driven leadership.
- In managers who have the willingness and courage to lead.
- In managers who build and run healthy teams.
- That leadership is a group sport.

We believe in purpose-driven leadership

In our managers, we look for strong managerial skills as well as the ability and desire to be a true leader. We expect managers to inspire and drive vision – that is how our teams are motivated to willingly engage and contribute to our purpose.

Managers lead by example, always taking into consideration our company values and mission. Growth is our mantra and our managers are right on the front lines, cultivating a growth mindset and encouraging innovation within their teams. Managers empower growth by providing frequent feedback and coaching to unlock band members' potential and opportunities to learn. In short, leadership at Spotify means guiding great teams that grow the business as well as growing themselves.

**We believe in managers who have
the willingness and courage to lead**

Managing at Spotify isn't for the faint of heart. Here, controlled chaos is the norm. Managers need to be authentic, strong and open to vulnerability in order to instil trust and stability whilst surrounded by constant change. Managers at Spotify make an active choice to lead and grow the business and fellow band members.

Our managers bring clarity to their teams, translating complexity into actionable insights and removing any roadblocks. They embrace polarities, identifying issues not as either/or but both/and. Most importantly, they stay flexible – able to adjust quickly to new circumstances, prioritising ruthlessly for the right impact.

Managers are courageous enough to take risks. They dare to let go of control and empower autonomy (within guardrails, of course). In order to enable their team to make informed decisions, managers share information transparently. Most importantly, they give their teams the freedom to fail, recognising that it's an inevitable outcome when pursuing innovation.

That doesn't mean they don't assume accountability or hold their teams accountable to fulfil their goals. Managers are courageous enough to set clear expectations and deliver honest feedback so as to drive results.

We believe in managers who build and run healthy teams

When it comes to team building, we strongly believe that a diversity of experience, perspectives and backgrounds leads to a better working environment for everyone and, subsequently, better business outcomes. Inclusive teams are more innovative and effective, promoting creativity and unique thinking.

Spotify leaders are instrumental in ensuring our everyday reality reflects those values. They guarantee all voices are heard and know how to navigate divergent opinions within their team. They lead with empathy and act to minimise politics. They promote clear and sincere communication, focused on building trust in the team. They build an inclusive culture where everyone feels empowered to be themselves, where everyone feels like they belong.

At Spotify, things move fast – speed is everything. So managers need to be resilient and know how to cultivate a sustainable mindset for their team and working environment.

We believe that leadership is a group sport

Working fast means acting with consent, not consensus. Even if the majority can't come to an agreement, it's important to keep moving, take a chance and execute. A good manager encourages debate and discussion, acknowledging that innovation can come from any direction. Listening is everything.

Our managers know that it is ideas, not bureaucracy, that drives us. We believe that leadership takes place alongside teams and we truly believe leadership is a group sport. We're all in it together – we don't have space for entitled egos.

By operating with the business' best interests at heart, managers recognise that the talent they nurture and grow in their teams doesn't belong to them – it's Spotify's. We get things done by collaborating across teams, sharing talent, prioritising mutual long-term goals and always operating in the interest of the greater good.

HOW WE MAKE THE MANAGER MANIFESTO COME ALIVE

Our Manager Manifesto is embedded in our daily work and is part of our ways of working and our processes. For example, we use it when we assess performance and when we reward our leaders. Conscious application in everyday life is what has made an impact (not just a new leadership pro-gramme, as that would not be enough and can so easily become a fad). Does this mean that all our managers live up to our entire manifesto all the time? No, it doesn't, and we're not looking for superhumans. We believe in learning, developing and growing even among our managers. However, if our managers have the four criteria from our Manager Manifesto in the back of their minds and they let them guide their day-to-day decisions, they are on the right track.

Culture & Values
– culture as a strategy

If you already are a values- and purpose-driven organisation (or are well on your way to becoming one), demonstrating great trust in your employees and consistently putting them first – congratulations! Most organisations don't have this situation and there's much work to be done. We've spoken many times in this book about how important culture is to all aspects of HR and how it must be reflected in everything you do. In this final chapter of the second part, we will demonstrate the link between culture and strategic, global HR and provide a picture of what our own 'culture journey' has looked like.

A major challenge in working with culture and values is that the people you are creating them for, i.e. your employees, will not always agree with your approach, understand what you are doing and why, or grasp how complex the work is. Your managers or your CEO won't always understand the work (sometimes visible, sometimes invisible) that underpins this intricate strategy either. Everyone seems to believe they know what a company culture is and many view themselves as experts on how to get it right.

Culture plays a huge role in every aspect of your HR work – strategic, operational and tactical. The same is true for the rest of the business as well. We spoke earlier about how a 'strong' culture is not necessarily the right culture. The 'right' culture is one that has grown from your roots, your business and your people. When challenging old truths, culture is the anchor. You need to be aware of this anchor and communicate about it in a way that causes your employees to care. In this new era, you will probably throw out processes that require a lot of administration and you will definitely try new things. If you have nothing to hold on to, you will feel fragmented and lost.

By defining your culture, you bring your people together, empowering them to focus and collaborate, and aiding the creation of an environment that is productive for the business and for each individual. Culture is what holds the organisation together – it allows your employees to feel a sense of belonging and community and to perform at their best, marching at the same pace, in the same direction, at the same time.

Culture is really only properly tested in adversity. Consider the notion – especially when you hear (as you will almost daily) about one company doing this and another doing that – where the employees have this experience, where they express themselves this way, where this benefit exists, and so on. When you start to follow suit, you will find yourself deviating from your strategy, your culture and your 'game plan' in the name of short-term quick fixes. The minute you dip your toe into this pool, you will have begun an unpleasant 'culture erosion' journey.

Identifying and defining your culture

Who are you and what drives you? Your culture is shaped by your purpose or mission, your people, your leadership style, your workplace and your way of working. It's underpinned by your values, which act as a foundation. Your culture is about how you want the company as a whole – and each individual – to behave. It's all the behaviours you see in your employees, how you make decisions, and all the norms and invisible rules that apply internally. Culture can be cultivated and shaped, but never fully controlled. You can have ambitions for the culture and set guidelines based on your values. This cannot be forced, it is a process that takes time.

It is likely that you will need to define your culture more clearly as you evolve. Your culture will evolve over time because it is the sum of your people. It *should* evolve – that change is healthy. Culture can never be completely erased and recreated from scratch, so working on it requires thought. Don't let your history stand in the way of the culture you want to create here and now. Don't be discouraged if you hear comments like "our culture was much stronger and better back then". Who really decides what 'stronger' and 'better' means? Clinging to the past has also never helped anyone succeed in the future.

Your values

Regarding values (core values) and culture: involve your employees. Make sure you have them by your side and that there is an authenticity or genuineness in what you do. Work on the values throughout the employee journey.

Swedes are famous for always wanting to reach a consensus and even though Spotify was founded in Sweden and definitely has aspects of Swedish culture in its roots, we talk more about *consent*. We accept that it's impossible to get 100% consensus, but we also champion the concept of giving every employee a voice and listening carefully to what they say. What is important to them? What are their values? What culture do they want at Spotify?

Once you have found a 'constant', or a red thread, you will not have to seek consensus for every decision. If there is a dialogue during the process of defining your values and you are open and transparent, trust will increase. If everything that happens in the organisation is clear to everyone, can be discussed by everyone and questioned by everyone – then you have a solid foundation to build on.

Such transparency and trust also creates a specific type of leadership. In a culture where everyone receives information at the same time, openly and transparently, the information is no longer only at the top level and therefore cannot be used as a means of power. Allowing smart people to get the same information at the same time from the same source makes it possible for an organisation to go all in, when the time is right. Or, as we say: *When we go, we go hard.*

As you begin your culture and values journey, you need to find the optimal way to communicate with and engage employees and create an environment where everyone feels safe to discuss, comment and even criticise. Employees must be able to find a way to relate to the culture. You must also have regular, formal communication platforms to check and change the culture.

Culture as a strategy

The internationally renowned management consultant Peter Drucker once observed that "culture eats strategy for breakfast."[10] This was a recognition of the importance of corporate culture to an organisation. However, just because culture is important, it does not mean that strategy is unimportant. Perhaps in this era we should instead ask – couldn't culture and strategy have breakfast together?

In the new era of HR, culture and strategy are intimately linked, they are interdependent. At Spotify, it has never been either/or. Culture should support strategy and strategy should support culture. One cannot flourish without the other.

We will now say a few words about the elements of a People Strategy that should go hand in hand to shape a culture. As you will notice, we have written more in depth about almost all these elements in their own dedicated chapters. See this as a way of tying them all together, and providing a summary (or repetition, if you like).

1. ATTRACTING AND RECRUITING TALENT

Yes, of course, recruitment and culture must fit like a glove. Flexibility must, however, also exist. The hand will grow and eventually need a bigger glove. Don't rush your recruitment strategy and start plugging all the holes right away. It's better to play it cool, look up and try to see the big picture, i.e. consider what culture and company you are trying to create and develop. It's like planning an important, long-distance trip by imagining that you have arrived at your destination – and then going back to the starting point. Write down all the different stops along the way and the things you need to do to get there. We call it the Harvard Business Review (HBR) method. You write the article that you imagine being published in a future issue of HBR, reporting that you've reached your nirvana (describing what that is), and detailing what you needed to do to get there – including the price of taking shortcuts.

Your employer branding strategy will be central to this work right from the start. It's never too late to adjust or adapt, of course, but most truly successful companies have a very clear picture of their employee value proposition (EVP) and how they wish to present it. Your EVP should be able to carry your culture and describe what's unique about it. It should be a reason for people to choose you (or not choose you). Don't forget that *when everything is 'wildly important', nothing is very important.* Stick to what you have, communicate, repeat and remind everyone what it is. Make sure it is actually true.

You cannot be attractive to the talent of the future if you are not attractive to the talent you have today. The essence is attracting and retaining the right people. We remind you again: engage in open and transparent (and frequent) communication with your employees. If done successfully, they will act as the ambassadors you want and need, and their stories about who you are will be genuine and meaningful. *This means that everything you do, everything you don't do and everything in between affects how you will be seen and how attractive you are.*

2. RETAINING TALENT

Culture attracts when you validate that you're the one telling your story, so that the right people come to you for the right reasons – not because of what others have decided are the characteristics of your brand or what your EVP is.

In many ways, attracting the right people is easier than keeping them. We've all heard and perhaps believed that "people join organisations and leave managers", meaning that people who leave don't do so because they want to get away from the organisation they work for – they leave a manager they don't want to work for. However, in any organisation with more than a handful of people, there is more than one manager, and many different roles. If you want to get away from a particular person – why leave and start all over again?

Your managers are a big part of their teams' work environment. Employees who stay do so for more reasons than their direct managers – if and when you live up to your original promise. If the picture you paint of your organisation and your culture is true – and you deliver on it – retaining your crew will be much simpler.

Does this sound too straightforward? For the majority of your workforce, it's no more complicated than that. If you are a good employer and are fair to your employees, all is well. Treat people with respect, communicate too much rather than too little, be consistent so that they feel they can trust you, and be convincing. No one is looking for perfection – perfection is usually boring. Most people would rather be part of something bigger than themselves. They want to feel that they are contributing to something meaningful, that they belong and that they are growing and developing. They want to be seen, heard and – yes – even loved, for what they can bring to the table if they receive support and trust.

3. LEADERSHIP

Every employee is important and shapes culture, although how leaders and managers behave has a particularly strong impact. You can talk about who you are and what you stand for, but if management doesn't behave in a way that matches what you say, it's nothing more than a sad reminder that the emperor is naked: everyone knows it, but few dare to talk about it – with devastating consequences. As an example: you talk about putting employees first and then clearly show that a lot of other things are more important. Or you claim to believe in diversity and then hire ten more people who 'fit in' because they are so similar to existing employees. Or you have managers who talk extensively about vulnerability, the importance of failure and learning, and then never venture out of their comfort zone. In such scenarios, sooner or later, your employees will 'vote with their feet' and leave and you will have to go through a costly phase of filling vacant positions because of your bad leaders.

As mentioned earlier, at Spotify, we have a Manager Manifesto. This manifesto is a promise to the organisation and employees about what our managers are expected to deliver. The leadership criteria are based on what our managers and employees have said is required both in the short and long term to be a successful leader at Spotify. We use our Manager Manifesto to recruit, develop, assess and sometimes even redeploy our managers.

In our experience, even in a non-hierarchical organisation, employees tend to do as leaders do, not as they say. In short, leaders must safeguard the culture by role modelling, promoting, driving and enabling it – all at the same time.

4. DIVERSITY, INCLUSION AND BELONGING

It is often said that what you decide to measure is what actually gets done. This is also true when it comes to diversity. More important than just showing great diversity metrics is working towards an inclusive culture, where all employees can perform at their best, make an impact and make a difference. In our case, such a culture is closely linked to our mission and our aim to remain innovative, which is also one of our core values.

Working towards greater diversity, inclusion and belonging is a commitment from senior management. It is essential that it is also an approach that comes from within. Everyone is responsible for the execution, even if there are teams and individuals that are working on it full-time. As diversity increases, inclusion decreases. At first. Diversity, Inclusion and Belonging (DIB) work is an investment and will probably slow you down, at least initially. Be open about it, *talk* about it. If you can have a discussion about the pros and cons of addressing these issues, your employees will better understand what you want to achieve and why and as a result, your culture will mature and evolve. DIB work will enrich you, create greater business value and help you create a healthy, profitable and sustainable culture – in addition to upholding your morals.

5. LEARNING AND DEVELOPMENT

One of the most important HR skills of the future is to 'build learning'. If you want to stay relevant and keep performing at your best, you can't kill your employees' desire to grow and develop. How do you remove the barriers to their drive and curiosity?

As you know by now, a growth mindset is the starting point or foundation of our learning and leadership philosophy. We know that we have highly motivated employees and that their motivation increases further if we treat them with respect and trust. We told you in the chapter on performance development that early on, we dared to question the idea that employees should be 'managed' and controlled through rigid, administratively heavy processes. Instead, we focused on a number of universal motivational factors: purpose, autonomy, competence development and belonging. Benevolence – which is about employees choosing to work in organisations where there is a higher purpose than just making money – is also a factor. Next, we offered tools, programmes, training – all sorts of development opportunities – so that our employees could drive their own development. This does not make our managers redundant, but it has led to a re-evaluation and redefinition of what a manager should focus on. This approach also emphasises the obvious: that no one will ever be as committed to your own personal growth as you are yourself! One thing is certain: development is hard, sometimes even painful. If it's not, it's not development, it's something else!

It takes time to change your thinking pattern. When you want to change a leader's mindset, it needs to be done gently. Support your managers and their team members in their journey towards a more modern and coaching approach, where managers challenge, support and develop their people by showing trust and presence. This will shape your culture.

6. COMPENSATION AND BENEFITS

If there is one aspect that speaks about your culture, it is how you reward your employees. Rewarding in different forms is a relevant way to strengthen and reinforce a culture. You can do this with small, sophisticated methods and large, complex and more creative methods. This is an area where you can connect all the dots and show both which behaviours you want to see more of and which you are less fond of.

When it comes to compensation and benefits, it's tempting to do what others are doing, but you risk losing your identity and there can be a lot of unexpected side effects. None of the colours in the HR palette are as sensitive as the compensation and rewards colour. A small change in shade in one area can have a huge impact on other areas.

What is 'fair' is difficult to determine, when the manager's discretion is, after all, decisive. It is not difficult to see that the outcome of a performance evaluation and/or compensation assessment depends on who conducts it. You should be open and transparent about how the system, processes and mechanisms are designed and explain the reasoning behind the compensation philosophy in a way that everyone can understand. How this ties in with your People Strategy and your company's values and culture is hugely important.

When designing your compensation mix, start from who you are as a company, what you want to be and what is important to you. Don't copy other organisations' reward systems. It doesn't matter if their methods are successful. Sure, get inspired, but direct copying? No, that's not a good idea.

Don't fall prey to the loudest individuals in your organisation who ask, tell or even demand that you add, change and/or remove something – because they have heard from a friend or read about something another employer is doing or has that they should also be entitled to. This is the worst thing you can do. If you take something important away, or add something that doesn't fit, there will be major (and often devastating) consequences. Trust your experience, your professionalism and your understanding of how 'everything fits together'. This includes not succumbing to the temptation to resort to quick, easy solutions – 'sugar rushes' – which will create a negative spiral. We humans have short memories and what made people happy a week ago will make them crave more! When it becomes part of the culture to complain or threaten your way to what you want – you're screwed. Soon enough, people will ask for the unreasonable, like a pink pony, just because they can...

Sorry, you will not get a pink pony! Instead, spend a lot of time thinking about how you can attract and retain the kind of people you want, keep them motivated, and reward performance and behaviour that is in line with what you are trying to achieve together.

7. STRATEGIC WORK

In most companies, *Strategy Operations* – the strategy team – does not fall under the remit of the CHRO. Maybe it should though? It is logical to think that everything related to people would benefit from being part of the same mission.

If it's clear to you that your managers' job is not to control your people, and if you really put your people first, then strategising is all about making sure that everyone is moving in the same direction, together, and that there is unity and commitment in this movement. At Spotify, we call this *The Spotify Rhythm*. It is here, in the Spotify Rhythm, that our vision, our focus areas, our goals and strategies meet – for all employees. Instead of directing employees, we inform, communicate and teach them about our rhythm and how to achieve our goals. It is not unusual for an organisation to have different cultures in different departments, or in different geographical locations. There must, however, be something that binds the different parts together – a 'social glue' that helps you work together and aim for the same star in a common effort.

Making as much information as possible available to all employees, being open about your strategies, initiatives and results, will increase employee motivation. No matter who you are and what role you have, you want to do your best, and influence the results and the business. No matter who you are, you want to be seen, heard and recognised for your contribution. Making strategy activities part of HR sends a very clear message about what the most important asset is.

Change management

People who say they love change are either lying or thinking mainly about the times they initiated or were driving the change themselves. When a change is forced upon you, and you have no say in it, or can't slow it down or avoid it, you will almost certainly dislike it – this is human nature. On the other hand, *people don't have to like a decision, they just have to be given the opportunity to understand it.*

There are no fully democratic decisions when running a business. You can, however, involve everyone by informing them about why, how and when a particular decision is made. Also, distinguish between those who are directly affected by the decision and those who are more indirectly affected. Talk to those directly affected and make sure they have a chance to absorb and process the decisions and react to the information they receive. There is also an argument for giving everyone the same information at the same time, from the same source and giving them a chance to speak, ask questions and get a better understanding of why the change should happen.

We've said it before – every organisation struggles with internal communication. That doesn't mean you can run away and avoid difficult conversations and tough decisions. Nor can you assume that most of the people involved will make a decision right away, because they won't. Instead, they'll be left in shock, processing the decision – or not. At worst, they will become worried and scared – and, therefore, angry and hurt – or behave in a seemingly illogical way. This can be avoided through conversation, communication and more communication. Sometimes it will suffice to say that you do not have more information to give at the current moment. Remaining silent and closed during a period of change is detrimental to both employees and the business. While some in the organisation will be annoyed that you are over-communicating the change, most will see it as a positive. Your employees are smart, they will understand that it is necessary. They'll also support the change *if they understand why it's happening* – even if they might prefer to stay with what they've become accustomed to and know inside out.

Change management and crisis management have many similarities (we will return to this in the next part of the book). Where they differ is mostly in the fact that at the beginning of a crisis there is little time and few data points. When planning an organisational change, a change in the way of working, or the implementation of new technology or processes, there is usually time and opportunity to explain and share your thoughts and plans. You can explain what the next steps are, what the timeline is and what would be considered a successful outcome. In a crisis situation, you need to act within minutes – and the sooner the better. It is optimal to have fewer people involved in the core team than to include many people with different opinions and ideas. Each person in the team should know what their role is.

Crisis and change are not the same thing – the circumstances and frameworks are different – but in both cases, people are forced to react to something that scares them, that they are unlikely to view positively. Therefore, the building blocks are the same in both cases. Most organisations that are good at managing change and understand that this is part of the process will also be good at managing crises. Largely because employees trust their leaders and know that the company is truly putting employees first and doing what needs to be done – with employee health and safety as a top priority.

Let the culture evolve

Many leaders, and perhaps even more founders, have fallen in love with their culture for one reason or another and don't want to see it evolve. Clinging tenaciously to yesterday's culture and forcing HR to rigidly hold to it is sending the message that any employee who joins the company after the culture has already been defined doesn't matter and that what they can bring to the table is unimportant.

We should all choose our workplace and manager carefully, because work is such a big part of life. It can take a toll on your mental health if your personal values are not in line with the values of the organisation where you work. The match doesn't have to be one hundred percent, but if it doesn't match at all, it can be devastating for the individual.

Therefore, if you work in HR, what you do with culture should always be based on a conscious decision. When setting or defining values (and desired behaviours), you should always involve all employees. If the process is not well thought out and inclusive, the result will be a paper product (or digital ditto) that feels outdated even before it is introduced. This is not a campaign and your values are not a slogan. It is an ongoing process where you give all your employees a voice. You must have the courage to test and evaluate your values and culture in a structured way.

As well as caring for and nurturing your culture, you should have a plan for what to measure, how, and how often – so you can decide when it's time to make a change and innovate.

SPOTIFY'S CULTURAL JOURNEY

At Spotify's inception, we were a technology-centric organisation. During the startup years, we followed an agile model that coloured our culture and core values. However, it became increasingly clear that this strong 'culture within the culture' excluded departments outside of technology or R&D, which grew in number as the company grew. The need for a common set of values, a shared culture, became the seed for a more product-driven organisation with a clear strategy and a shared vision and mission.

THE SCALE-UP PHASE

A scaling-up phase followed – and with it, a whole new set of challenges. This phase brought with it a high risk of things going badly wrong – whether the company's product or service was good or not, there was so much to think about, especially since this was a global journey. Everything, all the way down to the very core of the business, must be scalable, which often requires letting go of some of your old concepts of success in order to invest in new ones. Especially the aspects linked to leadership, organisational design and People Strategy.

It was at this stage of our 'culture journey' that we created and executed our Passion Tour (2014). We really went *all in* – it was like Lady Gaga was coming to town. We had a tour schedule, tickets, T-shirts, 'shows' (what we called the workshops) and a site where all staff could follow where the tour was and what was happening at each stop.

We designed our shows (workshops) to give everyone a chance to discuss, absorb and give feedback on our new vision and mission statement. All shows were facilitated by the same team from the HR department, to ensure they looked identical for all band members around the world.

We worked our way from our most remote offices to the largest in London and New York and then finished the tour at our headquarters in Stockholm.

The first part was primarily focused on communicating our (then new) vision and mission with all employees. We wanted to get real-time feedback and make any necessary adjustments so that the whole company would understand, support and be energised by our future desired state and higher purpose. The second part was to define our values. In short, we asked our employees: *What is important to you in order to do a good job while having fun and growing?*

We started in the more remote offices, not in the head office in Stockholm or the bigger offices in London or New York. We held these events in-person, even though it was time-consuming and involved a lot more work than just informing people about our vision, mission and values. Why did we do it this way? Well, because we had employees spread across different floors, offices, cities, countries (with different cultures), and you don't capture facial expressions, body language or cultural nuances if you're not there to facilitate the exercises in-person and ask questions. Being there in-person also gave another level of reassurance to employees, that we really wanted to listen to their thoughts. At that time, not many people in management positions understood our approach, let alone liked it. The tech departments suggested we transfer their values and culture to the rest of the organisation and many others rolled their eyes. Not all of them, but enough to make any HR team lose interest in inviting people to share their opinions. However, it was necessary for us to do it – and it is for you too. Giving people from all parts of the organisation a voice and letting them know that their opinions and feedback are being communicated directly to senior management (in real time) is invaluable. Employees will understand what leaders may not, and the company will benefit.

It is not easy. You have to be able to sell and promote your ideas, even though half the time your colleagues don't understand how much research, experience and hard work went into them. Instead, they think they know – better than you – how to solve issues just because they've read an article or talked to someone about a philosophy. Non-HR experts will never have full knowledge of the data, theories and philosophies on which you base your strategies, programmes, or even a single activity. It may take many years for them to understand why you did what you did and by then they won't remember how hard they fought or how loudly they pushed back against your ideas. They may not even realise how much those ideas have actually benefited them.

Courage and boldness are good and necessary in your work on culture. *Persistence* in that work is just as important.

THE BAND MANIFESTO

As Spotify continued to mature, it remained important for us to have a clear and shared view of our culture, our values and what it meant to be a Spotifier. We realised that we had often talked about and referred to 'The Spotify Way' but that we had never really defined what that meant. We are and have always been very focused on our culture and what happens within the organisation, but we hadn't talked much about the culture externally. As a result, others had tried to define it for us, with varying degrees of success. If you search 'Spotify culture' online, you can find a series of old videos about our agile practices and some news articles describing us – from the outside! We had our own way of doing things, but we had not succeeded in explaining what it is – or why it matters.

HOW THE MANIFESTO CAME ABOUT

For a few months in 2019, members of Spotify's HR leadership team joined our co-founder and CEO, Daniel Ek, in a series of conversations we called *Culture Jam Sessions*. We discussed what kind of company we wanted to be, how we had evolved over time and what kind of people we believed would thrive with us. Next, we floated our thoughts and ideas with a number of people from different parts of the organisation and then our Brand & Creative team (responsible for our brand and marketing) helped us sort through our thoughts, put them into concise words and visualise them.

The result was *The Band Manifesto*, a document that describes what Spotify is as a company and employer. We explained at the beginning of the book that we like to think of ourselves as a band. Just like the members of a band, we are interdependent and need to be in sync in order to create music. Just like a band that wants to get somewhere, we need a set of rules – yes, a manifesto – to help us see where we want to go and how to get there. The Band Manifesto explains our mission statement, our beliefs, our culture, our values and everything in between. It briefly describes who we are, what we stand for and what we want to achieve together.

We believe that this manifesto is relevant to all Spotifiers – whether they have worked with us for ten days or ten years. We wanted the manifesto to feel familiar, as neither our mission nor our values have changed.

During our 2014 Passion Tour, we involved all employees and gave them a voice, and a couple of years later we did a follow-up: *Passion Tour: The Encore*. For our new employees, we run culture and values workshops on an ongoing basis. In 2021, we let all employees 'test drive' our values and their definitions again in our *Band Reunion*.

THE BAND REUNION

It's natural for the culture to evolve and deepen with each new employee who joins us; it is still resting firmly on our core values. The fact that we hired over 1,400 new employees in the first year alone of the COVID-19 pandemic obviously had a huge impact on the entire company. We needed to keep reminding and educating our employees about our Swedish-influenced culture, our core values and our Manifesto.

In line with the Band Manifesto, and after a year of homework, we rolled out *The Band Reunion* – a platform where all leaders and employees could rediscover our values, culture and manifesto in a virtual, unique, engaging, playful and data-driven way.

The Band Reunion consisted of three parts:

- *The Rehearsal:* A content-rich interactive platform where our employees could explore content related to our manifesto. There was an interview with Daniel Ek and Katarina Berg, podcasts with our leaders and one of the HRBPs, several videos about our culture and, of course, the manifesto itself.

- *The Jam Session:* A 90-minute virtual workshop led by executives. The Jam Session, which is a workshop that is still being held, allows managers and teams to have a dialogue about Spotify's culture and values. It also serves as a reminder of why each of us chose to work at Spotify in the first place and what we want to achieve here.

- *Explore the Tour:* An interactive platform that collected all the data from Jam Sessions around the world, where all employees could look at the results and see how our culture and values are realised in different parts of the world.

We did not write our Band Manifesto for others to read, but so that we could all walk in step with each other. The manifesto should be seen in the light of what we just said: it cannot be copied. We use it to provide Spotifiers, job seekers and the rest of the world with a clear picture of our culture, our values and what it means to be a Spotifier. It is our story about ourselves. It should not feel out of the blue to anyone who knows us. It's not a change in direction or a change in values, but a clarification of things we've said before, or things we've felt but never really put into words.

PART 3

Part 3.
Bread and Butter
– the essence of HR work

Introduction by Dr Tomas Chamorro-Premuzic

It's only very high-end bread and butter that can get people excited about the foundational aspects of such basic food. And of course, simple things are the hardest to perfect, because you have very few parameters and too many constraints. In the words of Antoine de Saint-Exupery (most famous as the author of *The Little Prince*): "perfection is finally attained not when there is no longer anything to add, but when there is no longer anything to take away".[11]

It is with this context that I invite you to enjoy the next section of this book, which celebrates the importance of a solid foundation, and knowing and understanding that if everything does not rest on a solid foundation, it will fail gloriously. This concept of basics may sound counterintuitive, as the world of HR – just like the world in general – is infiltrated with complex new technologies, algorithmic euphoria, and both glorification and vilification of artificial rather than natural resources. However, there is always something misleading about complexity. If your point of view is that work (and people) are complex, then your goal is to try to explain them away rather than understand them.

Sure, the world is way more complex today than it has ever been, and certainly more sophisticated from a technological standpoint than it was in mediaeval times, or in early hunter-gatherer societies. But it is still inhabited by humans, and there are no salient biological or psychological differences between our needs and those of our ancestors. This includes work: it is essentially our bread and butter, or the vehicle we pursue to feed ourselves and our families. The fact that we can also find it enjoyable, meaningful, and instructive does not make work or humans any more special today than they were thousands of years ago.

I recall meeting a self-made billionaire in China a few years ago, who owned one of the biggest grocery chains in Shanghai. "Tell me something," he said, after I finished giving an overly complex lecture on the future of HR, "I like what you said and trust you, but can you explain something to me please?" Not without intrigue, and knowing who the man was, I asked him to continue. "Do I need this thing called 'HR'?" he asked. The man, and his mega-successful multibillion dollar venture, had no formal HR department or function. Naturally, this would lead many people in the western world to suspect that their employees were missing out on a great work experience, basic employee rights, the potential to unlock their potential, and perhaps even find the meaning of life. But what if they weren't? What if they could get that from somewhere else? Perhaps their managers and leaders? Perhaps they didn't expect it either? Also, why assume that HR can provide this, if most organisations have HR departments, yet people are still often disengaged, burned out, stagnating, and looking (if not hoping) for better alternatives? In short, what is the most foundational and immovable aspect of HR that cannot be taken away, and hence represents a state of conceptual perfection, at least according to Saint-Exupery?

I do not have the right answer to this question, but would encourage you to find it for your organisation. Starting with this question may help you articulate your basic HR philosophy, and guide you not just directionally, but also in strength or degree. Nobody knows what the future will bring because we have no data on it, but as the following chapters articulate, we CAN make logical interpretations of our present if we inspect the past: if you want to understand where you are going, it helps to know how you got here, which calls for a look at the relatively short history of HR.

This history is not equal for all, but it can be generalised as follows: HR actually started life as scientific management, when large organisations such as Ford turned their assembly lines into real life HR laboratories to apply the basic principles of scientific management (Friedrich Taylor and Fordism). In a way, this was very advanced: today we talk about a data revolution in HR and other areas, but science is data + theory and does not just predict but also explains replicable phenomena in a reliable and proven way. As you will see in this chapter, much of the current euphoria around people analytics is trying to replicate these early foundations of HR, albeit with much stronger and more granular tools and instruments. After this initial scientific discovery phase, HR became quite legal and bureaucratic, entering the administrative phase. The goal here was not to measure things or optimise for performance and productivity, but to protect employees. This laid the foundations of modern employee-centric HR, taken to another level in modern times, with companies (such as Spotify) wanting to offer consumer-like experiences to their employees: this is how you win the war for talent. And then came the spiritual or philosophical phase of HR, which is focussed on the war for talent. This kick-started the psychological quest for understanding and boosting talent, engagement, leadership, and thinking of employees as spiritual workaholics. It's basically scientific management + employee rights, with an injection of modern positive psych and the rise of employee wellbeing.

But as this part of the book shows, today we are in the technological phase of HR, where tools, tech and data can have a distracting, if not perverse, effect on people management practices. In this phase, we need more expertise than ever, but expertise is not enough. We also need skilled and curious HR leaders who are willing to learn and humble to know what they don't know. Without curiosity, your expertise has already become outdated, and without humility, you will develop imaginary cocoons of delusional confidence that will construct a distorted version of reality that makes you feel smart, as opposed to actually making you smart. The role of humans in this highly technological phase of HR is to prove their own value by adding something to the machines, and something to the data. Human expertise, just like the early scientist of Taylor's revolutionary days, is the ability to translate data into insights, and insights into action. We want a story that moves our minds and hearts into better ways of working, and that story won't be told by a chatbot.

This chapter tells the story of this age, vindicating all that has ever been precious and valuable about HR – in the current context. Yes, this is the new era of people-first but we also need to reconcile this with business-centricity. Today, most historical distinctions, such as work-life balance or intrinsic vs extrinsic motivation, are obsolete. Just like it is obsolete to see tensions between diversity and profits, or shareholder and stakeholder value. As this chapter notes, technology is always a means rather than an end: and no matter how fancy the toys, how cool and cutting-edge the gadgets, HR tech is like any other tech – an attempt to do 'more with less'. People are lazy, and this may be one of the most underrated human virtues: the desire to make things easier and simpler has spurred much innovation, not just in HR. Every tech ever invented has been driven by an attempt to free up human energies and creativity for something not yet automatable or doable by tech. HR techs are no different from today's dating apps: you can easily swipe right or left, but then you have to meet the person and decide if you want to date them; and then, perhaps, you have to marry them – and then the work starts.

Where will HR take us? As this chapter argues, this is not a technology question. The tail should not wag the dog. Looking for shiny new toys or technology to solve our existential problems is one of the biggest catastrophes (and most avoidable mistakes) of modern HR. No technology can substitute for great HR practices, because it is not just human resources that are being managed, but also humans who are tasked with the management. I hope that, like me, you will find this chapter of tremendous practical value before you decide to run into any of the popular destinations HR is being dragged into. If you are going fast in the wrong direction, you will only get lost quicker. Instead, pause, think, and ditch the 8-course meal in favour of the humble bread and butter. But make it the best bread and butter you have ever made, and don't give up on perfecting it. As for technology, use anything you want, but think of problems waiting for solutions rather than tech that is a solution waiting for a problem to be solved – which often causes many more problems too.

HR Tech
– technology as an enabler

The tools available to those of us working in HR are changing rapidly and whilst HR tech can be described as 'an area where innovation meets HR', it can also cause some confusion and paralysis in HR departments. In addition, HR managers are inundated with offers of different apps, systems and processes, as more and more developers and entrepreneurs come to the realisation that HR has ownership of budgets for these tools.

At Spotify we consider that HR tech includes digital workplaces, collaboration tools as well as a number of other tools. If you think about this broad definition, instead of just blindly believing what the salespeople say, it becomes clear that we're really talking about *HR systems* – the technology that connects everything you oversee in the HR function. At least that's the beginning of the story: you can't create, integrate or add more HR tech if the basic system is not solid. It will be very challenging to implement innovation projects if you don't have the right infrastructure and systems in place.

You have probably already been approached by consultants with no HR experience but a lot of marketing experience and a digital system to sell. They've asked you: "What will the future of talent acquisition, learning and development and HR work look like in a world of smarter artificial intelligence, chatbots, voice control and virtual reality?" They will follow up quickly with a claim that the answer to these questions is the new HR tool they are trying to sell. More often than not, it's a tool that doesn't support your team, help you recruit people who add to your culture, or help you focus on strategies that drive the business. They say their tools solve all your problems, save time, reduce workloads, engage employees and propel you into the digital future. In most (if not all) cases this just is not true. Don't get blindsided by sales tactics. Instead, go back to your roots. Of course, you can update your existing systems – digitising your HR system will be the most impactful investment you make when it comes to HR tech – but don't throw out the bread and butter, the core of HR work, just because there has been a technological revolution.

If you're a small business and don't have an HR system (and don't think you need one yet) – think long-term. This will help you get on the right track right from the start. If you get the optimal system in place, you can then tackle other innovation projects. You can really start to influence how much value you create for your business and your employees. Don't automatically go for the latest, greatest, 'all bells and whistles' system. You need to establish the need and the business case for solving it before you even start looking for a fancy system.

Driver or passenger?

Everyone in the HR team must understand that the system will not solve all their problems. The most successful integration of a digital HR system happens when the focus is on finding a system that supports your strategies, philosophies and ways of working. Don't make the mistake of believing that everything called 'tech' will allow you to sit back and relax. As our wise colleague Arvid Hedman says: "In our industry in particular – and in society in general – we are so fascinated by AI that we make fantastic assumptions about what AI can do for us. The consequence is that people (read: HR) may be pushed aside, we become immersed in technology. Don't get me wrong: there is a time and a place for advanced technology, but starting there is the wrong way to go." It's the HR department's knowledge of the organisation and your people, and understanding the balance and polarities that exist with that, which really results in the most value. Therefore, your systems need to mould to that. HR tech and machines won't be able to take your culture into account – this is the work that should be done by humans and supported by tech. Therefore, you must take your business, people and culture into account as you update your processes. It's paramount to ensure the entire team is aligned on the common goals. It's a great practice to keep checking back on these and map them to your future vision. Just as you choose your HR processes and ways of working with this in mind – strategically and in line with your culture – choose your system with this in mind. Then, any subsequent adjustments will be small and the system you've chosen will still make sense.

If you haven't defined your HR processes yet, or if your way of working needs updating, it would be a good idea to do this at the same time as choosing your system. This will reduce costs, and you can make sure everything fits together before making an investment. Doing everything at the same time also makes sense from a change management point of view. You don't end up in a situation where you are told that you can't make the change you want to make "because the system doesn't support it". Essentially, never forget that it is your knowledge and expertise and your organisation's business needs that have put you in the driver's seat, so it is a bad strategy to take a back seat.

Zoom in, zoom out

You may have already found ways of working, processes, common values and philosophies that the whole organisation signs up to and that HR owns and feels responsible for. There is more work to be done on the foundation itself. For example, it might be wise to map your processes and ways of working so that you have a good overview of what is actually being done, what can be ironed out and what is being done piecemeal. This step should be done both zoomed in (at a detailed level) and zoomed out, so that you look at the entire HR ecosystem.

Clear responsibilities are always preferable, but equally important, if not more so, is to understand the transition between the teams within your HR department. Be sure to look in all directions. Then look again. If you don't bring the pieces together into a whole, the organisation will feel the pain and make you aware of what is not working well and not supporting their way of working nor creating business value.

We can take learning as an example. You need to think about how you work with learning, how you design and deliver training programmes. Do you deliver training in the classroom and/or digitally? Is there any kind of approval required in order to participate? Do you use external providers? If so, how are they selected? So on and so forth. Such questions make it immediately clear that your central HR system needs to be adaptable to your learning strategy.

Again, no single system will be able to meet all your needs. You may need to integrate different e-learning tools or enable third parties to deliver training. Opening up your systems to more people, especially external providers, raises some pretty important questions. For example, how to limit the access of these external providers so that they can deliver what you want without compromising security. If, like Spotify, you have a global operation, you need to account for local legislation and cultural differences in your processes, which means the system needs to be able to adapt to such factors.

The HR system you choose should have functionality that allows you to reduce repetitive tasks, such as getting events and training sessions onto employees' calendars, or sending out surveys and integrating them with your internal communication systems.

Taking all of these factors into account means that this task is not easy. The most important thing is not to worry and get so overwhelmed that you start to believe the stories about easy-to-implement, or 'plug-n-play' systems that magically solve all of these problems without you needing to invest time and thought. Don't fall for it. Be aware that it will be difficult, but that applying your unique insight into your business, people and culture is the way to make the best informed choices. Don't imagine that this will be the last time you do a comprehensive analysis, select a new system and integrate it. Choosing the right technical solution will be one of those regular review items on your HR agenda. This is rudimentary in keeping you and the work you do for the business relevant.

Data and statistics

It is important that the system(s) you choose give you access to the data and statistics you need. You may want to see if there is a correlation between high performing employees and how they were recruited, or what training they have received. Or you may want to use psychometric data from the recruitment process to draw conclusions on how to make even better recruitment decisions in the future.

Our advice is to think about data beyond your *hiring funnel* (more on that in the next chapter), otherwise it becomes 'talent acquisition analytics' rather than people analytics. Both are good, but you can't possibly draw conclusions for the entire employee lifecycle, such as what investments to make or where to locate the next office, using recruitment data. Your *data warehouse* needs to be bigger than that to help you make bold but informed decisions and make sound business recommendations.

When choosing an HR system, you may reach a dead end if your vision of what you want to achieve is based on insufficient or even corrupt data. At best, this gives you a distorted picture or a limited basis – at worst it gives you a false sense of security. *Then you're really in trouble and likely to find yourself in the middle of nowhere – and nobody wants that!*

Writing a shopping list

How do you identify the essentials? Although it's laborious, you need to actually map out your entire HR landscape. The next step is to think about different stakeholders and what falls into the 'nice to have' and 'need to have' categories – some things are nice to have, others are absolutely necessary.

Again, don't think you can cover everything. Instead, think about the whole picture and not just the part that the HR system is supposed to solve. Think about how that part of your responsibility is connected to other parts of the employee experience, to see where consistency and seamless flow is important and where it makes sense to use a separate system that is not fully integrated, even if it is supported by the central HR system.

One (sometimes unexpected) bonus of thinking this through properly is that you can address any inefficient existing processes when introducing a new system. You will almost certainly identify more processes that would benefit from an update or could even be removed. It's like when you move house, you take the opportunity to purge – keeping some really good, useful things and throwing away the stuff you don't need anymore or rarely use, that is just taking up space (or time).

You need to prioritise your needs and be clear and tough (both with the system provider and with your colleagues in HR) about what is important to the business. This will require some compromises. Think about questions like: Does the motto 'simplicity and business value above all' apply, or can we manage a system that is better for the users (managers and employees) and slightly worse for the administrator (HR)? A key fact to keep in mind here is that you will never make everyone happy. However, the system needs to be functional and future-proofed, and to have the business and your employees in focus.

Don't forget to look at all the necessary aspects of corporate governance and internal control. For example, you need to keep track of who approves which changes. If you have a lot of multi-step controls, think about how you will get those responsible for them to prioritise this project, otherwise the processes will drag on for weeks or even months. Clear ownership, autonomy in decision-making and approval levels, as well as privacy protection are examples of things that should be on your 'shopping list'.

Being overwhelmed or dazzled

Once you know what you want the technology to do for you, it's time to go shopping. Here, it's a great idea to reach out for support from someone who is good at buying systems, from the purchasing department or even an external consultant. This should be a person with the right knowledge, who understands what you want and can help you make a requirements specification where you describe what you want the system to be able to do and support. You then meet with the suppliers that you think best meet your requirements.

We also recommend that you think through how the new responsibilities will be allocated, although this may depend on the system you end up buying. Don't forget the need for management and maintenance, for example. If you need to recruit system specialists, start this process as early as possible.

If you have a network of HR colleagues in other companies, take advantage of their experience to find out which system is best at doing what you want to do (now that you know what it is). This is not to say that you should copy another company's system, but you can learn a lot from what others say about both what has worked well and what has been unnecessarily difficult and downright painful. Also, plan time in the acquisition process to make comparisons with companies that already use the systems you are interested in (provided they use the system in the same way as you plan to).

Undeniably, there's a lot to think about and we haven't covered every aspect (see our 'words of wisdom' at the end of the chapter for further guidance). Even if you don't feel you need a particularly sophisticated system right now – think ahead, long-term. What do you need further down the road? The HR system should serve as a foundation for your way of working and your philosophy. It won't do the work for you, but it can make it easier and can even become a central part of your strategic work. As always when working on something big, it's good to conduct thorough groundwork.

Once you roll out the new system, make sure those affected understand why you are doing it, what you want to achieve and how it will help those who use it – and the organisation as a whole. After all, it's not just about making the system work, it's also about making sure users benefit from it – otherwise it's not a good investment. That's why it's wise to involve people outside of HR who can act as a sounding board, a cross-functional user group that gives their views on what they think is important from a managerial and employee perspective.

SOME TIPS FOR CHOOSING AN HR SYSTEM

We will end this chapter with a small guide, some concrete tips for choosing an HR system.

Choosing the System

1. CHOOSE PROJECT MANAGERS WITH CARE

Your preparations and your shopping list will never be better than your project manager makes them. The project manager must be a conscious decision maker and not your most junior team member, nor your typical technical expert. Using a senior project manager to reconcile, map, anchor and write the shopping list is central to a successful procurement process and integration. Cultivating relationships with stakeholders (stakeholder management) is no small task!

2. DON'T FORGET THE MAINTENANCE

Systems do not maintain or manage themselves! Someone has to take care of the system and all the data, processes and integrations. Make sure you have a person or team who has ownership, who knows what needs to be done and how. Bear in mind that systems that require employees and managers to participate in their management, such as manually entering data, are rarely managed well – people don't see the point of filling out forms. Don't create processes that rely on employees and managers spending time reporting.

Many HR systems sell 'self-serve' solutions, such as allowing managers to request salary changes for employees in the system, or allowing employees to change their own job titles. While this may work for some companies, it can also be tricky as everyone who inputs information needs to understand how the system is set up and why, as well as the structure behind the titles, and also know the HR terminology. It's easy to create a mess, corrupt data and cause the whole system to be unusable. That's when a mess quickly becomes a disaster!

3. DON'T BE CHEAP

When you see the price tag of an HR system like the one we're talking about here, it can be a shock – but we can pretty much guarantee that it will pay off.

Cheap alternatives that don't support all your processes are rarely worth the money. Sure, HR systems can be expensive, but we encourage you to change your angle of thought: compare the system with the systems that other companies use, not with the minor HR tools you've looked at before. We're talking about a comprehensive infrastructure system and that will have a significant price tag.

Consider your future development needs when looking at the cost. Management is one thing, expanding and developing the system is another. If the system costs a lot up-front, further development and customisation will probably be included, while with cheaper systems the supplier will probably wait until your desired changes have been requested from all their other customers as well, or you will need to pay extra.

4. DO NOT LOOK FOR THE ULTIMATE SOLUTION

Don't expect to find a solution that can cover all your needs. There are systems that cover most HR areas, such as recruitment, employee engagement, employment data, learning and development, performance management, compensation and benefits, salary reviews, internal mobility and absence management, etc. Don't try to solve everything – focus on the fact that the basics are in place and that other systems can be integrated.

Many will promise that they can solve all your problems. They may well believe it themselves, because they are experts in how to implement the extensive and complex system they offer – and they are very keen to make a deal. Remember that you know your business best and you are the HR experts. Don't allow for a situation where you've already signed a contract and started the implementation when you realise that the vendor can't keep all their promises.

Moreover, more is not always better. You don't want to buy an overly complicated system with a lot of cool features and modules, even if you are completely enchanted by the salesperson's impressive demonstration. The logic of 'bigger is better' does not apply here. Rather, it's an opportunity to think about who you are, where you're going, and what you really need and expect. Don't buy that space rocket when all you really need is a smart TV.

If something looks good, you automatically become interested in it. Many of us have been guilty of buying what looks coolest. Don't get caught in that trap this time. Don't compromise on functionality. As we all know, all that glitters is not gold. A system with a lot of features is usually just cluttered. It's better to have an appetising user interface. Think: intuitive, functional and clear.

Choosing the Right Supplier

In addition to thinking about the system itself, also consider the supplier. Here are some aspects to consider:

- How does the supplier work with data security, privacy and other current or future regulations?

- Do they offer support for change management?

- How does the support from the supplier work – can they support administrators, employees and perhaps staff/managers during working hours, or are their customer support and employees on the other side of the world?

- What user training do they offer?

- What are the dependencies on the supplier and any partners? Do you need help from consultants to adapt things to your business?

- How will the system be updated with new versions/customisations? Do you need to hire consultants to make your system adaptations work after each update?

- How does the provider charge for the system, what is included in the price?

- How long will the implementation take? What do you need to do and what do the supplier and any partners need to do during the implementation?

Checklist for Project Implementation

Once the decision is made and the system is purchased, it's time to start the implementation, in collaboration with the supplier. Get a project team that covers all areas in place. The team can be larger or smaller depending on the size of the company and the system being purchased. For slightly larger projects, be sure to set up a project team that includes:

- Project Manager.

- Those who will use the system every day.

- Future system administrators.

- Experts in technology implementation, design and integration.

- Those who know HR but also understand the technology and can explain to the technicians what they want to achieve with each part.

- A 'sponsor' – someone with a mandate to make quick decisions along the way (because the group will need to make such decisions on more than one occasion).

- Representatives of your users (managers and employees within the organisation, for example).

- Those who will need data and reports from the system.

- Communicators.

- Trainers.

- Lawyers/purchasing department.

- Internal controllers.

Choosing a system and then implementing it is a massive task and it's easy to get overwhelmed. First, lay the foundations and agree on the processes. This will give you direction and guidelines, and make decision-making much easier. It will also increase the likelihood that you will choose a system that is truly right for you. You won't be as tempted to copy someone else and you won't be blinded by the latest trend or buzzwords thrown around by the vendor.

People Analytics
– data as a foundation
for HR work

Congratulations – you've made it to the data part of the book! If you're only going to read one chapter, let it be this one! No, that's a bit of a stretch – but using people analytics (PA) correctly is, in the new era of HR, the difference between being good and being *great*.

First, a clarification – what is people analytics? It has been said that 'data is the new oil'. It sounds like something a consultancy firm came up with during a brainstorming meeting. The analogy is not entirely wrong though, because this new raw material is creating a new industry and new profitability for those who are most successful in extracting it. The same goes for HR – if you own a lot of data, you are rich in business opportunities.

Maybe you've seen the movie *Van Wilder*, where Ryan Reynolds says, "write that down". We'll let Ryan join us in this chapter – and now comes the first 'write that down' moment – do you have your pen ready? *Have you noticed that, even though people started talking about the importance of people analytics around 2018, it seems that most people still don't treat it as important?*

Of course, if you work in HR, you can't say that people analytics *isn't* important – it's listed in every industry magazine as one of the things you really need to focus on. We don't want to sound like we're rooting for a people analytics revolution, yet it's pretty amazing that the HR professionals who are actively using data are still very much in the minority.

If you are new to the HR profession – make people analytics the core of your approach. If you've already been working in HR for a while and feel that your people analytics isn't as deep as it should be, even when you really challenge yourself and insist that it's important – you should quickly, or 'faster than lightning', become *data informed*, and let data and data analysis become the foundation of your work.

HR is where the marketing industry was 20-30 years ago in terms of understanding and leveraging data and this is the area where we can see the huge increase in efficiency. HR is going through the same evolution and it's already becoming apparent which HR teams are on that boat and which are still reporting the classic old KPIs.

If you think of the employee experience and employer brand as a product you sell to your customers – that is, your teams – how can you sell more successfully? This is where people analytics can help, in the same way that data helps marketers sell products to consumers. It's an essential tool for understanding your people, whether it's recruitment, engagement, performance development, or any other aspect.

The better we understand all the intricacies of our people, the better we can meet their needs. *Write that down!*

How to make people analytics the foundation of HR work?

We believe that all of us working in HR have an obligation to learn how to deal with data in order to develop our function and our profession. This does not mean that we all have to become experts in the field, or even excel. We do all need to be open to using data as the foundation of our solutions and offerings for the business.

A negative attitude towards data is one of the biggest obstacles to understanding both the business and employees. As an HR specialist, to place something you don't understand at the core of what you do is to make yourself extremely vulnerable. Just like with other areas: you will need to be bold and let your guard down.

When it comes to people analytics, many organisations feel that they need to close the 'skills gap' first and foremost. In our experience, the problem is rarely a lack of knowledge about people analytics, since this can be learned. Instead, our profession is hampered by a strange kind of humility. Relatively few HR professionals consider themselves experts in storytelling and many are unaccustomed to having to explain relationships in such a way that can persuade the organisation to walk a new path in a specific area. Storytelling is an important skill, perhaps even essential, for successful HR work in the new era.

Both the HR and People Analytics teams need to approach the subject from the perspective of garnering insights about the business that will help the people, and vice versa. The HR experts think about the business as a whole, or even represent the business in this collaboration. The PA team has the ability to deeply interpret, analyse and extract the important things from the datasets that will bring us closer to an informed decision. This is how the competences of the HR palette complement each other in the best possible way!

Being a great analyst, or part of a great analytics department, is not about having technical skills. It is about the ability to imagine that you are in the same position as the person who has reached out for help and to use a creative approach to data to solve the problem. If you were that person, sitting in a room with your stakeholders, how would you present your arguments? What problems do you really want to solve? What questions are you worried will be asked? Where do you think you will be challenged?

Okay, here we go again – here's another 'write that down' opportunity: *making data and analytics the bedrock of HR work requires a change in mindset.*

Both the classic HR skills and the 'newer' ones linked to people analytics need to focus on the business and what is best for the big picture by looking at the parts, trends and tendencies. After all, HR work in general, and people analytics work in particular, aims to gather insights about the business that can help employees, and insights about employees that can help the business.

The first thing to ask is what data you have, or how your analysis of data can improve your understanding of the business. If you start at this point, data will be the basis of your future solutions.

How to develop your people analytics skills?

Maybe you have a People Analytics function in HR that knows what it is doing but in reality this is not the case for most organisations. Let's take a step back and say a few words about how to get good at people analytics and what key areas to focus on.

We mentioned a moment ago that data is called 'the new oil'. A better metaphor – which is especially relevant when trying to understand how to build your capabilities in this area – is to think of data, especially employee-related data, as *water*. A while back, we were asked: "If you think of HR as the human body, what part would the people analytics function be?" And here you might be tempted to answer 'the brain'. If the answer doesn't have to be an organ or body part, then our answer would undoubtedly be *water*. Water can create energy, speed up movement and generate great impact when it accumulates. We can build on this analogy in our explanation of how to lay the foundation for a strong people analytics capability in HR.

Principles for working with water

We will now simplify the challenges in some areas rather crudely, but highlight what we believe is central to success. These 'principles for working with water' will act as an anchor to help you prioritise when distractions are plentiful.

PRINCIPLE 1: DO NOT DROWN!

Today, data is rarely hard to come by – in fact, you often have more data than you can handle, and you don't know what to do with it. This can give a false sense of security. It's a bit like a PowerPoint presentation with lots of text on each slide. For those creating the presentation, it's nice to know that you 'have it all' – but no one will understand your point. Too much data has the same effect: no one knows where to start.

To avoid drowning, start at the shallow end. Don't assume that all data has the same value, because it doesn't. You need to prioritise the data points that provide the most value and help you convince your stakeholders.

First, there's basic HR data on employees: how many people you employ, who reports to whom, how much they are paid, how long they have worked for the company, gender, age, and where in the business they work. This is not a complete list, but without a strong grip on this kind of data, you won't be able to swim at all.

You will spend an inordinate amount of time explaining the difference between the numbers and lose all credibility in the eyes of your stakeholders.

A close second is recruitment data: job vacancies, how long recruitment processes take, data related to the health of your *hiring funnel* and pipelines, which offers have been made, which offers have been declined, which people are hired and from where. Again, not an exhaustive list.

The point is that these two datasets affect the managers of the business in their daily work. If you don't understand these numbers and can't answer questions about them, you'll never be able to move past the inflatables.

PRINCIPLE 2: DO NOT WATER THE LAWN WITH BOTTLED WATER
Data quality – sometimes you hear 'rubbish in, rubbish out'. This statement does not really help us. It doesn't tell us how complex the issue is or where to begin to solve the problem. In reality, data is rarely perfect. You don't water your lawn with bottled water – that would be idiotic – *write that down.*

Read the theory, make sure you understand it – and be pragmatic when implementing it. Remember that you have to rely on people, with all their flaws. As long as people are feeding data into the system, it will never be completely reliable.

This is in line with Principle 1: prioritise your data points, write them down and critically assess how accurate the numbers need to be. Of course, the ideal is always 100% – but you'll be surprised how many don't have to be this precise. Next, move on to Principle 3.

PRINCIPLE 3: CLEAN WATER AT THE SOURCE

Once you have written your list of data points and the reliability required, make a plan on how to 'clean' the data so that it is reliable enough. Here, you need to think at the right scale. In every company and industry, there are shortcuts to solving data quality problems. They usually exist in some analyst's spreadsheet, are based on 57 *vlookups* (searches inside spreadsheets) and take about 27 minutes to process. This is a reality that many have to accept, but it can also only be considered a short-term solution to what is likely to be a long-term problem.

Therefore, think at the right scale. Go back to the original systems, to the water source, where the original data came from, and find a way to solve the problems that reduce reliability at the starting point. This is a long process and you will certainly not be able to solve all of the issues. The ones you can solve, though, will be solved permanently. No duct tape, no elaborate spreadsheet formula – a scalable solution.

At Spotify, we have brought the people responsible for our HRIS (our core HR system) under the same roof as the People Analytics team. Since People Analytics gets so much data from HRIS, it makes us faster and actually better, as the feedback between the teams flows more smoothly when they belong to the same HR sub-department. The People Analytics team informs the systems team of issues that have emerged during data analysis and the systems team then uses its technical knowledge to develop permanent solutions. Again – a pragmatic approach. Most importantly, the focus is on long-term problem solving.

The last thing to mention under this principle is that you need standards and governance. This not only improves reliability but creates a common language. Nobody likes system hierarchies

– they are boring and time-consuming to maintain – but they are the building blocks that move your business towards a common understanding of the truth. Decide what the source is so you are able to keep the water clean. It is astonishing how much working time is spent discussing numbers, just because the numbers have been defined in different ways. If you don't take this into account and prioritise the basics – good luck with the conversations about why the full time equivalent (FTE) figure is not the same as the number of employees.

PRINCIPLE 4: MAKE WATER AVAILABLE
Never underestimate the importance of packaging the results of your data processes in an accessible and appealing way. To build on the water equation, you need a tap – preferably one that people can get water from themselves.

Here are the biggest costs in your people analytics journey. As we noted in the previous chapter, there is no shortage of vendors willing to take your money and they all have excellent arguments for why their solution is the best. Again, there is no perfect solution. Instead, focus on what you most want to get out of the solution, who will use the solution, what skills they have in using data, and how far you have progressed in your journey. A big mistake made time and time again in this area is just to throw money at the problem. Some people buy the nicest, most expensive gold taps without anyone knowing how to get the water to flow out of them. Insanity!

'Consumerization' of the data experience

We've now said a few words about what people analytics is, why it's important, how you can make it the foundation of everything you do and what building blocks are needed to establish a successful PA function. In this final section, we focus on what will perhaps be the most important development, not only in people analytics but in all types of analytics, in all industries. We can call it the 'consumerization' of data.

Some would argue that this has already happened. If you look at the plethora of business intelligence tools on the market, with their endless features and sleek interfaces, it's clear that the market has changed. In reality, the tools are still aimed at people who are already familiar with data, not the average user, so the change we are witnessing is just the tip of the iceberg. The truth is that principles 1–3 don't really interest your stakeholders that much. They assume that those things have already been taken care of. How you package the results you show your stakeholders (whether managers, employees, CEOs or anyone else) is the most crucial.

To develop this theory of consumerization of the data experience in people analytics, we can make the following three assumptions.

1. PEOPLE ARE LAZY

We are creatures of habit who like to follow the law of least resistance. There are too many examples to list here, so we'll settle for one: When you search for something online, how often do you click through to the second page? Not very often, right? You probably change your search terms instead, hoping to get a good hit at the top next time. Technology outside the workplace has changed what we expect to get at work too. In other words, if it's not practical, we don't use it.

2. WE EAT WITH OUR EYES

Our perception of something is greatly influenced by what we *see*. This is one of the reasons why restaurants invest so much in the environment (decor, table setting, etc.). If they have done it really well, you will have decided that the food is good before you even taste it. Similarly, we consume data in environments that shape our view of the quality of the results. Let's say you show an ugly chart with important data points on the one hand, and a great looking chart that says nothing on the other. If you ask ten people which chart was most insightful, most, if not all, will point to the pretty one. The trick is to combine them.

3. 'GOOD ENOUGH' IS NOT ENOUGH

Excellence, or a desire to do something really, really well, is an attitude and a habit. Aristotle said that "we are what we constantly do". Our simple, pragmatic interpretation of this statement is that we should strive to establish credibility in the quality of our output. How do we create consistently good evidence/results, whether it's a simple report or a complex analysis? The answer is not 'by being satisfied that what we deliver is pretty good'. You need to create a culture within the team where *excellence* is the accepted standard, not *good enough*. The user will soon see through the fancy presentations if there is no substance to the content.

What does all this mean? Well, it means that people analytics can be of enormous benefit to your business and your employees. You have to mean it when you say it's important and you have to understand why. It also means that you have to set bold priorities. It's a balancing act – you don't want to get overwhelmed and drown, but you need to get into deep enough water to explore the real opportunities. Finding that balance will allow you to use the power of your data and the insights it can provide – a new resource in the new era of HR. By all means, don't forget the basics. That's our last *write that down* message.

The Future of People Analytics

What we've walked you through above is the basics of people analytics and how to build the right foundations from which to grow. Like any area, people analytics is evolving, and evolving fast. Our take on that evolution isn't necessarily the same as everyone else's.

We have a strong belief that the long-term success of people analytics is far more subtle than many others may think. Big, one-off projects that are heralded as best practice are just too deliberate in our opinion. We think people analytics can be considered a true success when it's so deeply woven into how an HR function is working that you don't know it's there. We see this new age as analytical output that is deeply integrated within a product suite that is both driving the core employee experience and improving the effectiveness of HR. This marks a shift in the people analytics team's output from being wholly focussed on analysis, to becoming products which analysis is a part of. We really mean actual products, not some 'productization' spin that you'll hear elsewhere.

PEOPLE ANALYTICS PRODUCTS THAT IMPROVE EMPLOYEE EXPERIENCE AND HR EFFECTIVENESS AT SPOTIFY

DISCO – WHERE DATA COMES TO DANCE

If we roughly simplify what the consumer product created by Spotify does, it connects listeners with audio content they like and makes it easy for them to find new things based on data and past behaviour. The secret is in *how* we do it. We've all had the experience of opening Spotify and either seeing new music from a favourite artist or getting suggestions for a song we've never heard but then happily play on repeat for a month. (Same with podcasts, of course.) Could we recreate that experience with HR data?

We wanted to create a true consumer experience to connect our customers – and by that, we mean everyone at Spotify – with data we knew they wanted to see, and even suggest data they didn't know they would be interested in. In practice, we wanted to do a Spotify for Spotify when it comes to people analytics. We call it *Disco*. A place where data comes to dance!

To build Disco, we used all the content you've already read about in this chapter. We focused on the design and user experience and then started to tackle a wide range of data for each employee at Spotify. We wanted to build an overview for each employee, displaying all the steps along the way, from when the candidate first applies for a position to when they leave the company, so that we could answer any question from the employee's data. We can go back to the four water principles: with this end goal, we needed to prioritise which datasets to focus on first and create a roadmap for which others to introduce, and when (Principle 1). Then we needed to review the quality of the data sources (Principle 2). The next step was to establish a common language and address data quality issues at the source (Principle 3). Last, but not least, we needed to make the results available in the most optimal way (Principle 4).

We've created a Disco app that is customised for each user in such a way that they can access all the employee-related metrics that are important to their role. We've tried to be a little creative with the language: a 'song' is a metric, an 'album' is a group of similar metrics related to a particular theme, such as compensation, and a 'playlist' is a way of structuring a dashboard. There are, of course, many technical subtleties in how the system works, but it is these overarching principles that are the heart and soul of Disco.

We are *informed* by data – we are not driven by it. At Spotify, we love data, so it's perhaps not surprising that we see people analytics as the water that moves our boat forwards. However, we make a clear distinction between being driven by numbers or data, and making informed decisions based on the data we collect and how it relates to each other.

BOUNCE – A PLACE TO GO, KNOW AND DO

Describing what Bounce is is actually tricky. Not because it has some obscure use case, or it's so complex that you couldn't work out what it is. As with anything new, it's human nature to compare it to something that we're already familiar with in order to help understand it.

One way we could describe Bounce is as a new type of intranet. We all know what an intranet is and no one has ever got excited when they hear the term. It's the cousin of the internet, where information goes to retire. We could describe it as an employee experience platform that brings together disparate apps to give employees a single portal and knowledge management interface. There's been a plethora of these recently in the market; the majority are a little functional-looking and don't provide the most inspiring user experience. We could describe Bounce as a new type of employee comms platform, but that gives it a very singular use case. The reality is that Bounce is all three, but not simultaneously. Bounce creates its own new space that we believe will become the standard.

What is this new space? Well, Bounce is Spotify for the workplace in a certain sense. What do we mean by that? Well, at our last investor day we introduced the idea of the Spotify machine. Put simply, the machine has three horizontal functions. We have a platform layer, which is the Spotify technology platform. We have the Spotify experience layer, which is all the applications, surfaces, mobile apps, cars and desktops. Then we have a personalisation layer, which is how we decide what content to recommend to what user. These three horizontals act as a synchronisation function. We then have the verticals: music, podcasts and – most recently – audiobooks, which are all very different content types. Now, what these three horizontal functions, or synchronisation functions, do is eat through all of the complexity that the different content types produce so that that complexity doesn't end up with the end user. The end user is left with a single platform that has all of these different content types that work in harmony and co-exist in a way that produces a great user experience. In turn, each of those content types takes advantage of the capabilities of the platform, e.g. personalisation, ubiquity, etc.

Bounce is the Spotify machine built for workplace content. The horizontals in Bounce are a platform layer that connects to any internal system that not only consumes its content but can also write and edit content directly in the system. Think of all those times when you've needed to do something and had to open up different tabs or screens to read instructions on one and enter the information in another. That is now a thing of the past. The experience layer gives the same user experience regardless of content type. Just think about how significant that is for a second. Think of your HR platform, your knowledge platform, your comms platform, etc., and how different they all are. Now imagine using them and they all feel like the same system. That's what Bounce can do. The last layer we have is the personalisation layer. Not only is there all of this different content, with a single user experience, but it's personalised at an individual level so the experience is optimised for each individual employee. This personalisation is not present on some superficial level – every piece of workplace content is optimised to make sure it is seen by the people who need to see it, when they need to see it. That could be when someone joins the band or starts a new role, or is about to go on parental leave, or a timely communication that's specific for your business unit. The list is endless.

And what is at the core of all of this? People Analytics.

The future of people analytics is not an input into a decision, it's the personalisation engine of your organisation. It just needed a platform. We take all of the information we have on our employees and use it to optimise their experience at work. If a band member needs to go somewhere, Bounce gets them there fast. If they need to know something, Bounce curates the content specifically for them so they don't need to go looking. If they need to complete something, Bounce gives them a consistent user experience, regardless of the task. Bounce is the future state of people analytics that you won't find at the end of a consultant's maturity curve.

Strategic Workforce Planning
– the right person in the right job at the right time

When business leaders rank risk factors, lack of talent and lack of skills that match the business strategy are often high on the list. Many want to get better at workforce *planning*, i.e. ensuring that the business has access to employees with the right skills in the right job at the right moment (in both the short and long term). Why do so many organisations struggle with these issues?

Those of us in HR have depended on good workforce planning for all aspects of our work – strategic, operational and tactical. There are numerous models to choose from and they are better or worse suited to different phases and different businesses. It is the decisions behind them, i.e. what to optimise for, that need to be fully thought through, because with every choice come risks that need to be managed. At best, the planning of competence supply can be done without an overly large and heavy process, with the added administration and manual work that takes time and energy away from managers and HR.

The importance of being pragmatic in your HR work isn't often discussed, yet it's one of the things that separates really successful HR departments from mediocre ones. So do make sure you have enough skills to be pragmatic and to dare to make those bold moves that can sometimes even be a bit contradictory. This will help you to predict what needs you have or will have, and when and where.

Only then will you be able to see where in the world you can find the talent you need and what to look for in terms of talent *density* (clustering of a profession and/or skills). Other factors that may come into play when choosing where to have a presence can be salary levels, labour law, and how proactive or reactive you dare to be when it comes to, for example, opening a new office in a new city and in a new market.

Workforce planning is not something you do once a year and then create a document in the belief that you have become strategic overnight. We see strategic workforce planning as an ongoing, dynamic process that ties together current and future talent management and development strategies.

How can you plan for something that is constantly changing? Traditionally, companies have often had a three-to-five year time horizon for their strategic talent management. In the past, HR teams could count on greater stability and be more confident that what they plan for today will come to fruition in the future. This scenario has not been the case at Spotify and it is generally becoming less and less common. Spotify's rapid growth forced us to adapt our HR work, let go of old models and be more agile and responsive.

If change is a normal state of affairs for you too, you need to find your own way of planning your skills supply strategically. The plan itself is perhaps mostly an illusion. It's the planning that's important and that is where the magic happens. You should link different activities, measurements and time horizons to it. As long as there is ambition, as well as method and reflection in your workforce planning, then the timespan is not so important. See it as an ongoing process, with no finish line. A dynamic skills supply should ensure that your current and future business needs reflect the skills of your employees.

In order to take a strategic approach, there needs to be trust between colleagues in the HR department and within the business as a whole. If this exists, which can take some time to establish, it becomes much easier for the HR team to manage operational activities such as recruitment, onboarding, performance development and succession planning, to name a few aspects.

This mission, just like several others in this new era, can feel overwhelming. Stick to what you are trying to achieve. Again, don't copy someone else's model. Try to find your own way of creating plans that the rest of the HR organisation and business can rely on.

A lot of problems arise when HR is not seen as a partner but is treated as a kiosk where the business tries to 'order' what it thinks it needs. The supply of skills must reflect the ambition and goals of the business. In many cases, and even for us at Spotify, the big 'workforce exercise' happens once a year and coincides with the budget and headcount process. As mentioned, workforce planning should be a constant work in progress where it's just as important to be able to manage the accelerator as it is to manage the brake.

In a state of hyper growth, many managers will believe that the only solution is to hire more people. It is important to be bold and resilient here, because more employees is not always the only, best or most effective solution to meet increased productivity demands. This is where *pruning* comes in. Trimming the sails does not make the sailboat move more slowly, nor does it necessarily require more people. What it does require is the knowledge of how to do more in a different way. You will meet many managers who have read up on various theories and models but who in practice have no experience of either skills management or of which organisational model to use during a start-up phase, a scale-up phase or a more mature phase. They will still have a lot of opinions and maybe even suggest that you should bring in consultants – in your area of expertise. Our advice is: learn to deal with it, take it easy and demonstrate that this is exactly the kind of knowledge you have, both in theory and in practice.

THE SIX PHASES OF SPOTIFY'S WORKFORCE PLANNING FRAMEWORK

Spotify has grown rapidly over the years and we have recruited at a high rate, so we have had to approach the issue of skills supply in our own way.

Our *workforce planning journey*, i.e. how to get a firmer grip on talent management, started when more and more of our managers started using the term (even if they didn't fully understand all parts of it). The senior leadership team, HRBPs, line managers, the real estate team (who plan for office capacity) and, last but not least, the recruitment team were all looking for better workforce planning for a variety of reasons. We witnessed major consequences taking place due to the lack of proper planning.

Workforce planning is a vast area and since it touches on most areas of HR, the task can completely take over all others. It was therefore important for us to first form a definition and agree on what we mean by workforce planning in our context – what it is and what it is not – so that we in HR, our colleagues in finance and all the managers were talking about the same thing.

To guide that discussion, we developed a framework with six different phases. They show where the different functions and business units are on their respective journeys. With this framework, it became much easier for us in HR to identify where to put our focus, support and training. We will describe these six phases in more detail here.

1. FINANCE AND HR: THE DYNAMIC DUO

If your CFO and your HR manager have the same set of principles and the same vision, you will be able to create solid plans for strategic talent management and a well-oiled and well-functioning organisation, or 'employ-ment machinery'. Without such a partnership, it becomes really difficult.

If you're only going to take one step in your workforce planning journey, invest in this relationship. The collaboration will become smoother when the HR and Finance teams know who does what, and do so with the same set of standards. This 'dynamic duo' can then create business value.

In the early days of Spotify, there was no such collaboration. At the end of the budget process, the HR team was presented with a long list of new roles. A wish list that was, in short, unrealistic. Managers weren't getting the talent they wanted and needed and in the worst-case scenario, business plans had to be redone. It was a painful process for everyone involved. To avoid this, the relationship between HR and finance had to be strengthened and developed. It is crucial that transparency and trust exists between the teams. There is tremendous power in this duo, when it finds the right balance to support the business. This requires respecting each other's skills and understanding what the people in the other department are experts in and how the functions can complement each other.

We in HR see workforce planning as an *investment*, while a controller sees it as a *cost*. You need to create a space where these two perspectives can meet and find a common voice that both challenges and supports the business. Build close relationships between FP&A (Financial Planning & Analysis) and HRBPs and be prepared that the time you invest here is unlikely to create immediate value – nor will you receive much praise. Just when you think your planning cycle is getting really good, new challenges will come your way and you will face new criticism. Rest assured, howev-er, that if you understand each other's competencies (HR and finance) in relation to workforce planning, the duality of your respective roles will be very important for the growth of your business. If you can meet and find a common voice, true magic can occur – a golden process.

This step involves cost containment, succession planning, upskilling and reskilling. With rapid growth, the starting point is often to constantly recruit, and recruit a lot. Whatever your situation, the goal should always be to build healthy, diverse and productive teams. You have an important role to play here, because the easiest thing for everyone involved to do is to recruit more of what you already have. Like for like.

HR needs to constantly be on top of everything related to recruitment. Your recruitment planning needs to be based on, and *informed* by, data, not *driven* by data. If it is driven by data, there is a risk that recruitment becomes an exercise in putting out fires rather than strategic action. This is an important distinction that every HR team needs to be aware of.

Don't forget the expertise of the recruiters: the Talent Acquisition team. Experts in sourcing, interviewing and negotiating with external talent, they must also be humble, transparent, communicative and confident. Humble enough to understand the real recruitment needs of the business, transparent with their data and insights, communicative (so they can explain the EVP and outline the culture and remuneration model) and brave enough to set realistic expectations. They also need to be able to speak up when necessary. Hiring managers ideally want to get talent into the company yesterday. In an environment where the focus is on rapid growth, HR in general and the Talent Acquisition team in particular need to be resilient and not fearful of their stakeholders.

There was a time when Spotify's HRBP and TA teams had to almost automate the recruitment process in many different business areas. We simply had to prioritise hard. We developed a very forced process, with quarterly cycles, and prioritised the business-critical roles in all areas. These roles needed to match both the capacity of the Talent Acquisition team and our financial planning. Maybe it sounds trivial, but having a process for this was immensely helpful for our recruiters. Our Head of

Talent Acquisition found it much easier to plan our recruitment capacity and their own workforce. They had confirmation from the leadership team that their time was spent on the most important work and we could manage expectations together. This built on the work done in Phase 1, as there was close cooperation between the HRBPs, Talent Acquisition leaders and the finance department.

3. TALENT ACQUISITION – DATA

Most managers want access to the right talent immediately. Especially in companies that are growing very fast and do not yet have established processes for their strategic talent management. The solution is to drive the recruitment plan proactively, using insights from datasets. Your recruitment data may not be flawless from the start, but that doesn't have to be a problem. The data still points to relevant areas, so you can discuss how to prioritise your recruitment resources and set a realistic recruitment plan. What is realistic doesn't always have to be linked to your ability to recruit, it could just as easily be that managers don't have time to sit and interview people all day or spend most of their time introducing new employees. Or perhaps that you don't have the capacity to onboard many new people at the same time.

Using data to ensure that hiring managers and under-staffed teams are informed and feel included builds trust and strengthens the partnership. A headcount budget is an estimate, a forecast. It takes time to bring in the right talent at the right time, in the right position and with diversity in mind. When you do succeed, you can reap the sweet fruits of your labour. If you have the time.

The key ingredient in this recipe is an HR team that is bold and dares to own the narrative, i.e. to be process and conceptual experts and have the ability to communicate. In the best of all worlds, the TA team is in control of its recruitment forecast and can drive the story alongside HRBPs and the finance team. Unknown variables – attrition, reorganisations, difficult-to-fill roles, and so on – can mean that a recruitment plan needs to be adjusted throughout the year. Partnering with hiring managers and sharing your data builds trust and creates a sense of common ground.

At Spotify, HR owns all *people data* and therefore also the associated talent acquisition report on how things are progressing, what actions are needed and other analysis. We trust our recruiters across the business and we succeed or fail together. We also recognise that our Talent Acquisition team plays a strategic role in filling critical roles, in the company's ability to evolve our platform, and in continually improving our strategic workforce planning. Having reliable data and Talent Acquisition and HRBPs acting as one creates business value and is a collaboration that is both effective and fun. When this starts to happen, it's a sign that things are moving in the right direction. The HRBP and Talent Acquisition teams are working side by side with their key stakeholders and you can move on to the next phase of your journey to become even more strategic in your workforce planning.

4. WORKFORCE ANALYTICS

When the HRBP and the business leaders discuss their recruitment plan, many questions arise. For example: How should we increase the rate of internal hiring? What is our need for more senior talent? How do we ensure more diversity in our recruitments? The list can be long. In an organisation where many people know a lot about a lot, and are curious and well-read, it is easy to be bombarded with a plethora of questions that it is best to be prepared for.

Those of us working in HR at Spotify need to appreciate both theory and practice, research and development. We need to like data and also be able to analyse and navigate all the new research findings. At the same time, we must be able to keep a cool head, to have confidence in our skills and experience, and to ask *why*. Where does this data come from? Is it really objective information, or rather an anecdote to get a wish to satisfy a short-term need? Why do we need to adjust our philosophy, our People Strategy, and how does this drive the business forwards?

Business acumen and the ability to hypothesise are important for HR professionals. Whether a business area already has a well-developed talent management plan or is in the early stages of creating one, HR should facilitate that process so that the focus is on the right metrics for the right reasons.

The goal here is to find some KPIs that are important over time – this is your *workforce analytics*. The simpler and clearer these indicators are, the better. Of course, the simplest is often the hardest, so it's easy to get lost in all the questions about data and different perspectives. You can easily panic and struggle to get hold of the data, analyse it and build a story around it. Once the story is created, stakeholders may have already moved on to the next topic that has subsequently become much more important. It's key that your workforce analytics practices are consistent over time, support your company's growth, make business sense and are based on your vision of how you want to operate as an organisation. Just as the business tries to stick to a few key objectives and indicators linked to them, HR should try to find the most central data points for the People Strategy. Then you can dive into those data points and build out initiatives and programmes and – more importantly – guide the right kind of discussions. Otherwise, it will be easy for the conversations and discussions to derail.

If there is no clear talent management plan in place, you should work on it in parallel. This is not a linear process and it is important to choose a long-term direction and accept some chaos and deviations along the way.

5. OPERATIONAL WORKFORCE PLANNING

Once you've completed phases 1-4, you can take your first steps on the bridge that will take you beyond basic workforce planning to a place where you can minimise *talent risk* and engage in more operational workforce planning.

HR departments often plan for a certain rhythm, with a few building blocks in place each year. When you look at these building blocks separately, they can appear to be mere hygiene factors – examples include development talks and compensation reviews. It is easy to be overwhelmed by 'hygiene tasks'. One way to avoid this is to link what is requested to talent risks – i.e. look first and foremost at the information you receive that relates to the risk of losing people with critical skills.

Succession planning is an example of a building block that is both operational and highly strategic. It can be built into many other activities that take place during the regular planning cycle. If your succession planning is linked to a vision of how you want to minimise talent risks, it also becomes more strategic, even if this happens during more mundane activities. The HR team needs to carry out a risk analysis to find the right balance. We can go so far as to say that if you don't minimise your talent risks on an ongoing basis, it doesn't matter how good your strategic workforce plan is. Minimising these risks allows you to focus on and follow up on needs that arise 'out of rhythm' – which are often business-critical or in areas that move the business and its strategies forwards.

6. STRATEGIC WORKFORCE PLANNING

You have arrived! You have reached the final phase: where your workforce planning becomes strategic, or – in other words – where the organisation's competence needs are aligned with your employees' competences and you don't only have an idea of how to optimise your talent supply, promotion and organisational design, but have created a well-functioning 'talent ecosystem'.

Celebrate it and remember that it is a dynamic and ongoing process. Even if you have reached your goal, don't forget that you need to constantly adapt, manage your relationships and plan, to ensure that your existing and future strategies are aligned with your employees' competencies.

It's important to recognise that different leadership teams work in different ways and that their time is precious. Strategic workforce planning is best done when it's integrated with what is already on the agenda. Look for links to what is already in focus. Don't forget to embed, embed and embed. Communicate, communicate and communicate! There should also be links between this and organisational design, and more operationally oriented discussions regarding succession planning. Keeping the five previous phases in mind and holding a focused meeting where the leadership team selects a few beliefs, principles and priority areas related to competence supply all together. This is an effective way to get started. Do remember – there is no universal solution!

Feel free to use methods and frameworks, but don't become slaves to them. Instead, dare to adapt how you do the work and find your own path. A large portion of pragmatism mixed with an equally large portion of method is what is required. Since an overall process and method cannot always be shoehorned in exactly the same way throughout the organisation, be prepared to adjust approaches even between business areas. Most importantly, don't give any advantages to any one part of the organisation without justification.

This is good and has served us well, but it naturally applies to growth. We can both sense and are beginning to crack the door open to the next phase – when we leave the scale-up phase and enter a more mature phase. Then, this last piece of advice will also apply to us. We will need to let go of what has worked, change our approach, and have a model that is better suited for a mature organisation when it comes to strategic workforce planning.

Change management – leading change

More than two and a half thousand years have passed since Heraclitus observed that nothing in the world is permanent except change. Today, change is taking place at an even faster pace. What would a Greek philosopher think of the modern world and this new era in HR?

In today's world of work, you need to be good at *change management*. For us at Spotify, it's so central that it forms the entire basis of our Band Manifesto. We've talked before about 'controlled chaos', how it's an accepted state of affairs at Spotify and an important part of the way we work. We've built our entire identity around a high rate of change. It's not for everyone. Even for those who can and want to work in such an environment and culture, rapid and constant change can be uncomfortable and tiring. Those in HR who work in change management need to be bold and in order to adapt quickly, they need to be able to manage change in a way that works for both the business and employees. It's impossible to be a change agent if you don't like change yourself.

Get to know your business

Leading change is very much about anticipating and often proactively proposing a change, perhaps even before the majority understands why it is important. In order to be successful, HR professionals should be a strategic and trusted partner to the leadership team, with detailed knowledge of the company's business, strategy, goals and objectives. The organisation is a living organism and you need to understand its structure, history and people in order to be an effective change leader.

You must also understand and believe in the change that you will be involved in driving. Here, your trust capital is crucial for the majority to quickly understand why the change will happen, when and how. Additionally, when the organisation changes, it may be wise for you to adjust your HR organisation to best support the new situation. Reflecting the change creates credibility and also gives you extra speed and power to turn the last sceptics. After all, you will have experienced what the change means yourself.

The basis of our philosophy is that in the new era of HR, we cannot rely solely on traditional HR skills (*HR acumen*), we must also have a deep understanding and knowledge of the business (*business acumen*). Otherwise, we can never carry through a long-term and successful *people-first approach*. This close relationship with the business is non-negotiable. This is where you as HR professionals should remember that your role is to support, develop, challenge and push. You need to question mindsets that don't belong in your culture and organisational theories and beliefs, or designs that simply don't fit your needs.

There is often a strong relationship between HR and the parts of the business you work with most. Remember that no matter which area your role focuses on, if you are involved in change management, you must have good relationships with managers, leaders and teams in all parts of the business and at all levels. Even if you are not planning a major change, it takes time to build strong, trusting relationships where you can play your different roles properly – so start straight away. Build relationships by having recurring meetings with managers and leaders, once a week or every two weeks. Make sure you have regular check-ins with your colleagues in each area of responsibility. Remember that we work in the 'trust business' and that we must constantly educate ourselves to get an up-to-date picture of the structure, challenges and opportunities of our people, the product and the financial results. Remember that HR is the only department, apart from the CEO and the finance department, that has an overview of the whole business. Moreover, HR is neutral, in the sense that it has no hidden business agenda of its own. What you do and propose is what you think is best for the business as a whole, in each given moment and phase.

If you do not have a seat at the change table, something is wrong. You should, because your knowledge of the business is a valuable input to business decisions. You are experts in organisational design and organisational change, to name just two areas relevant to change management. Surprisingly, organisations often bring in consultants when it is time to restructure. Don't do that. They don't know your organisation as well as you do. They are likely to present various theories and models and show off an occasional four grid box, all very professionally, at a senior leadership retreat. However, they lack knowledge about the 'invisible contracts' in the organisation. They don't know what's working even though, in theory, it shouldn't. They don't understand that something that has brought you here will not take you to the next phase. They don't know which relationships are critical to efficiency and productivity. They won't be the ones implementing the change in practice, either in the organisation or administratively, when it comes to what needs to be moved behind the curtain – in HR, finance, legal and other support teams – in order for everything to run as smoothly as possible and taking every single important detail into account. They will also not be present to accept the consequences of the change they propose. They will stand brashly in front of the next CEO and tell them what they did with and for you.

Overview and Insight

When there is a need for change within the organisation, you – who have deep knowledge and understanding of the strategy and have built strong, trusting relationships with the whole organisation – will be among the first to see that change is coming, or is needed. This will give you a hint of upcoming strategy changes, allowing you to be proactive in your change management planning. As an HR professional, you are in a unique position to flag that certain strategic changes need to be made in order for the business to be better equipped to achieve new goals.

There can be many reasons why a change is required, so always start by asking yourself what problem you are trying to solve. The problem doesn't have to be something negative, such as poor business performance. It could also be that you are growing so fast that your organisational model is no longer as effective. Define your challenge and the problem you want to solve and what your objectives are. Then define the intended actions and/or the intended organisational design. The key is to create a structure based on what you want to achieve from a business perspective.

Your overview and proactivity and your clear objectives also give you a good guide for change and for the new organisational structure. No model is good for everything, all designs have their pros and cons. However, HR's neutral position means that decisions are made based on the goals of the business and not necessarily on the strengths and shortcomings of existing managers. Not even in the existing design. A professional HR team will be able to identify the goal at an early stage, in terms of:

- the change that is needed,
- the new organisational structure and/or new ways of working,
- the capabilities needed in the future and the process and communication plan that best prepares the business for rapid and effective change.

It can mean a total transformation – or just a minor adjustment.

The DIBB model

When deciding what to change and when, use a simple model so that everyone involved and affected understands the problem you are trying to solve. In many situations, the DIBB (*Data, Insight, Belief, Bet*) model works well. Acquire the information (*data*) you need and see what *insights* you can get from that data, what conclusions you can draw. Based on your data and your insights – both internal and external – write down what you think this will mean (*belief*). Then decide what you want to do, what you '*bet*' you can achieve (*bet*). Most people and organisations draw the same conclusions from the same data and information, so make sure some of your bets are '*contrarian bets*'. Dare to be radically different. In this bold new era, innovation is not just for R&D, it is also for HR.

Do it wholeheartedly

When making a change, do it properly! Organisational change takes time and energy and can have a negative impact on productivity and employee engagement. This can be seen both when creating the new organisational design and when implementing it. Therefore, it is important to think through the problem in detail. Also, think as long-term as possible when creating the new structure. It is tempting to redesign because there is dissatisfaction or frustration in the organisation, but this course of action would be short-sighted. Rather, find out where the dissatisfaction comes from and address the root cause.

One of the most common reasons for organisational change in more traditional and mature organisations is poor performance. Here, you should consider whether you will create even more chaos by attacking poor profitability with a 'pick and choose' strategy. When all the parts (employees) are in the air and will land in a mess in unknown places, productivity, loyalty, security and well-being rarely increase.

Change as a normal state

We remind all our band members that *change is our constant*, that *growth is our mantra* and that we operate in *controlled chaos*. They hear it before they even sign their employment contract and they are reminded of it during their introduction and, of course, once they are in the organisation. People who really don't like change, who have a strong need for security and predictability, who want clearly defined roles that stay the same, and who thrive when the organisational form remains constant, may well not want to join us. They will struggle with the constant change that comes from progress and growing and developing. So be open about who you are and clear about what to expect when working with you. If the organisation is constantly changing, be honest about this in your communication from the beginning – in the contact with the candidate during the recruitment process – and then continue to emphasise it throughout the employee's journey with you. For example, be wary of using attributes that signal low levels of change, such as organisational charts and job descriptions. Instead, if you can visualise and communicate a constantly evolving and changing organisation, it will help everyone see that change is inevitable. Yes, even something that is sought after. The sooner they can deal with the discomfort that change always brings, the better.

Don't forget that the vast majority of us have selective memory and don't really like change unless we have initiated it ourselves. So again – remind, remind, remind! *Hit, re-hit and remind!*

Communication, communication, communication

Decisions regarding change have been made with business objectives in mind, which is how it should be. As you carry out the change, you need to remember that it affects your employees, so the change communication should be employee-centric. Your employees don't have to *like* the change, but they must be able to accept it and they must be given the opportunity to understand it. Don't rely on your business acumen here, but on your expertise as a behavioural scientist. Think about how you can best involve and inform your employees and create a space for dialogue about what will happen and why.

Some thoughts when crafting your communication: Where will you be as an organisation in a few years and is your planned organisational structure the way to get there? Do the managers who will lead in the new structure have the right skills and is the number of decision-making levels within the organisation reasonable? What effect will the change have on cross-organisational forums, roles and responsibilities?

It is easy to plan a change in silos, forgetting how the work outside the silos will be conducted, or even how straightforward reporting structures actually work in practice. Again, it is important to know your organisation. What is the impact of the change? Some of your external stakeholders may need to be informed about or even involved in planning the change. For example, if you are changing a product, or changing the nature of your customer service function, you will probably need to communicate this both externally and internally.

To guarantee that everyone affected by the change is informed effectively, we recommend that you create a communication plan, including a schedule of dates, times, responsible people, target groups, etc., and share this plan within your team. Don't forget to include information about when the change will take place.

When it's time to communicate, do it in the right order (we'll come back to that in a moment) and make sure that all communication takes place within a reasonable and fairly short time frame. Expect information to spread quickly within the company once you start communicating. There is a high risk of misunderstandings and wrong assumptions being made that will prevent the change from gaining support and therefore being successful. At worst, it can lead to unnecessary stress for all involved. You want to avoid this at all costs.

In terms of communicating in the *right order*, the managers who will be directly affected by the change must first be informed. Ideally, they should have been part of the dialogue from the very beginning so that the change doesn't come as a surprise – in a perfect world, they will have even suggested it. Regardless of who initiated the change, you need to equip managers with a narrative that is easy to understand and absorb, and ensure that they are on board and understand the goal and purpose of the change. Consistent communication, sticking to the same message, even having a script, minimises unnecessary anxiety among those affected.

Now that managers have been informed and are on board, the next step is to schedule one-on-one meetings with the team members who will be directly affected. Perhaps the change will mean having a new manager, or a partially different area of responsibility due to a new organisational or reporting structure.

Only after these meetings have taken place can you move on to the next step, which is broader communication with the rest of the organisation. This communication should be in writing and go out through the company's various communications channels. For major changes, oral communication from senior leadership is often most effective. This can take place at a department level meeting, at an *All Hands*, or with everyone in the company at a *town hall* meeting if the change affects the organisation as a whole.

Try to anticipate questions about the change and create a document with these questions and answers so that you are prepared. Some people need some time to process the information before they have relevant questions to ask. Giving them access to a document with key questions and answers will help them gain an understanding on their own terms. Transparency is very important here, so while some questions may be difficult, you need to be as open as possible about why you've made the decisions you've made.

If the change involves a major shift in strategy or, for example, a merger with another company, you should follow up the communication with training sessions within the organisation explaining the meaning of the new strategy and how you have structured the organisation.

The right timing

Think about the timing of the change and make sure it doesn't clash with a major event in the organisation, such as a product launch. Don't communicate or carry out a reorganisation on a weekend or holiday – make sure you have a number of days set aside during the week to answer questions and provide information. If the time frame is too tight, you will create unnecessary anxiety among your employees.

Investing so much time in communication and setting a schedule may seem overly ambitious, but we can guarantee that those who follow a time-bound communication plan during a change period can start working on the new strategy much faster than those who do not. It makes sense if you put yourself in the employee's shoes. If you were to get a new role or a new manager, we bet you would rather be informed about the change, and how it might affect you, from your current manager than read about it in an email or hear about it through rumours. It's much more time-efficient to set up a thorough communication plan than to deal with rumours and reactions from employees who haven't been adequately kept in the loop, or are upset about the disrespect shown by the lack of communication.

The working group

As for the working group, not everyone should be brought into it. It is not a group that needs many voices and opinions. Because you have established close relationships with people across the organisation, you have already gathered the information you need from the 'real world'. In many organisations, there is a perception that all employees can contribute wise views on an organisational change and how it should be implemented. This is not true. An overly large or improperly constituted working group leads to subjective decisions and runs the real risk of sensitive information being leaked at the wrong time, before it has been finalised. Successful change management requires smaller working groups with representatives from the different parts of the business most affected by the change and people with a mandate to make decisions. Sometimes the group is as small as just the CEO and CHRO in the first stage, and then expanded to include relevant business unit heads depending on where in the organisation the change is to take place.

The project plan

Once you've assembled the working group, it's time for a step-by-step strategy. Create a project plan where you identify the responsibilities of the different members of the group and set dates for the implementation of the different parts of the project.

A summary of change management (introducing a new operating model):

- Define the problem you are trying to solve, taking into account the business strategy, the objectives and the outcome you want to see.
- Determine what your new operating model should look like to give your organisation the best possible starting point for realising your business strategy.
- Try to anticipate possible risks, problems and dissatisfaction that may arise when introducing a new operating model and plan how to deal with them.
- Draw the map of the new organisation and identify what capabilities are needed in it and where you have gaps.
- Match existing staff to the new structure and roles.
- Create a communication plan, including who (internal and possible external partners) needs to be informed about the change and when.

To manage change effectively, structure the work as you would any other complex project. Build sufficient time into the plan. Each organisational structure will have its own dependencies and structural variations that need to be discussed and adapted before choosing your final solution. The last thing you want is to make wrong decisions simply because you've run out of time.

Change – the only constant

In a constantly changing organisation, it is important to reflect on what happened and why, especially when things don't go as planned. Next time you can learn how to tackle similar problems in a better way (learning from failure). That's why we are strong advocates of *retrospective* – catch-up meetings with your team to discuss what worked well and what can be improved. We also recommend creating measurement points to evaluate the results and get a picture of productivity and employee motivation levels after a change has taken place. You should also measure how quickly the change was carried through, from idea to implementation, from communication to new ways of working.

Once you decide that you need to make a change – don't hesitate. It's often better to make a significant change all in one go than to do it in phases. It's easy to think that doing a little at a time is less painful, but our experience tells us that it's better to rip the plaster off in one go. Do it slowly, and the pain will last longer. A well-executed big change will ultimately be more effective and successful than many small, incremental changes. In addition, be prepared to make difficult decisions once the change has been made. Perhaps you realised that there are too many levels of decision-making to effectively achieve your organisation's goals, or certain roles became redundant as you redrew the organisational chart, or employee roles changed because you discontinued a certain product or shifted your focus from one strategy to another. Whatever the underlying reason, our experience is that decisions will gain a completely different acceptance within the organisation if you are open and transparent about the idea behind them, in comparison to not being able to explain them. Clarity about the purpose of the change is crucial for successful implementation. As usual, it is important that you can answer the question: What business problem are we trying to solve?

Great change management is about finding the balance between prioritising business and prioritising people. Both must be nurtured, guided and given space to develop. This type of work is gradual – it is a form of metamorphosis that happens as the organisation evolves.

Ultimately, being bold when it comes to change and change management is both rewarding and challenging. You shouldn't move *too* fast, but moving too slow can be devastating.

CHANGE MANAGEMENT AT SPOTIFY

In a business like ours, where 'constant change' and 'controlled chaos' are part of our everyday life, there are many examples of change management. We focus on constantly evolving and keeping up with – or preferably ahead of – the changes in our surrounding landscape, whether the perspective is artists and creators, users and listeners, or employees and organisation. To be that adaptable, we need to lead change in a thoughtful and effective way. Let's talk about two instances where this has been the case.

CHANGE MANAGEMENT DURING RESTRUCTURING

We were going through a reorganisation that affected two of our business areas in particular. However, with the planned change, most of our band members would keep the same manager and work on the same things as before the change. The change was more focused on how functions would be merged and form units instead. We also wanted to take the opportunity to centralise marketing in the company, after it had been scattered across three business units. The change could be seen as confusing, but it was an obvious decision at that stage of Spotify's development (having good business acumen and deep knowledge of the roles of departments, managers and teams). We saw an opportunity and a business need linked to productivity and efficiency in how we worked – a way to continue to grow in a qualitative way and still retain our customers.

The decision was made after several discussions and iterations between a few unit and functional leaders and the CHRO, with the blessing of our CEO. The change affected more than 1,200 individuals globally at the time, so of course we needed a solid change plan. We created a small team, with two of our senior HRBPs working in tandem as change managers. Having a small group enabled the team to work closely together, without the risk of sensitive information being leaked. We then discussed, planned and prepared all communications within the team.

We wanted to clarify the purpose behind the change and answer the questions that we knew from experience would come up. More specifically, we chose a waterfall communication plan in this case, to ensure that we communicated in face-to-face meetings with all directly affected managers and employees, all affected teams, all stakeholders and the rest of the organisation – and in the right order. We also identified the people – informal leaders who were important to bring on board – those who undoubtedly needed to get first-hand information. We knew it was necessary for them to 1) feel comfortable, and 2) support and promote the upcoming changes.

Before we carried through the reorganisation, we had outlined all interactions – 110 of them. At an early stage of the process, we had prepared a number of important communication elements, such as developing a template for presentations so that we would be communicating in the same way and sending spokespeople and status information to the CEO and the CHRO who initiated the change. A small but important detail was that we planned the communication in multiple time zones, as the reorganisation affected managers and teams all over the world. We planned in detail (hours and minutes) who would contact whom and when, and who would follow up immediately afterwards. We also created guidelines and guides for several managers, including HRBPs, so that they could give employees the support they needed while providing consistent information to reduce any concerns.

Within three days, after more than 75 meetings, broad communication to everyone in the company and smaller departmental meetings with the relevant teams, we got the word out about the new organisation, including the new reporting structure.

Of course, the process did not end there. The following weeks and months were devoted to continued follow-up, confirming business objectives and ensuring that all employees still felt a sense of belonging, understood the purpose of the change and had continued development opportunities. We also wanted to make sure that business and customer relationships were not negatively affected by the organisational changes.

The five weeks invested in preparation and three days of carrying through the change paid off. The solid partnership and collaboration, the thoughtful communication, the clarity of purpose, the focus on people, the well-being of the organisation and the strategic business decisions became the basis for even better performance and increased customer satisfaction.

The fact that we can change large parts or the whole company in just a few days is quite unique and a bit of a superpower of this HR team. However, it's not impossible to do. It requires practice, clarity and communication. It's also a team effort.

MORE CHOICE FOR EVERYONE!

One of the philosophical approaches behind Spotify's success is freedom and flexibility. Our customers have the freedom to choose when and where to listen and what to listen to. It sounds obvious today, but many people were not fully convinced of our business model when the company was founded.

In the HR world, many people still think that it's better to have everything centrally controlled than to let people make their own decisions. Our customers wouldn't appreciate it if we forced them to listen to our curated playlists all day, just as our managers and employees don't appreciate total direction and control. We believe it's right to give our employees the same freedom as we give our customers, although translated into a workplace context.

In the conservative pay and benefits landscape, greater freedom, trust and flexibility are not expected. This is our second example of a change that led to greater choice for our employees and also challenged old structures.

We told you earlier in the book that we decided to introduce an incentive mix, offering employees an incentive sum that they could then choose how to invest. We based this initiative on the idea that our employees know themselves best and can take responsibility for their own decisions.

The change was implemented with relatively little fuss (thanks to the hard work of the Compensation & Benefits team in particular, and because we had put a lot of emphasis on explaining why we were doing it and how employees would be affected). When we switched to the incentive mix, we switched from one paradigm to another and that in itself was a challenge. You can't have two systems active at the same time. As soon as people realise that something they perceive as better is happening, they will try to speed up the change. Or at least argue that they personally should be moved to the new system, even if it has not yet been implemented. We had made changes to the incentive structure before and learned the hard way that even our most senior employees couldn't work in an existing system if they knew something better was coming. Why would they, when it's part of their role to constantly focus on what they believe is best for the employees and the company? With that in mind, we chose (perhaps surprisingly) to under-communicate in the early stages of this particular change, in order to ensure a consistent implementation, until the change could be implemented.

Leading the kind of change we have given examples of here is not about following traditional change management models to the letter. It's about taking the plunge and actually making the changes required, changes that everyone can understand the logic behind. This inevitably involves some follow-up, fine-tuning – and further supporting and sincerely apologising to anyone who felt they were under-informed and under-trained at the moment of change. There are usually not as many people as you might think who feel this way. When you can give a clear answer to the question *why*, most people are patient with the fact that not all the pieces of the *how* are in place on day one.

We've seen how important it is to have the courage to believe that everything is possible. We did what we did because we knew it was right for our business, because trust and autonomy are the pillars of our culture and because we are convinced that we have smart people who know what's best for them.

Labour Law
– a pragmatic approach to labour and employment law

You might think that labour law is the dullest part of HR. Not in this new era it's not! Labour and employment law acts as a bridge between employee and employer, shaping the relationship between them. It sounds very formal and, whilst everyone should absolutely respect the role that labour law plays, it doesn't have to be your gospel, nor should it be seen as something mysterious or scary. Legislation should never be something you hide behind – especially when you should be driving your business forwards, addressing underperforming employees, or elevating employees to further success.

When working in HR, regardless of your field, it's a great advantage to be familiar with labour and employment law, because we all come into contact with these rules to a lesser or greater extent. Some see laws and regulations as a necessary evil – something that limits them in their work. At the other end of the spectrum, there are those who live and breathe labour and employment law and use it as an excuse to maintain rigid structures. Then there are those who do everything they can to comply with all the requirements of the law – but mostly to cover their backs. Of course, labour law was created to protect our workers and ensure decent working conditions for all, and its importance cannot be overstated, but again – don't hide behind it when making decisions.

With a full focus on creating strategies that truly benefit both the employees and the business, you rarely need to fall into either of these extremes. The key is to stay within the benchmarks of the law, but not at the expense of the business or employees. You have to find a way to be pragmatic, for the benefit of everyone. To do that, you simply have to know what the law stipulates.

Compliance

Those who are worried about breaking a law or a rule should keep this in mind: in reality, we know that we won't be able to do everything exactly as regulated – it is simply not possible. Legislators don't always have the time to update laws as society and technology evolve. Moreover, laws are written based on local conditions and what is reasonable at a given time. Working in a global company can mean encountering conflicting laws. Instead of trying to cover every possible eventuality and juggling a whole bunch of different laws, try to find a balance. Try to understand why the law was made in the first place and use that insight as a basis for decision-making when creating your company policies. Without such freedom of interpretation and without a sense of doing what is right and reasonable, you will end up buried in marathon interpretation exercises, long processes and administration that ultimately benefit no one. Of course, this does not mean that you should drop the idea of accountability and focus on total non-compliance. Try to prioritise so that the HR team spends its time on things that support the business and employees – meaning things that help the company achieve its goals. Instead of being 'compliance-driven', be purpose-driven and focus on doing what's right for everyone involved.

Don't forget to think about consequences – and about what is best for the majority. Let's take the example of allowing employees to bring their dog to the office (this is not a labour or employment law issue, but it demonstrates how to make a decision with the majority in mind). For dog owners, such an option would probably be welcomed, as it would greatly facilitate their everyday life. What are the consequences though? What about employees who are allergic to dogs? Or those who are afraid of these four-legged friends? Someone else may feel uncomfortable with a lot of dog hair in the office. Even if we isolate a part of the office for a team that is in favour of this set-up, what about new team members – or people who need to interact with the team? What about customers and partners who can no longer be in the office without getting sick? The list goes on and on. You can never make everyone happy, so this is an example of when you should choose to do what is best for the majority instead of making dog owners and dog lovers happy. Besides, what about cat owners, chameleon owners and guinea pig owners...?

Values-driven work in the field of
labour and employment law

Start from scratch and build your philosophy globally, based on your culture and what you stand for. You can make local adaptations, if required, at a later stage. Working conditions and the like should be linked to your core values, not primarily to what the law says. If you are a good, attractive employer, you are almost certainly on the right side of the law. How else will you attract and retain all your good people if you don't do right by them?

With your current practices and methods – or because of past, negative experiences – it may be difficult to shift to this new way of thinking. Again – be bold! Dare to look at things from new perspectives, especially if you want to stand out as an employer. Sure, you can make comparisons with other companies and ask around the network for advice and examples of different interpretations of laws and regulations, but most importantly, have the courage to think innovatively and pragmatically. Don't hold on to outdated thinking and the way things work today. Be bold, especially if you come up with an idea that would protect your employees' rights, and is also based on modern technology and an understanding of how the world and organisations work today.

You don't want to break the law, so make sure you know the legal requirements in different regions. From this starting point, you can create a checklist (like the one below) to help you map out how things work in different parts of the world and how well they fit into your global philosophy. Determine whether there are areas where it makes sense to do the bare minimum for compliance and where it makes sense to choose a different solution for the sake of a win-win situation.

Then you just have to get on with it. The devil is always in the details and you need to nail those details in every area. Discuss different scenarios within the team, ask lots of questions and cover the topic from every angle. Always go back to your philosophy and explore what you want to give your employees and why. Zoom in and then zoom out again.

Once upon a time, a good employer was one that acted in accordance with labour law and had a collective agreement. Today, when the battle for talent is at its peak, the ability to attract and retain good people is the real currency. You can't just be a good employer – you have to be a great employer! The truth is that laws and regulations are not always up to date with the current reality.

Politicians, unions and other bodies have often not kept up with global, borderless technology and a constantly connected workforce, although they may have tried.

If you decide to be a sought-after, purpose-driven, trustworthy and values-driven employer and want to do what is right for your employees, you have most likely already raised the bar compared to any collective agreement. Being purpose- and value-driven means that you follow the rules, but also brings about an awareness that you can't hold on to ideas that are over fifty years old. There are rules and practices that were created in a different time and for activities that have little in common with ours, when the relationship between employer and employee was very different from today's reality. In the past, the employer held all of the power. Today you need to do the right thing by your employees, be open and transparent, offer exciting and challenging tasks and constant skills development in all its forms. Otherwise, your people will first be loud, then they'll be dissatisfied and lose motivation, and sooner or later, they'll simply resign to join an employer who has the sense to take care of their most important resource.

Legal expertise

Take legal help when needed. However, when buying the services of an external consultant, remember that lawyers have a code of ethics that they have to follow and therefore they have to repeat exactly what the law says. They are not in the business of interpreting the law and finding a good balance that benefits the business or employees. Many will not understand what you mean if you ask about risks and consequences. Often, grey areas exist in labour and employment law as well. Speaking of which, talk to an expert. If you try to involve an external consultant in weighing up the risks, it's likely that you will end up thinking in circles. Every follow-up question you ask will only make the final invoice bigger.

So, before you start working with an external labour and employment law expert, think about how to formulate your questions. Don't ask yes/no questions, rather pose questions that open up a topic and can give you ideas. Ask how things usually work and what the regulations are in this area. Or present your global philosophy and ask the lawyers for advice on how to adapt it to local conditions. This approach of evaluating the risks and understanding the consequences can help you, if you choose to do things in a non-traditional way. You will get more nuanced answers that can give you a clearer picture.

Sometimes, you can take the risk of breaking a rule in good conscience, but only when you understand the full purpose of the legislation and *agree with* the intention behind it. Contradictory? Yes, but hopefully the following example will clarify. A law, clause or rule was once intended to protect employees, but it may have outlived its usefulness as society changed, technology developed and people adapted the way they live, work and behave. It may be that the legal protection is no longer needed, or even frustrates those it was originally designed to protect. When you deviate and understand the consequences, it may be worth the risk and it's unlikely that any employee will complain about your breach, as it's likely to be in line with what they want too. If there are consequences, it's a risk you're willing to take and you will have no difficulty explaining why you've done what you've done, either to employees or to the outside world.

That's exactly what we did at Spotify when we introduced our *Flexible Public Holiday* policy. To explain how it works – an individual can choose to work at Christmas and instead take a day off during Diwali, Pride week or any other day that means a lot to them. As long as the employee and their manager agree that there are no negative consequences for the team and that the workload won't be too heavy for other colleagues, the switch can be made. In most countries, it is a legal requirement not to work on public holidays, so formally, we do not follow the law. We are willing to take the risk of consequences, because this is not something we force on any of our employees but a choice they make themselves – it's more like a voluntary benefit. We offer our employees something *they* want, not what those who made the law once thought was right. We fully comply with the purpose or spirit of the law, but allow each employee to do what suits their values, beliefs, culture and/or interests.

Communication

If you have truly considered the best interests of your employees and the business, you have probably made some decisions that may seem controversial to 'compliance-driven' people. For some employees, it may be unclear what your policies are and how they benefit them. Therefore, you also need to spend time and effort on communication. Write down the guidelines you have decided on and start creating your own *playbook*, your employee handbook. Make sure you have guidelines for both employees and managers. Ideally, you can use a customisable Content Management System (CMS) to ensure that your philosophies, guidelines and instructions are structured and accessible to all employees in a seamless way. A very practical piece of advice on this: steer clear of uploading a lot of documents, presentations and other files – in order to avoid problems related to searches, links, mobile readability and the like. Instead, build the content into the system itself and it will be easier to keep it updated.

You may decide to make your managers' guidelines and the various local rules available to everyone. This will allow employees to see what is happening in other countries and, more importantly, it will help you stick to your core philosophy and ensure that your approach is market-driven and, at the same time, fair. The fact that all information is available to everyone and not only to managers creates a sense of calm and increases trust in both HR and management.

Aim for simplicity and clarity for everyone involved. Write clear, concise texts, cut out what is superfluous and keep what is really used and needed. The same goes for your contracts. Create global templates where you peel away everything that is unnecessary – without letting go of what you believe in. Long, complicated employment contracts in difficult legal language only serve to create unnecessary uncertainty at the beginning of your relationship with new employees.

Be bold, take risks, influence

With this approach to labour and employment law, you are likely to face some resistance from lawyers, but if you start digging into why the resistance exists, the arguments soon fade. The right thing to do is to do the right thing: identify your minimum requirements, think about what the law was intended to do when it was written and draw on your core values to find philosophies that can be used to create simple, useful policies.

This could turn into a political battle – you are trying to incorporate an area driven by *compliance*, a rule-based way of thinking and working, into an environment where transparency and openness are highly valued. Don't give up! Remember not to be too stubborn. Pick your battles and don't make it a goal in itself to always question each and every rule. Although some of them may seem unnecessarily complex, the consequences of circumventing them can be significant. Think carefully, ask questions and investigate further. You will find practical solutions that benefit both the business and the people. Don't buy any arguments or be silenced by comments such as 'the law is there for a reason' and 'we can't do that because we'd be breaking the law'. In a constantly connected and interconnected world, some old laws inevitably become obsolete.

SPOTIFY'S GLOBAL EMPLOYMENT AGREEMENT

The first year that we hired more than 1,000 people in one year, our recruiters spent a total of 285 working hours drafting offers and contracts. At that time, we were hiring in 23 different countries, with more to come. This meant that we had to keep track of and adapt to 23 different sets of labour laws. We had to take into account the human factor here – the likelihood was quite high that we would miss something somewhere and create contracts that somehow broke the law.

Labour and employment laws are national, not international, so using the same employment contract in all countries has been considered impossible by many HR departments. At Spotify, we believe this is a truth that should be challenged. We've proven that it can be, through our Global Employment Agreement.

WHY ONE STANDARD EMPLOYMENT CONTRACT?

As usual, we started by asking *why?* What would be the point of one standard agreement template? We didn't want to challenge old truths just for the sake of it, so we came up with a list of reasons:

- Some agreements are only a few pages long, others are as long as a novel. This makes it difficult for us in HR, and for our employees, to get an overview.

- If there are many different agreements, there's also a lot of room for discussion, interpretation and negotiation when presenting an offer to a candidate. This means that many people need to be involved in each recruitment (the recruiter may not be fully aware of everything that applies locally).

- Much of the information in the contracts is generic and repeats legislation or company guidelines.

- Having clauses that are open to negotiation results in each individual employment contract being worded in a unique way, making it impossible to change certain company policies without holding negotiations with many individuals.

- Having the same agreement worldwide makes it easier to automate the process.

- Simplified contracts can have a positive impact on the candidate experience. A more readable and understandable contract also allows recruiters to be more confident when explaining it to the prospective employee.

In short, simplifying the process and making it faster, more scalable, globally consistent, more efficient, and of better quality, seemed an obvious choice.

GETTING STARTED

To start the process of converting all our local agreements into a common global template, our HR specialist team (driving the project) created a working group with expertise from several other teams in the HR function, such as Talent Acquisition, Compensation & Benefits, HRIS (HR Information Systems) and HRBPs, as well as with our internal Employment Law team. First, we mapped out what is required in all the countries where we have employees. We used existing agreements to collect such information. Then, from a values-driven perspective, we started mapping out the minimum requirements we wanted in all markets.

We took a closer look at the elements of an employment contract – what do the candidate and the employer actually agree on? Here, we could see some common denominators. The contract clarifies:

- the role for which the candidate is being recruited,
- the place where the candidate is employed,
- compensation, and
- the first day of employment (and the last day if it is fixed-term).

Because our approach is values-driven, we were able to standardise most parts of the contract. At Spotify, we don't treat our employees differently depending on the level of the corporate hierarchy they are in. There are areas that in another organisation would be negotiable, but are not at Spotify – therefore, we could also consider these as common denominators. They are:

- vacation,
- working hours, and
- notice period.

All good in theory, but here we encountered the first difficulty. In some countries, we *had to* create different levels – it is stated in law or in trade union collective agreements that employees, at certain levels, are entitled to overtime pay and that this right cannot be negotiated away.

The important lesson here was that we didn't give up or let this challenge halt our plans. We reminded ourselves why we were doing what we were doing, that it would be of great importance for our employees and our business. We accepted the situation and focused on standardising the rest of the agreements. Then we realised that this didn't actually affect many contracts, just a handful.

MORE SCRUTINY

The next step was to examine the agreements in detail. The working group took a deep dive into what else could be removed and what should remain.

We agreed to remove the parts of the agreement that we considered to be generic, where we had policies/guidelines in place and where employees would need regular reminders. We made sure to update the guidelines so that they were in line with our core values, fulfilled their legal purpose and managed relevant risks. At the same time, we made sure to integrate the guidelines into the onboarding of new employees, ensuring that they were familiar with them from the beginning of their employment.

We also removed parts that were only found in certain agreements and were considered unnecessary, such as guidelines on travel and expenses that in practice apply to all employees across the company. These were things that didn't really fit in either a policy or an agreement, but existed for historical reasons.

Finally, we identified the parts of the contracts that we did *not* want to remove – the parts that we felt had a valid place in an employment contract. Although some aspects were covered by legislation in certain places in the world, we wanted to include them in all our contracts. We included these areas:

- intellectual property rights,
- confidentiality, and
- non-solicitation.

Here, another small obstacle on our path to fully unified global employment contracts was highlighted: non-compete clauses. We believe that people come to us because they want to and because they believe in our purpose, our journey and our goals. This is why we believe – and our employment contracts reflect this – that as long as they are employed by us, they are bound by the contract and the loyalty it represents. This is why we only have specific non-compete clauses in the contracts of those who work in particularly competitive positions, and mostly in the US.

This work resulted in a four-page agreement. Only a few contracts have to differ slightly due to local legislation – the basis is the same and the deviations are minor for a handful of employees.

The next step was for us to ensure we were managing risks, so we turned to our trusted suppliers for some help. We asked: If we implement this contract in this location, what risks are we taking as an employer and what could the consequences be? Their answers provided us with insights that allowed us to make rational decisions about how to proceed. As an employer, we ended up in a risk situation in only a few places. It was not our employees who were at risk and the risks were – frankly – so far-fetched that we decided to go ahead with the agreement.

This has paid off. It's easy for candidates to understand the contract and it's clear in the recruitment process that we only negotiate certain individual terms, and that the others are non-negotiable. This makes conversations with candidates easy and our recruiters have fewer questions and can focus on what they do best.

From the perspective of the HR team, things have become much easier. Everyone can rest assured that the basis of all contracts is identical. For HR, this means we have simplified and made it easier to find what we are looking for in a contract, even in a language we don't understand.

The single employment contract has allowed us to take the next step towards automating the final stage of the recruitment process: producing a contract and sending it to the candidate without having to complete anything manually. This also facilitates compliance, as the human error factor is less likely to interfere. We can also automate the process when someone changes roles within the company.

We should not hide the fact that it took a lot of work and discussions to get to this point. When you compare that effort with the time and effort we would otherwise have spent discussing these issues during recruitment processes, and in negotiations with employees who have wording in their contracts that is not in line with newly adopted policies, it's clear that it was well worth the effort.

Attrition, Exiting & Offboarding – healthy attrition and well-managed exits

Let's tell the truth about exits. This is something that many people find difficult because we are really talking about ending a relationship – and who likes that? For many, it's an emotionally charged situation whether the termination is forced or voluntary. Attrition is, however, inevitable and can be both beneficial and healthy. Also, leaving doesn't always mean that something is wrong or has been bad. People sometimes need new challenges and new opportunities to develop. Organisations also need a breath of fresh air, new blood, new energy, new experience and new ideas.

Traditionally, companies have had one of two different mindsets: people first or company first. If you put people – your employees – first, you tend to focus more on gratitude for the time the employee has given to the company. Such companies often put culture, learning and development on the agenda and actively work to retain their talented employees. They are also more likely to work on their *why* – i.e. be purpose-driven. In organisations that put the company first, the tendency is to think that the employee should just keep working, and understand that they are a small piece in the bigger machinery and feel grateful that they have a job at all. These companies often focus more on financial or business goals and push their employees until they are no longer useful to the business.

As you know by now, we at Spotify are more in favour of the first approach, *people first*. A company with the right and relevant culture for the business, which understands that proud people perform.

As HR professionals, we have to be somewhat cool or rational when it comes to people leaving. Otherwise, we are easily overwhelmed by emotions when talented people choose to move on and seek new challenges outside the organisation. The same approach also applies when employees leave, but not of their own free will. In such situations, empathy and compassion are still hugely important. It is also important to have the courage to be clear in your communication, know your labour and employment law, and do right by the person who is leaving. It's not at all unusual for what's best for the employee and what's best for the organisation to coincide, even during a separation. The strategy for retaining employees and dealing with terminations requires both honesty and empathy.

People will leave, in all workplaces. Therefore, how the exit process will be executed, whatever the reason behind it, is something you need to have a clear plan for. The exit process is of a proactive nature, as strange as it may sound. Your philosophy, your approach and the activities that are part of an exit must be well thought out, adapted and implemented *before* your employees start thinking about changing employers and before you end up in a situation where you go your separate ways. Once someone has started thinking about leaving, it's often too late to do anything to make them stay. If the termination is initiated by the employer, well, then a lot of conversations, action plans and follow-up should have already taken place. The process should have been carefully documented for the sake of both parties and, therefore, should come as no surprise.

In order to create an optimal process, you need to be proactive and strategic and you should have a clear idea of which people you are particularly keen to retain. This may include people with business-critical skills that you would be very unfortunate to lose. You may spontaneously think that the best thing for the business would be for *everyone* to stay, zero percent attrition, but you'll quickly realise what a crazy idea that is. Not only is it an unachievable goal, but it's highly unlikely that every single employee is exactly the right person, in exactly the right role, in exactly the right place. Of course, we want to have low attrition and to strive for anything else would be counterproductive, but we also have to be realistic. Otherwise, you may encounter problems when your employees leave and you can't manage the situation well.

There's a lot to consider here and it's HR's job to think strategically, equipping the organisation with a plan and the managers with the right skills to follow the plan in a coherent, structured, dignified and emotionally balanced way.

A job, not a love affair

It's not only the person leaving the company who can experience strong emotions – we're all human. Often, when an employee wants to end their employment themselves, managers react as if the person is 'breaking up' with them. They may be hurt and a little hostile towards the employee during the final days. After working closely in a team and perhaps spending many hours solving problems together, strong bonds may have been formed. Therefore, it's not uncommon for the manager (especially if they are at an early stage in their career) to take it personally when a team member resigns. The manager may feel abandoned and betrayed and think:

"Have I failed as a manager? Will more people leave now?" These are important questions and maybe you can learn something from asking them, but termination should not be taken personally. We train our managers to be coaches or mentors, but as soon as someone quits, this notion seems to disappear. Remind them to try to be happy for team members who are moving on in their careers. Advise your managers to congratulate them on their new job, if applicable, and to wish them continued success and take pride in the fact that they and the organisation have found, developed and trained another talent that is attractive in the job market.

It is the manager's job to make each employee's journey as rewarding and meaningful as possible – for both the employee and the company. We talked earlier about acting much like a gardener and helping your employees to grow. It's a sign of success when an employee moves on to a new challenge – preferably within the same organisation, if possible. It's also okay to be sad and the best thing a manager can do is to share their feelings with their employee (without blame). This helps the employee understand that they have done their job well and that the manager cares.

A piece of advice: don't make endings more difficult than they need to be by building a culture where you call each other 'family'. It's easy to do – we're all on a journey together, we have fun together and there are many parallels that make the analogy feel natural. Don't encourage your employees to see each other as family, because you don't choose your family – but you can choose your boss, your colleagues and your workplace. Therefore, you can also choose to leave them.

Termination

HR can do a lot to support managers who need to fire someone. It may be necessary to terminate the employment if an employee is underperforming, not acting in line with your values, or behaving inappropriately. It may also be necessary due to redundancy.

Whatever the circumstances, the formula of honesty + empathy = dignity is well worth remembering. As an employer, you have power and influence, and your decisions affect the lives of individuals. Throughout the process, show that you are aware of this and treat people with respect. Here, honesty and time are your friends. Don't rush the process. A few days here or there don't matter in the end. Of course, you want to move forwards, but remember that you're already on the other side of the change curve, while the employee is only at the beginning.

The employee's manager has almost certainly been considering it for some time and may have already discussed termination with their own manager and with you in HR. The manager has probably had time to think about it carefully and come to the conclusion that this is the optimal next step. The employee who is dismissed normally reacts in one of two different ways. There are those who understand that this is about to happen, because they've been told repeatedly what needs to be changed, improved or stopped. They've received support, training and perhaps both verbal and written warnings, and an action plan with a timeline. Quite often, they react with relief. There are others who are surprised, stating that they didn't realise the seriousness of the situation and will now do everything that has been discussed and is expected of them. Both reactions are of course perfectly natural and human. If the employee has consistently failed to do their job properly or to deliver on time, it's not surprising that they are eventually dismissed. On the other hand, an employee may turn out to have insufficient skills to do their job – for example, because they've been promoted above their skill level or because technology has developed so quickly that they haven't kept up. In the vast majority of cases of a 'lack of competence', you as an employer have been involved and complicit. This could be because you promoted someone to a role they were not yet ready for, or able to perform satisfactorily, or because they hadn't been given sufficient opportunities to learn new skills or gather new knowledge. In such cases, termination is a very strange conclusion. This is more about 'dressing' your employees and managers with the right skills and making sure that you don't promote to reward long and faithful service but on the basis of competence and potential.

In the extremely rare cases where an employee simply doesn't want to perform the tasks assigned to them, it is a case of refusal to work. In situations where someone breaks a law, uses violence or harasses another colleague in the workplace – well, this should of course be reported and investigated, and may result in a termination. Whatever the reason for splitting up, expect the co-worker to be in a state of shock, denial and/or anger. How well you have communicated and implemented the termination won't change these emotions. Also, expect the employee to remember very little of what was said at the first meeting, apart from the fact that they no longer have a job. Sometimes, they don't even remember that part. This is perfectly natural, part of the human way of dealing with big, shocking changes. It's therefore of the utmost importance that you don't wrap things up or be vague and unclear to try to soften the message. In your attempt to be nice, you are not. Dismissals and recruitments are similar in that they can be handled well or badly, they can be handled with dignity or indignity. You know you've handled the termination well when you meet former employees a few years later and they thank you, both for the way the process was handled and because they were helped to make a fresh start elsewhere.

Dismissals typically include a severance package to ensure that the employee has time to process the change, regroup and find the next equivalent opportunity without suffering too much financially. This is not an area where you as an employer should cut corners. Set up a structure that makes it easy for you to be fair to those who are made redundant. Perhaps you should have an outplacement programme to help employees find a new, suitable job as soon as possible.

Don't focus too much on 'winning' negotiations. There are no winners here – in a dismissal, both parties lose because it was not the desired outcome from the start. If you go into the process with this view, both parties are likely to feel that they have had their say.

Dismissal is always sensitive, but remember that an employee who is stuck in a role where they're not successful or where they're constantly underperforming is probably not happy at work. This affects the employee's life and it's your responsibility to be honest about it. Remember that the person being dismissed is a future ambassador (and potential customer), regardless of the reason for leaving. Most importantly, they are fellow human beings and should be treated as such.

Redundancy – how to be a strategic partner

Sometimes, you reorganise to meet new business needs. Perhaps a part of your business is not doing as well as intended, or you realise that completely different skills are needed in the future, or – as sometimes happens for us at Spotify – you have grown so much that the old structure is not sufficient for the next phase. Hopefully, you can find new positions within the organisation for the affected employees but this isn't always possible. In such circumstances, there's a shortage of work and you have a redundancy situation at hand.

In the event of major changes and redundancies due to lack of work, HR must act as a strategic partner for the business and keep a cool head. By that we don't mean that HR first and foremost comes in and makes decisions about who can stay and who can leave. That is not a strategic approach.

Sometimes, difficult decisions have to be made to keep the business alive in the long term, or in order to deal with a crisis. Every possible way forwards must be balanced in both the short and long term. For example, companies that choose to reduce sales and marketing departments when times are tough may find themselves in a position where they have to lay off even more people because sales are falling. Those who lay off people who create and improve products may, as a consequence, have to lay off sales people later on because they can't sell an inferior product. It's best to think about it from all angles and make sure you don't make short-term or panic-led decisions. Keep the consequences front of mind! Here we return to the fact that HR must know the business. You need to be able to assess, guide and advise the business on decisions related to the employees.

It can be better to lay off many employees from the start rather than just a few at a time. This can be painful, but is the best way to ensure the survival of the business. You make a major, necessary intervention instead of 'dabbling'. With early, open and transparent communication to the entire organisation, you minimise the damage to employee confidence, pride, safety and focus. In short, as we noted in the chapter on change management, doing as little as possible is not always best. If you keep picking at a scab, you run the risk of bleeding to death because the wound keeps tearing open. Even if it feels more empathetic to take small measures in the hope of minimising the number of people negatively affected, the risk is that you will have to continue taking such measures – and this affects both those who leave and those who stay in a very negative way. It doesn't improve the situation and we don't recommend this course of action.

All decisions on organisational change create 'debt'. It often takes time for the new organisation to settle in, find its rhythm, build new ways of working and start delivering value. That's why it's important that you make thoughtful decisions and see them through. Both employees who leave and employees who stay will have strong feelings about what has happened and will remember how you handled it. It's easy to think that a proven shortage of work or redundancy is the easiest type of termination to communicate, because no one needs to take it quite so personally. The individuals affected are still human beings and most of them have probably enjoyed their workplace, their tasks and their colleagues. You should at least assume that they will be as hurt, scared, shocked, angry and disappointed as they would be if there was a different reason for the termination.

Therefore, make sure to keep all conversations private, giving those concerned time to react and come back with questions, as well as space to express their thoughts and feelings. Don't rush into the practicalities and next steps. You have just pulled the rug out from under their feet; they may feel that they are now losing part of their identity, as well as their source of livelihood.

That said, when redundancy is unavoidable, make sure that your decisions focus less on individuals and more on the skills the business needs. Strange as it may sound, it will be fairer for those affected and you won't be depriving the business of key skills. You want to minimise the risk of having to get out the cheese slicer. Do your analysis and be prepared to fight for neutral decisions. Managers will fight for their employees and the decisions you make should not be driven by who is most upset and vocal, or by convenience. Be honest and make sure everyone understands the reasons and can accept the rationale behind your decisions. Being cool and collected in these situations is the warmest thing you can be!

Counteroffer – employment is no place for bidding wars

A manager receives an invitation to a meeting, without an agenda, from a key member of his team. It's unusual and a bit worrying. The manager's fears are confirmed at the meeting: the employee has received an offer from a competitor and is considering quitting. The offer is financially better than what the employee is currently earning and the challenge fits like a glove. The employee states that they might consider staying if the employer can match the new offer. It is easy for the manager to think short-term in this situation. They need the employee right now. The employee is important to the organisation and the manager wants them to stay. It is also more convenient not to have to recruit and introduce a new skill. In our experience, counteroffers never work in the long run. If an employee has started talking to other employers, they have already mentally prepared themselves to change jobs. Once that process has started, it is almost impossible to bring it to a stop. A counter-offer may make the employee stay for a few months, but usually they will leave soon enough anyway. It also creates a risk that there will be a constant discussion about compensation in the organisation. In such cases, ask your managers to consider whether they could have retained the employee by giving them new challenges within the company. If the answer is yes, this is a valuable lesson for the organisation. If the answer is no and there was nothing the manager could have done – just let it go.

When employees start talking about money as if it were the only driving force, it's a sign that they're done and want to move on, regardless of what you offer. Don't be reactive! If nothing is missing and an employee comes to a manager after receiving an alternative offer, guide the manager to be supportive by congratulating the employee and wishing them good luck in their new workplace. If you give your employees fair, market-based compensation – and maybe even more than that – and have a well-developed and relevant compensation and benefits strategy, don't fight to keep the occasional outlier.

Frankly, many people talk about compensation without understanding the mechanisms behind it. Of course, unfair compensation leads to leavers, but so does a lack of employee understanding of the company's compensation philosophy. We recommend that you spend time teaching your employees about your philosophy, strategy, the fixed and variable components and how the complexity and responsibility of a role affects total compensation.

We know it may sound harsh and uncomfortable, but look at the situation from another angle. If you make a counter-offer, you are also sending a signal to the rest of the company that the only way to increase your salary is to threaten bids from competitors. You create incentives for such behaviour. If you play the defence game and give in to this type of discussion, you will end up with a storm in a teacup. You have just opened up for compensation negotiations all year round instead of an annual compensation review. You will not have a compensation model that allows you to link your compensation philosophy to your purpose or values. You'll be constantly reacting to those who scream the loudest and you'll end up with mercenary employees.

If you do a good job – if you are a successful company and a good employer – you will have a strong and clear employer brand. This, in turn, means that your employees will receive offers all the time, probably with better pay (how else would another organisation get them to change jobs?). If you allow these kinds of conversations outside of the annual compensation review, then you will never talk about anything other than compensation and no one will ever be satisfied. Your managers will have to deal with even more unpredictability than they do already. You will be distracted from focusing on creating a work environment where employees feel seen and heard, where they can develop, where they feel a sense of belonging and autonomy with accountability.

Overall, pay your employees fairly and focus on creating an organisational culture and work environment that makes them want to stay, makes them feel that all-important sense of belonging and gives them ample opportunity to develop and grow. Compensation is not always motivating – in fact, it can become the opposite.

Offboarding

Onboarding is an extremely important part of your culture – and the same goes for offboarding. First impressions matter, last impressions last. This is highly relevant to our personal lives as well as in the employer-employee relationship. We all have a tendency to evaluate people based on the last encounter we had with them.

Just as an employer often remembers how an employee ends their employment, the person leaving will evaluate the employer based on how they experienced their exit. It doesn't matter if you paid them well, or gave them the biggest challenge of their life and empowered them to grow in every way if you then treated them badly when they left.

We've also noted several times that all leavers are potential ambassadors for the company and can also be future customers, or in some cases 'boomerangers' (we'll come back to that in a moment). They are an important part of your employer branding and also part of a network where there may well be people you want to attract and who will definitely then ask them how they experienced their time with your organisation.

Boomerang

A 'boomeranger' is a person who leaves the company and then returns (or wants to return). Here, it is wise to choose a strategy, even if this has not happened to you yet, because it is important to be consistent. For example, most companies have a relatively large number of positions for people who are at the beginning of their career (entry level positions). It is not uncommon for these employees to reach a point where they can be better challenged and developed in another company. They may be ready to take on more responsibility and you may not have such a role to offer them at that time. In such circumstances, it can be positive for both the business and the employee to reunite at a later stage.

Whichever approach you choose, remember that the person left you for a reason. It could be that the former employee was unhappy with something but decides to return because the proverbial grass was not greener on the other side. It is also worth bearing in mind that both the company and the individual are likely to have changed in the meantime. Allow your prospective boomerangers to go through the whole recruitment process again, to make sure you're still a good fit for each other. Our experience tells us that the reason for the split – and which party initiates the dialogue – matters to a potential boomerang hiring decision.

The notice period

Notice periods primarily exist to protect the employee. The person who resigns has a safety net in the form of a guaranteed income for a predetermined period of time. This also protects your organisation. If a person with key skills leaves the company, you will have advance notice and can plan for a handover, replacement, or reorganisation. There is often not enough time to find, hire and onboard someone new before the employee has left, highlighting the importance of succession planning and being proactive with your pipeline for critical roles.

For most organisations, it is reasonable to use local legislation as a basis or starting point. Then look at your different roles in terms of how crucial they are to your success and make deliberate departures from local legislation where necessary for the sake of the business. This may include having longer notice periods for people with certain skills or in senior roles that are difficult to fill.

At Spotify, as mentioned, we now have uniform employment contracts. Simplicity and consistency are good foundations. Even if you don't follow our lead and use the same type of contract throughout your organisation, avoid having unique contracts and notice periods on an *individual* level. Create a system with the same notice period for all but senior management. This makes negotiations easier and ensures fair treatment within the organisation. Fairness is important to get employees to trust the system you use. You can make individual exceptions when someone has decided to leave and you have assessed the business needs of that person.

Non-compete clauses

Non-compete clauses should be used with care. There are some clear advantages but also some disadvantages. The important thing is to remember why non-compete clauses exist. They are not just used for the sake of it. Take care of the business but don't forget to be human and show respect.

There are only certain roles (probably only a few) that require non-compete clauses. Make a list of these roles and ensure that there is always a non-compete clause in their contracts.

Some of the benefits are:

1. PROTECTION

In some positions, employees have access to highly sensitive information that could be valuable to competitors. You need protection to prevent such information from being shared if an employee goes to work for a competitor.

2. THE POSSIBILITY TO DEROGATE

In many countries (jurisdictions), you can unilaterally waive a time-based quarantine (non-compete) if, at the time of termination, you decide that the extra protection is not required. In this case, you will not have to pay compensation for it.

3. EASIER TO PROVE

Breaches of non-compete agreements are generally easier to prove than breaches of confidentiality obligations. Since liquidated damages are available for breaches of non-compete agreements, they can be an effective tool to prevent employees from working for a competitor and taking your sensitive information to them.

Some of the disadvantages are:

1. COSTS

In many countries, you have to compensate an employee for post-contractual bankruptcy restrictions. The costs are often in the range of 50-60% of the employee's previous monthly salary and can be higher than that.

2. CAN BE QUESTIONED

Many companies ignore the non-compete clauses at the time of termination (where possible), which means they do not get the protection they need. The clause then becomes mostly cosmetic, raising questions about whether it should have been included in the first place.

3. CANNOT BE WAIVED IN SOME COUNTRIES/REGIONS

In some jurisdictions, non-compete clauses cannot be unilaterally waived, which means that if the employee demands it, you may have to pay for a non-compete after the contract period, even if you don't see a need for it. Since you are likely to want to waive such clauses (see above), there is a risk that you will have to pay a lot of compensation for something you do not need or plan to use.

You have to decide what you believe in. Be aware that what you do has a ripple effect. Consider the limitations on individuals' ability to change jobs. If you want to be able to hire people from your competitors, it is not a good idea to have non-compete clauses when they are not really needed. Your competitors are likely to do the same and you will create a standard within your ecosystem. This reduces talent mobility, which hurts everyone. Focus on how to retain your employees through culture instead of trying to lock them in with non-compete clauses.

Proactive measures

You have accepted that attrition is inevitable – sometimes someone wants to leave and you'll have to accept that. Sometimes you want someone to leave, or you find yourself in a situation where someone (or several people) need to leave. That said, no one wants a high staff turnover. To be a strategic partner for business, HR must be able to work anywhere in the organisation in order to solve problems that manifest themselves in attrition, whether high or low. Of course, you need to identify the problems and understand them before trying to solve them. Being well informed and having access to the right data is the most objective way to do this, but there are some traps. You need to choose how to measure based on your own context. Rolling measurement periods work best for companies undergoing rapid growth, while fixed measurement periods work for companies with more stable attrition. It is also important to choose the right interval. If you only measure on an annual basis, you won't be able to act quickly; if you measure monthly, you'll miss seasonal variation. The trick is to remove as much natural variation as possible and still receive relevant data that you can react to immediately. Think about how you choose to measure.

It's also important to know whether attrition is forced or voluntary and whether it is regrettable or not. This will help you understand if things like reorganisation or lack of work are behind your figures, or if a large number of people are being let go due to underperformance, which could indicate misplaced expectations and lack of communication from managers. Similarly, a high rate of voluntary attrition can point to other reasons, such as a lack of development opportunities or the wrong remuneration philosophy.

Healthy attrition

When deciding what constitutes healthy attrition for your organisation, you want the majority of those leaving to be 'non-critical turnover', i.e. individuals who lack the skills needed for the future or who do not behave in line with your values.

When setting the comparative figure, there are some factors you should take into account:

- Consider the previous growth rate of the company. If you have grown a lot already and have invested in talent attraction, recruitment, onboarding and development, you should aim for a lower attrition rate. You have gained new perspectives through your new recruits and need more long-term employees for stability.

- Look at industry benchmarks to relate your attrition to and consider the demographics of your workforce. Think about your business and the specific skills and time investment required for someone to go from new hire status to fully productive. For example, a call centre can be expected to have higher turnover than a technology organisation that creates intricate, customised products.
- Duration. If people quit within six months or even a year of being hired, it is often because of mismatched expectations.
- Avoid looking at averages. Attrition may look good at company level but be too high or low in some parts of the organisation. It is HR's job to find those parts, understand the causes and suggest ways to deal with them. Preferably before they occur.
- Remember that the goal is not necessarily to retain all employees. Keep the right people – where both parties gain something from the relationship.

Find the trigger points

Once you have found a healthy attrition rate, you need to start measuring and finding ways to embed analysis points in the information you collect. We believe that exit interviews and surveys are the best way to get a good picture of the reason for the departure. Build a survey into your offboarding process and try to collect information on why employees leave. Think about what you want to understand when creating the survey and remember that in order to solve a problem, you need to be able to identify it. What you are looking for here is the cause of turnover, so that you can reduce it and increase the length of employment.

If your HR organisation works closely with the business, such surveys will confirm what you already know. The question, therefore, is: how can they be used? We believe that exit interviews are most useful when you want to study 'regrettable turnover' and understand why employees leave. If you embed questions in the survey that you have asked before, in employee surveys during their employment, you can see how the employee's attitude has changed over time. Then – and this is the most important part – you should compare this with other data points you have in HR to better understand what made the person start thinking about doing something else, outside the company. You can then use these insights to predict future departures and work proactively so that your best employees never consider opening emails from external recruiters, or even think about looking for a new job.

Exit interviews

It's often not possible to manage exit interviews centrally. One option is for managers to collect information and send it to HR, although this is both biassed and very costly.

Sometimes, interviews can be a temporary tool used to understand a certain situation. For example, if a sales team in Spain has twice the regrettable turnover rate of other teams in Europe, exit interviews can be used to understand what can be done to reduce the number of resignations there. They can also be used for a key competency group, department or other group – for example, the CEO wants to have conversations with all departing senior managers to understand the needs of the organisation.

While we do not encourage HR teams to rely on exit interviews as a permanent source of information to identify and solve turnover-related problems, we would still encourage managers to conduct exit interviews, as they can be a useful guide for future improvements.

Focus on people and operations

Most importantly, try to keep things simple, standardise your approach to ensure fair treatment and show a combination of courage and empathy when talking to departing employees. By being thoughtful about how you measure turnover and why employees leave, you can begin to address the root of any problems you may have. A little bit of attrition is good, 'talent drain' is downright bad.

WHEN IT'S TIME TO SAY GOODBYE

At Spotify, we make it a rule to be honest and tell the unvarnished truth when it comes to employee performance. We don't think we're doing anyone a favour by not telling it like it is, or waiting and hoping things will work themselves out. Most people also want to be treated as adults. Moreover, not giving feedback on underperformance is a way of saying that employees' performance, attendance or contributions don't really matter – that you don't see them or care about them.

Talking to someone about how they perform the tasks they are employed to do – and are competent to do – should not be an awkward conversation. It should, of course, be done with respect and empathy. At Spotify, we don't hope that anyone who doesn't live up to expectations will resign voluntarily. There's a lot to be done before that happens.

At Spotify, we are constantly working to create a safe environment, where clarity and 'honesty with care' is something everyone can expect and deserves. This includes ongoing verbal feedback about what works and what doesn't, as well as a discussion about what needs to be done differently.

THE MOST DIFFICULT OF CALLS – INVOLUNTARY TERMINATIONS

If we have reached the point where termination of employment is the only option, we always do it in a well-planned way. While we often talk about our *controlled chaos*, this does not apply to dismissals. We have carefully planned the different steps in the process before a notice of termination is issued, out of respect for the individual. These are people and colleagues.

Our HRBPs or HR specialists always conduct involuntary terminations to ensure that the process is carried out correctly, that the right parties are involved and that the manager is well prepared when it's time for the conversation. Warmth, clarity and integrity are important cornerstones of the conversation and we as HR can quality assure the conversation, especially with managers who don't have experience of this type of conversation. It needs to be handled with the utmost care for the individual.

The first part of the meeting often only takes a few minutes; we get straight to the point and give the notice of termination. If the decision has already been made and we're going to inform the employee, it's unhelpful to return to previous discussions, when we've tried to get the employee on the right track. We listen and confirm that we hear what the employee is saying but clarify that the decision has been made, so that we don't get stuck in a loop. Usually, the manager will leave the meeting quite soon after the decision is communicated, so that the employee has a moment to process the information together with the HRBP. We have seen that when we give our employees time to let the message sink in and ask questions, it makes it easier to process. It goes without saying that we should show care first and foremost for those who have been dismissed. It's also important to ensure that the employee's colleagues in the team are doing well under the circumstances. It's common to feel stressed and worry about your own employment when someone in your team is terminated for whatever reason.

DEALING WITH THE MYTH OF VOLUNTARY ATTRITION

When someone or multiple people leave the company, especially if they're key players, this will raise questions internally. What's behind it? Will more people leave? Sometimes this starts to be discussed externally as well, at least if the company is heavily covered in the media. This is another reason why it's valuable to have as clear a picture as possible of the potential reasons for the voluntary attrition and whether there are patterns that we should pay attention to.

Based on data and information from internal and external sources (such as people analytics data, exit interviews, global trends and the macroeconomic situation), we regularly compile an *attrition report*. The aim is partly to find out what the exact reason is for employees leaving. Is it a 'see you later' or a final goodbye? Are we still friends? It's done also partly to be able to answer how and if we as a company are affected by various global trends. Are we seeing *The Great Resignation* in our company too, or are our attrition figures quite stable? We need to be able to handle the tail of claims, conclusions and anecdotes that tend to arise in the wake of someone leaving.

We also do these analyses to better inform our workforce planning. We make sure we have as much data at hand as possible and can remind the organisation that we know exactly why and at what percentage we consider our staff turnover to be a problem, how we deal with it, but also why we consider it healthy and natural.

PART 4

Part 4.
A New Era, New Skills & New Remits

Introduction by Katarina Berg

In the new era of HR, 'people first' is a key guiding principle, but not the only one. We see a shift towards a broader view of what HR is and can be, towards a more holistic focus on the business as a whole. It's a paradigm shift that those of us working in HR can choose to embrace, or not. With this also comes a new and more strategic role for the HR department. A role where we no longer just have to put out fires from morning to night and where we are no longer invited to the party at five past twelve, but from the very start.

It is not a big-bang revolution, rather a natural evolution. If you want to join in, you will benefit from a more explicit strategy to adapt to a new way of working and a post-pandemic leadership and organisational model. You will need to ask yourself what HR work should really entail and find new ways of thinking and working. You'll need to be proactive, flexible, adaptable and fast. You'll need to spend your time on what really makes a difference. Also, you will need to embrace technology.

The new era of HR in part requires different skills and competences than before, different muscles. Don't wait to exercise them. If you want to know what else you can do, add some new skills and functions to your team. In the new era, it will also be important to develop and organise your teams in such a way that you don't lose momentum in execution. Maybe you should be even more embedded in the business? Maybe there are more roles and teams that should be under HR?

At Spotify, we believe in relevant remits and have stated that change is our only constant. With that philosophy, we have gathered everything related to employees under one hat, the People Constituency, worn by the CHRO. As Global Head of HR, I, Katarina, am responsible not only for HR but also for Strategy Operations, Equity & Impact and Global Workplace Services. These functions include Diversity, Equity, Inclusion & Belonging (DEIB), Sustainability, Social Impact, Real Estate, Design & Build, Facility, IT, Office Management, Travel & Business Protection. My team is therefore also responsible for business protection and crisis management (people-related), in all areas related to employees and physical buildings. These functions, which have not traditionally been within the CHRO remit, will be discussed in the fourth and final part of this book. These responsibilities are expected to shift though, just as there was a period of responsibility for Brand & Creative. Areas such as Strategy Operations may move out to make room for other responsibilities. That is the modus operandi at Spotify, ensuring that the span of control remains relevant for both the business and the individual.

The HR organisation at Spotify

At Spotify, HR is the central midfielder in the People Constituency team set-up. On either flank we have Company Strategy Operations and Global Workplace Services. The HR function consists of a few hundred employees divided into different HR teams with specialist and generalist roles. If you imagine an organisational chart, the specialist teams are viewed horizontally. They are: Learning &

Development (L&D), including Talent Growth (known as Green-House), Total Compensation & HR Insights (Pay & Reward, HRIS and People Analytics), Talent Acquisition (TA), Equity & Impact (DIB + Sustainability + Social Impact) and Community X. Then we have the verticals of the org chart reflecting how Spotify and the business is designed. There, our Human Resources Business Partners (HRBPs) operate in a way that is similar to HR managers or even CHROs in most organisations, given the size of their remits. They have a place in the respective management teams they support, and they are supported by HR specialists who are divided into a global central team and team members who follow the HRBP support in the organisation.

In this new era, HR professionals need to learn new things, acquire new skills and take on new tasks. There will be challenges, but it will also be exciting and fun. When we let go of the old and push through what we really believe in – for the sake of our people, our business and society at large – the work also feels more meaningful.

Crisis Management
– the role of HR
in crisis management

Constant, rapid change and an increasing number of unexpected and disruptive events create a sense of instability and uncertainty, which in turn affects people's physical and mental health. It is therefore increasingly important for organisations to take a strategic approach to crisis management. A crisis can come in many forms. It can be triggered by a single dramatic event or accident, by threats, violence or deaths in the workplace, by acts of terrorism, natural disasters and much more. Employees can both cause a crisis and experience one. Once upon a time, one person or department could have crisis management as one task among many – those days are gone. Crisis management is about more than just limiting financial or brand damage to your organisation, it's about the safety of your employees.

To navigate a crisis, you need a stable foundation to rest on: your culture and core values. This is where the HR team really comes into its own, as we saw clearly at Spotify during the COVID-19 pandemic. You are behavioural scientists and your work is people and company culture – every day. Since crisis is about people, the now essential crisis teams and crisis management strategies of this new era find a home in HR.

You must, of course, always try to strike a balance between what is right for the business and what is right for the employees.

With our people-first approach, these two interests are rarely in conflict with each other. In time-pressured, complicated situations, where you need to make decisions without having all the facts or information, you are strongly supported by your company purpose (mission), your values and your culture. It helps you fly straight and fast, even if the instruments are down and it's pitch black outside.

The team

To begin with, it's important to build a clear but flexible structure for the crisis management team. When it comes to crisis management, it's rarely good to have too many people involved, but there should be enough team members to ensure global coverage. Then, no matter the time of day, there is someone, somewhere in the world, who is awake and ready to act. Our basic philosophy is that too many cooks make a very bad soup. With a small, tight team, communication is clearer and more consistent, flexibility is greater and the pace is faster. It also reduces the risk of duplication, which in turn reduces the risk of confusion in what is likely to be a chaotic situation from the start. The few selected team members form the core of the team and are the ones who make the decisions.

Make sure that the members of the crisis team have a mandate to make decisions. This will increase the sense of security for your employees. Spotify's Crisis Management team includes the CHRO as a representative of the leadership team, who ultimately makes the decisions based on the team's proposal on how to handle a situation. This saves the team from having to wait for a larger team to agree on what to do. If you can create a similar solution in your company, it will speed up the decision-making process and help you both to ensure the safety of your employees more quickly and to better manage uncertainty and fear. In a large-scale crisis, there is no time or place for office politics. Every minute counts: getting messages out quickly and continuously, and creating a quick approval of decisions, can be directly decisive – maybe even save lives!

At Spotify, we talk about the team structure using the terms the 'inner circle' and the 'outer circle'. In our case, the inner circle, consisting of four or five people, makes 95% of all decisions affecting the whole organisation. The remaining 5% are the big decisions where the CEO needs to have a say and decisions are made there just as quickly. The small team then needs an 'outer circle', which can implement the agreed actions. Depending on the type of crisis, colleagues working in local offices, HRBP and HR specialists, travel, security, communication and/or legal are part of the outer circle. The leadership team is informed just before or at the same time as the whole organisation. This way of working requires courage and maturity in both functions and individuals and it has repeatedly proved successful. Unfortunately, we have had to practise in real life on several occasions.

We suggest that you keep other functions and departments out of the crisis management team so that they can, as far as possible, continue with 'business as usual'. Make sure they are continuously updated, but allow them to focus on ensuring that no further damage is done to the organisation in terms of finances or productivity. Otherwise, you may end up with a secondary crisis, on top of the one being managed. Of course, this does not apply in cases where the epicentre of the crisis is in the business itself.

Speed

When your team is made aware of a situation, you should come together within minutes to determine whether it is really a crisis or 'just' something important that needs to be dealt with immediately. In fact, this is one of the most important tools in the crisis management toolbox. If it is a real crisis, what you do in the first minutes and hours will determine the outcome of your work as a whole. Keeping up the pace and gathering information, without resorting to sensationalism or becoming impulse-driven, is crucial to your focus and results. Calling what has happened a 'crisis' lets the core team (the inner circle) know that everyone needs to be involved. Everyone should know what their role is, what to do and what checklists to follow.

If you don't get up to speed quickly enough, you may never quite catch up with what's happening, which means your employees may receive information that is delayed, inaccurate or too scarce. At that point, lack of trust can become a problem and suddenly, the team has two crises to deal with: the real one and the one about internal communication. Be quick – both to call something a crisis and to call something a non-crisis. If it is a crisis, be sure to follow the written and rehearsed plan.

Change of guards

Being part of a crisis team that may have to deal with death, war, terrorist attacks and more is extremely demanding and can negatively affect the health and well-being of team members. Regardless of the type of crisis and whether the trauma occurs in the organisation or in your own team, you need to plan for a change of guards, the relief of team members. Crisis work can go on for a long time and in the worst case, one crisis can follow another, or even worse – two or more crises occur at the same time.

Make sure you have a solid crisis management plan and a plan for change of guards. Rotating team members in and out of the core team – the inner circle – can be essential. If this is not done, you run the risk of making worse and worse decisions the longer the crisis goes on, and of members suffering from fatigue, both from prolonged and sustained stress and from the sheer weight of responsibility on their shoulders.

It makes sense for HR to take the lead in a crisis, which doesn't mean that crisis management should be a full-time job for someone in HR. It is very important that each member of the core team has time to recharge their batteries and take a break. Therefore, everyone on the team needs to be aware of their own well-being so that they can be relieved when needed. This means that another member of the core team must be ready to step in. We have practised changing the whole inner circle at the same time, although we have seen that in practice, it can work well to replace individuals who need relief. If you are leading a crisis team, watch out for signs of stress, anxiety or depression and make sure everyone gets the support and breaks they need to carry out their tasks without breaking down.

Actually taking a break from this intense work can be difficult – because what you do is really important. You are making a difference and you want to keep helping. At the same time, you can run out of energy, with your body telling you to stop. Not getting enough hours of sleep can be devastating. Debriefing and defusing, relieving the pressure through professional and peer support, getting a chance to 'talk it out', is also important – as is understanding that those who have been heavily involved in crisis management may feel depressed and hopeless when the crisis is over, or when the situation is defused and they can catch their breath. Many of us have heard of post-traumatic stress disorder (PTSD), but we often forget that we can suffer from it ourselves.

Communication

In a crisis, the most effective solution to reduce employee worry, anxiety and stress is often simple: communicate, communicate, communicate. Even if there is nothing new to say, say just that.

The impact of showing that you are listening should also not be underestimated. It shows your employees that you take their concerns and feelings seriously. In times of uncertainty, it is also extremely important for leaders to show vulnerability. Have the courage to address the uncomfortable feelings that may emerge during crises – such as sadness, depression, stress or loneliness – on your internal communication platforms. This gives your employees a place and a platform to communicate and guides them to the right resources. Never underestimate the importance of showing sympathy, empathy and compassion when communicating during difficult times. If there is a risk of your employees feeling panic or fear, the best remedy is to show them that their safety and well-being is important to their employer.

In the chaos of a crisis, contradictory messages can emerge, creating uncertainty in the workplace. It becomes important to counteract the fear and anxiety that uncertainty brings. Do everything you can to create an emotionally safe environment.

In short, regularly over-communicating with your employees in an honest, transparent, empathetic and clear way will counteract a lot of uncertainty in your organisation. It's not exactly brain surgery, but it's still easier said than done.

Culture and values

A crisis situation often leads to a new reality for your business or your employees. As HR professionals and experts in people and behaviour, you can rely on your knowledge to navigate for your employees.

In this new era of HR, a purpose-driven and values-driven approach will give you, your business and your people a solid foundation to stand on even in difficult, uncertain and contradictory times. Even for rapidly changing organisations outside of times of crisis, a 'new reality' can be extremely challenging.

In a time of change and adaptation, people look for stability. If you already have a clear culture and clear values, you can use them to support you, to create familiarity as you adapt to new circumstances. Those organisations that can embrace change, and balance it with their understanding of their people and business, will emerge the strongest from a crisis. However, don't fall into the trap of introducing new values to suit the situation, as this will not help you create stability. Look at your 'cultural DNA' and stick to the core values you already have.

Although you shouldn't introduce new values in times of crisis, you may need new ways of working, or realise that parts of your culture need to evolve. If so, do this gradually and always take into account your cultural roots. It's important that both your new employees and your long-serving staff recognise what is emerging. Let them be part of the work. We've said it before but it bears repeating – your people are your culture, and the culture is your people. Giving them a voice, listening to them and allowing them to help shape your values and culture is crucial.

In a crisis, values are put to the test. A company that lives by its values is in a much better position to survive a crisis (short or long term) than one that does not. Take care of your employees and their well-being and do what you can to make them feel as safe as possible under the circumstances. Remind them of the company's purpose and provide guidance and support on how they should act, and they will run the business for you.

Putting an end to it

If it is important to define when a crisis has started, it is also important to define when it is over. Especially for the crisis team – both the inner and outer circle – who may have been working day and night for some time. Waiting too long to end the crisis situation and let everyone know that you are returning to observation or normality can be detrimental. Saying this, loud and clear, is extremely important from a psychological perspective. It means that the debriefing process can begin, so that recovery, and in some cases, exhaustion and depression, can be managed outside the current crisis situation. By all means, don't forget to do a *retrospective*, as discussed earlier in the book. Take time to reflect on what happened, to learn from what went well and what didn't go so well, to see what you can do better during the next crisis. A clear ending is essential.

CRISIS MANAGEMENT DURING COVID-19

Few events in modern times have had such a transformative effect on work life as the COVID-19 pandemic. It had a huge impact on our personal lives and health and also on how we interact, on technology and the way we work. In these very special circumstances, we all had to rewrite the instruction book on how to run a business. At Spotify, this task was largely delegated to the crisis management team.

The crisis management team at Spotify was created as a formal team after the tragic bombings in Paris in 2015, when our HR and leadership teams struggled to keep all our staff and visitors in Paris safe. The incident revealed several gaps in our security plan for contacting employees during emergencies and helping them get to safety. Neither communication nor coordination worked satisfactorily. Multiple people attempting to reach the same individuals at the same time made the reconciliation lists unreliable and it took us a long time to contact everyone we needed to reach. However, what worked well was the communication to the rest of the workforce (those not directly involved in the incident).

We learned a lot from that event and perhaps most importantly: if you want to be able to act quickly and communicate in a coordinated way in a crisis, you need a small, centralised team to manage the crisis situation. We need to get all the benevolent (and sometimes sensation-driven) hands out of the cookie jar. In the case of Paris, if there were fewer of us, we would most likely have been able to act faster and verify the most important aspect – that all employees were safe. To put it simply, when it comes to running a crisis management team, less is more. It gives the team the power of agility and autonomy to make quick decisions in real time.

Most of the crises that we had dealt with before the pandemic had been linked to natural disasters, acts of terrorism and other local events that put the safety of employees at risk. These situations usually had a clear beginning and a clear end. They were tragic and difficult, but the time the crisis team had to deal with them was relatively short. The exception was the terrorist attack in Stockholm when one of our own was murdered and the Crisis Management team had to handle the crisis around the clock for over a week, providing subsequent information, support and assistance.

COVID-19 was something completely different and new. It was crisis management around the clock for a very long time. We had not practised or been prepared for it, especially the impact it would have on the mental health of the core team. We worked together, stayed in touch, supported each other and got through it all as a team, with the common goal that all our employees around the world would understand our strategy and approach to dealing with the pandemic. They would receive frequent and continuous updates, and the information was based on data from authorities and experts (no own interpretations). We kept a warm and human tone. We wanted to avoid our people feeling alone in a precarious situation where no one really had any answers to begin with.

In early January 2020, when COVID-19 struck, we created a simple strategy to deal with the situation. We fundamentally agreed that we would always focus on the safety and well-being of our bandmates. We also agreed that all decisions made during the pandemic had to be communicated in a transparent and timely manner to all employees. This could help increase confidence in the crisis team at a time when our staff were at their most fearful and anxious.

Throughout the pandemic (March 2020-May 2023), the crisis team also focused on reducing uncertainty for our employees by proactively resourcing and planning for the challenges that employees faced as we all adapted to life with COVID-19 as part of our everyday realities.

In early March 2020, we asked all staff to start working from home. As an early adopter of requesting people work from home, we realised that an overnight shift to remote working would create many short-term and long-term challenges. Therefore, we immediately went into an emergency planning mode to address, for example, the costs of IT equipment for home working and ergonomic setup at home. We also planned for a scalable food programme. We shifted all social events and training from physical to virtual solutions and had a much greater focus on health and well-being.

We learned as we went along and we had the support of the leadership team and a clear objective: the safety of our employees was the top priority. This included turning two floors of our Stockholm office into a temporary virus testing centre.

Early on in the pandemic and with no playbook to use, we were operating 100% in reactive mode. We worked closely with our travel and strategy teams, contacted local authorities and health organisations and tried, like the rest of the world, to understand what 'this' was and how long it would last. Over time, our crisis team shifted from 24/7 crisis management to a more proactive approach. When we realised that there was no clear end in sight, we started shifting the topics of our daily conversations from reactive crisis management issues to conversations about preventive actions concerning the health and well-being of our employees. We focused on topics such as the future of work and the long-term impact of remote working on employees. We accepted that the pandemic had made many things more complicated and more challenging. While the increased complexity was in many cases beyond our control, we chose to focus on one area where we as an employer could create a better environment for our employees. It was by offering them the most precious thing they had: time. For many, it was personal time – for others, it was shared social time.

We trusted our employees around the world to create a working environment that best served them and the forced remote work during the pandemic. We also knew that people's circumstances were very different. There is a big difference between living alone in a small apartment, isolated and with work as the meaningful hub of your life, and living in a house with a large family where everyone is suddenly at home all the time and several children are being home-schooled. In many countries there was a complete lockdown, while in Sweden there was no strict lockdown and more freedom, as long as people kept a reasonable distance from each other. In other words, there were many parameters to consider. What we wanted to do was to strengthen the sense of *One culture, One company* – that we were going through this together.

We empowered our employees with the freedom to do things in a way that worked for them, based on their home situation, and we encouraged them to take time off when needed to create a good work-life balance. They took responsibility for planning their own time, deciding when to work and how. However, for many of our employees, creating space for rest and recovery was a real challenge and it turned out that many of them still wanted support and advice, and even clear directives from their employer. One example of how we responded to this was to quickly put together a dynamic offering of training and discussion forums for employees and managers on relevant topics, in a way that was adapted to everyone being based at home.

The Trust Barometer, conducted by Edelman in 2020,[12] found that people trusted their employer the most when it came to getting updates and guidance on what needed to be done regarding COVID-19. 63% of respondents said they trusted their employer's communication, compared to 58% for a government website and 51% for a traditional media site. Although this is only one source, it shows, as does our experience, the great responsibility we have as a company. It underlines the importance of successful crisis management – for the culture, the business and, most importantly, for the health and well-being of employees.

The fact that the team trusted each other and had reached a point where we could literally finish one another's sentences because we were so in sync and confident with each other also made it easier to deal with a prolonged crisis. It is quite amazing how a crisis like this can quickly bond a team. We would not have been able to achieve what we did without the bond and trust we had as a small but effective Crisis Management team.

Today, we have ensured that members of the HR team can relieve each other in the role of crisis management leaders, as we now better understand what the prolonged pressure and lack of sleep that often comes with the role can do. We need to make sure we protect the well-being of our HR staff as well. We also now recognise that the core team, the inner circle, don't have to be the most senior people, but those who are most adept at dealing with crises. They need to be those who are clear and communicative, those who are least impulsive and those who are geographically located to cover all time zones.

Global Strategy Operations

Company Strategy Operations – the process of planning, setting goals and monitoring the business – may seem alien to anyone working in HR. If you've absorbed what we've written so far in this book, you might agree that it's inefficient to let HR operate in its own little universe. Moreover, you're probably already working on strategic questions about how to make the whole organisation more efficient and productive. As Martin Lorentzon, one of the founders of Spotify, says: "Strategy is the sum of all decisions in the business."

Strategy work is, of course, nothing new. However, it is unusual for Strategy Operations to be located within the People Constituency, in Spotify's case under the CHRO. In this new era, where employees are truly seen as the most important resource and where HR professionals know the business inside and out – and therefore, increasingly enable it – it makes perfect sense for the organisation's major artery to be part of a function that has insight into the entire company and acts a bit like... Switzerland.

The Strategy Operations team should be an objective and trusted partner for all those involved in strategic issues in the organisation. The team acts on a mandate from the CEO and always has the best interests of the business at heart. They look at the whole picture rather than focusing on any particular leader, department or business unit. They are 'strategic facilitators' and will be neutral, without an agenda and without a lot of preconceived ideas about how things 'should' be done or work.

They are responsible for the optimal functioning of the company's processes and the ability of the business to deliver on key strategic initiatives. Their role is to monitor initiatives and targets, create a relevant reporting and monitoring system, communicate with the whole organisation and keep everyone engaged. They should identify and remove any obstacles that arise and aim to continually improve efficiency across the organisation.

Like mushrooms after rain

A long-held belief is that teams that work on strategic and even operational issues must have knowledge of the specific areas in which they operate, with a detailed understanding of each unit's needs. It's a notion that should be challenged: after all, in a fast-growing, purpose-driven organisation, the strategic focus is on the CEO, management and core business, not the support functions. A strategy that is not realised, however, is nothing more than a hallucination, no matter how well formulated. It is when the organisation, i.e. the managers and employees, start producing efficiently and feel engaged and happy that they can deliver over time. So if *growth* is your mantra, for the business and for employees, the location of this function is crucial.

If you are growing like mushrooms after rain – rapidly, whether you are in a start-up phase or scaling up – it makes sense to have all parts of your company coordinated by one unit. Think about what that function means for you. In our case, for the last six years it has been HR. If you allow the company's Strategy Operations to be part of the CHRO's remit, HR and Strategy Operations can ensure that there is consistency in the communication of goals, target achievement, direction and quarterly results. You create conditions where there can be less friction and fewer interruptions and distractions in what needs to be shipped, delivered and performed. Then you can do something very few companies manage – grow by adding a large number of new employees without losing focus, momentum, joy, morale or quality.

A lot of it is about making sure the whole organisation is pulling in the same direction and at the same pace. To achieve this status, you must have an *operating model*, which is simple and understandable to everyone. In our case, we call it the *Spotify Rhythm*. This game plan explains our purpose and mission, our current *bets*, our annual goals and our long-term focus areas. The idea is simply to provide a clear picture of where we want to go and how we will get there. Every employee should be able to understand how their daily work can affect the final goal and how they contribute to it. Of course, not all employees work on big, strategic and business-critical objectives every day, but everyone should know how what they do is crucial to the business as a whole.

The most effective way to ensure and anchor a strategic direction that benefits the business is to develop the follow-up of the strategy work in parallel with your People Strategy. Such a strategic direction makes you fantastically fast and allows for enormous impact when the organisation has to deliver its goals.

The power of 'we'

We can think of the Strategy Operations team's job as translating the CEO's vision and strategy in such a way that every single employee has an understanding of, and commitment to, the direction and goals. When done correctly, each new employee will get up to speed faster. Each person can focus on their own impact first and you have a foolproof system to remove obstacles and set the direction of the work.

A model like this is particularly effective in a purpose- and values-driven organisation. The culture and core values show the employees who you are – the company's identity or personality, if you like. An *Operating System* (OS) consists of some commonly agreed principles and is intended to simplify the employees' joint work for greater effect. All parts should then be put together to realise the organisation's goals and vision in the best possible way.

This means that the operational business strategy must go hand in hand with the culture and core values and also have a close and natural connection to your workforce planning that is owned and driven by HR. It's impossible to plan for the future of your workforce without knowing the direction of your company and its strategic initiatives.

It is also important that the Strategy Operations team has close relationships with the people in the organisation who are involved in change management. Any large-scale change in the company should be carried through thoughtfully and in line with the company's overall strategy. As we mentioned in the chapter on change management, change managers must have foresight and knowledge of the business. Their work on organisation design must be reflected in the strategy – and vice versa.

Both workforce planning (mainly HRBP & Finance) and change management practitioners must be able to rely on their colleagues working closely with Company Strategy Operations for an agile overview of today's minimum requirements and tomorrow's (and future) resource needs.

SPOTIFY RHYTHM – GETTING EVERYONE TO PULL IN THE SAME DIRECTION, AT THE SAME TIME

At Spotify, it makes perfect sense that we regularly talk to our employees about strategy and the challenges facing the company – it is in line with our core values, our culture and who we say we are and want to be. For example, we share our quarterly reports, the content of our strategy days and the outcome of our goal prioritisation meetings. It also makes sense to clearly link our mission, our strategies and goals and our operating model – what we call the Spotify Rhythm – to our employee focus.

At Spotify, we often hire 'on potential' and not on the basis of past performance or what school or university someone went to. We always have to proactively think about what skills we will need in the future. With this in mind, having a handful of smooth and fast processes is a positive thing. It becomes even more important to ensure that everyone understands what we want to achieve together and our strategy for doing so. It's as simple as making sure that policies are easy for all employees to understand (easy to read, easy to interpret, effective). We look closely at our different organisational elements and sometimes pair them in a new way. In our case, in a way that shows even more clearly that employees come first.

In order to carry through changes of the kind discussed in this book, there is nothing wrong with understanding the rules of the game (step one) and preferably following them for a while (step two), and then developing and changing them (step three). Skipping the first two steps, as an individual or organisation, can cause the best of ideas to fall flat, even if in practice they should increase efficiency and productivity, simplify processes and deliver more business value.

Let's take a concrete example: at Spotify, we were influenced by *lean* and *agile* thinking and models, especially in the early stages of our history. In the two following phases, we dared to be a little rebellious about how we structure our teams. Some traditionalists would probably frown upon this, claiming that our way doesn't work, or is unnecessarily complicated. By following our own path, we have managed to get new results from existing teams.

In order to be able and willing to propose something radically different, you need to understand the unwritten rules of the organisation, which can otherwise act as a tripwire. You also need to understand the resistance that comes when you redistribute a certain amount of power. Returning to the example of *lean*, this model and way of working is in fact little or not at all about the past, or about who makes decisions or enjoys internal power. It's more about continuous improvement and the end customer experience.

At Spotify, we have placed Strategy Operations and HR close together, under the responsibility of the CHRO. This helps us to see the big picture and 'connect the dots', which in turn avoids a lot of frustration, clumsy handovers and unnecessary misunderstandings. Of course, this model is not the only possible solution and may not suit everyone. Compared to when Strategy Operations was in R&D or Content, there is now less administration, fewer processes, and the overly complicated reporting templates have been greatly simplified.

Social Impact
& Sustainability

We see a new (but long-awaited) approach emerging, with a strong focus on the responsibility of companies for their impact on society from an Environmental, Social and Governance (ESG) perspective. It's time for everyone to take sustainability and social impact seriously and to realise that people are at the heart of these topics. At present, every organisation needs to develop powerful strategies, designed to have a long-term impact, and to actually put them into action.

When tackling the topic of sustainability, it's easy to think about physical products and manufacturing, or about labour-intensive supply chains in some faraway country. In today's reality, every organisation, regardless of sector, needs to understand sustainability and climate change, and their impact on the business and employees. As an HR professional, this area cannot be set aside or delegated to someone else. Let's take Spotify as an example – why is sustainability important to us? First of all, because we actually have an impact on the world around us, both environmentally and socially. This impact is not insignificant and will grow as the company grows. We strive to be a responsible and inclusive part of society – not just for our employees, creators and the industry – but for the good of the whole world. The technology on which our business is based allows us to reach beyond all borders and because we reach large parts of the globe, we have the opportunity to make a noticeable difference.

That's why we are also determined to incorporate sustainability into everything we do. We try to raise awareness of these issues, we share our knowledge and we take action to help solve social and sustainability challenges around the world. We also know that our employees, both current and future, care about sustainability and want to work for a company that has a positive impact on the world.

More than just 'green'

For many years, sustainability was mostly about managing external perceptions – was the company 'green' in the sense of being environmentally friendly? People liked to talk loudly about sustainability and the work they were doing. In practice, they let individual employees or a small team with few resources do the actual work. If they made an effort, it was mostly because they wanted to avoid breaking laws and regulations and for the purpose of positive PR. There were also companies that squeezed a bit of eco-friendliness into their messages, as a kind of symbolic Corporate Social Responsibility (CSR) strategy. Compliance – making sure the organisation follows laws and regulations – is far from enough. We must work to maximise the positive impact we can have, not just do the minimum. Therefore, we need to incorporate principles related to positive social impact and sustainability into everything, including HR. That's why we recommend that in this new era, you should take the time to explore the synergies that are at hand when you cross-fertilise the responsibilities and work that

HR and the Social Impact team already deliver. Take advantage of what you know about change management in order to implement mechanisms that make the whole organisation 'think sustainable' when defining business strategies and making decisions. A simple first step is to always ask the question: How might this affect the rest of the world? This will rarely be a decisive factor, but should always be taken into account.

It is important that you demonstrate genuine responsibility in your social impact and sustainable development strategy. This may mean that the strategy needs to be aligned with other key HR strategies, such as those related to diversity, inclusion and belonging. This is where the world is headed, which is why we suggest that sustainability has a home within the HR department. After all, it's people who create real, large-scale change. A McKinsey study shows that organisations that address sustainability to achieve their business purpose and goals (because it aligns with their core values, or to make a real, positive difference on a particular issue) are more likely to create value, such as increased profits, reduced costs, or higher employee engagement, through their sustainability programmes.[13]

Create a strategy

When creating your strategy, define a roadmap that will enable you to:

- Run your business in a responsible and sustainable way, while being aware of the impact you have. This may include reducing emissions or waste, promoting social justice, finding the right suppliers and partners, and then engaging employees on these issues. You should also comply with local laws and regulations, reduce your negative impact on the environment and protect human rights.

- Help solve the world's problems, drive change beyond your own business and be a force for good, in line with your core values and purpose. Try to find the most effective way to do this. If you use your business model instead of doing sustainability work in a 'bubble', it will create more value than charity. Although charity work is important, supporting organisations with gifts and donations is not enough. For us at Spotify, it's been about using our platform and reach to drive change.

If you're feeling a bit overwhelmed and don't know where to start – take the UN Sustainable Development Goals (SDGs)[14] as a framework to set your strategy and examine where you stand in relation to the goals.

Change your mindset

Truly living the strategy is about replacing an old question with a new one, moving from 'how can we stop being part of the problem?' to 'how can we become part of the solution?' We believe this requires a shift in thinking – we need to learn to deal with the fact that things can be contradictory and still work and that one does not necessarily exclude the other. At Spotify, we talk about 'embracing the complex and mastering polarities'. Don't pit profit and sustainability (or other positive change) against each other. Don't think that working on these issues should be done 'on the side' – it needs to be integrated into all aspects of day-to-day operations and incorporated into the HR department's annual roadmap, goals and key performance indicators.

To operate in a sustainable way, you need to ensure that all parts of your organisation strive to minimise the negative environmental and social impact you have on your surroundings. This includes everything from how you manage your offices to how you deal with office waste, how you choose suppliers, and how you interact with each other (and everything in between). For example, Spotify's customer offering is not a physical product and as a media company, we need to think about the power of our platform and how we can use it to have the greatest possible positive impact. The question 'how can we become part of the solution?' serves as a guide.

Impact and prioritisation

Integrating sustainability into the HR department's roadmap is a journey in itself, as many companies have realised by now. One that we all need to be part of. Sustainability is good for business, so make it part of the culture and engage employees, customers and business partners in your 'sustainability agenda'. It needs to be a strategic priority because it requires a lot of thinking to create the necessary momentum. We're not talking about product development (although that's good), but rather being thoughtful and focused about how to apply sustainability principles to everything you do.

The smartest thing to do when it comes to issues like sustainability and social impact is to put energy into finding the right focus and to be thoughtful. In other words, define what 'impact' is first and prioritise in the next step. Think about what is most relevant to the world, your business and your stakeholders. Consider how you are uniquely positioned to create change. Make sure to take a holistic approach and look at the issue from multiple perspectives, with all your stakeholders and audiences in mind: employees, customers, partners and others.

At Spotify, we have established clear, focused priorities (for example, related to climate change), and set bold targets that are updated every year. On climate, our goal is to reach net zero emissions by 2030. We have also developed key performance indicators (in this case, greenhouse gas emissions from different parts of the business and the value chain, both in absolute and relative terms, electricity consumption, share of renewable electricity, etc.). Progress is communicated to our employees at the same time as the company's financial reports are.

Employee engagement and community

As in any other area, you need to understand where you are today, what you want to achieve and how you can get there. A snapshot will help you see the impact you have on your surroundings from a social and environmental perspective. A company like Spotify, while not based on physical products, will – from an environmental perspective – emit greenhouse gases (our buildings, our travel, and our users' streaming all lead to emissions!). In terms of social development, with our huge media platform, we have a big responsibility (we will describe this in more detail at the end of the chapter).

In the vast majority of organisations, employees are the biggest target group you can influence when it comes to awareness and positive climate change, or they *can* be. Whether you are a purpose-driven organisation or not, we can guarantee that your employees, current and future, care about these issues and want to work for a company that is determined to have a positive impact on the world.

It's worth dwelling on this idea for a while. It's impossible to see your own private impact on the world in one light and the impact you have through the company you work for in another. You can't define an individual's impact that way, either environmentally or socially. That's why you need to help employees see their own impact. Whether they are passionate about the issue or not, you will make it understandable and engaging for more employees if you make their individual impact as clear as possible. This is the key to employee-driven change.

Tap into your most loyal advocates: employees who feel included and at home in your company culture. The sense of belonging created when an individual's values align with the company's core values is incredibly powerful. We know that we can spark engagement and drive by creating understanding and awareness. Doing so with a basis in your company's purpose creates community among your employees around their core issues. Creating, developing and cultivating such a community can be a game changer. Like your employer brand and employee value proposition, your approach to social impact and sustainability must be genuine. Employees should recognise themselves. The company's work in this area, including its positions and objectives, should be consistent with its culture and identity.

Sustainability efforts are not short-term campaigns but long-term investments and initiatives, which must be strongly linked to the company's core values and purpose. The aim is to encourage employee engagement, as well as a sense of pride and shared responsibility.

This doesn't mean that you should spend time on *everyone's* pet issues. Think about which initiatives are most clearly aligned with your core values, and create interest groups linked to those specific issues. Choose focus and depth over breadth and superficiality.

The supply chain and partners

Employee engagement is key to successful sustainability efforts. There is another opportunity to drive change in sustainability and social impact: the supply chain. It's not just about travelling less, or being carbon neutral in terms of office waste and recycling. It's about creating truly sustainable workplaces. This includes how your office space is designed and built, who your electricity suppliers are and what food you offer, among many other aspects. Also think about your business practices, such as supplier codes of conduct, anti-corruption policies, and risk awareness and management. Map, evaluate and select the areas where you can have a real, meaningful impact. Then set clear, measurable and relevant targets.

The only way to succeed is to try to make an impact through collaboration. Individual companies can do a lot on their own to improve their sustainability indicators, but many face challenges that span entire sectors or regions. Reducing plastic waste requires the involvement of an entire sector, not just one company. Industry associations and non-profit organisations focus on bringing companies together to create new standards, promote technological innovation and advocate for improved policies.

Where does social impact and sustainability fit in the organisation?

There are differences of opinion about where in a company's organisational structure the sustainability teams actually belong. In many cases, this has led to unfocused and fragmented solutions. However well-intentioned, the result was a lack of clear direction. Sustainability and social development is a topic that benefits from a positive approach and change being made to create a movement and have real impact. In order not to spread efforts over too large an area and to ensure that all activities and initiatives are coordinated and lead to the same goal, all aspects of this topic should be brought together in a single team.

In our experience, there is a lot to be gained from coordinating teams working on social impact, sustainability, diversity, inclusion and belonging. Whichever constellation you choose, the important thing is that 1) your efforts support your core values, 2) you do good for the communities in which you operate, and 3) you really push your sustainability agenda in line with your commitments.

For those of us who work in a purpose-driven organisation and whose employees are very solution-oriented, driven and committed – the answer is simple. The HR department is undoubtedly the best home for social impact and sustainability.

PLAY YOUR PART – AN EXAMPLE OF HOW SPOTIFY ENGAGES EMPLOYEES AND USERS IN SUSTAINABILITY MATTERS

At Spotify, much of the focus of our social impact and sustainability strategy is on our product. As a global media platform, we have used the same methods as in other parts of our business, experimenting when we see an opportunity or discover a need. We implement, assess impact, iterate and expand.

In 2020, we created a hub on the platform called *Play Your Part*, focusing on civil society and voting in the US. Here, users were invited to engage, learn and act. In 2021, we expanded *Play Your Part* to activate more people on climate issues, using the same basic steps: *engage, learn, act*. Our data, and our desire to use our platform to highlight the issues we care about, prompted us to use the hub to expand our reach on sustainability, social impact and climate change issues.

ENGAGE – LEARN – ACT

Let's start from the beginning. Voting can be quite confusing, especially for a first-time voter. In the US, laws vary widely between states and it's not always easy to find clear, accurate information. In 2020, amidst the pandemic and political instability, voting was still more challenging. At Spotify, we want our users, creators, and employees alike to feel empowered, seen and heard. An important way to make your voice heard is to vote, which inspired us to build the first version of *Play Your Part* on the Spotify platform. It was filled with content to give voters important information for the 2020 elections. We didn't include party political messages, just pure information – a broad initiative where people trusted by voters raised important societal issues. We created playlists with podcasts from different thinkers, to inform and encourage people to vote. This covered the 'engage' and 'learn' parts of our approach.

Play Your Part allowed our users to find information on how to register (a requirement for voting) by geographical location, alongside playlists and a library of political podcasts. To make it easier for people to take the step to register, we made sure that one click was enough to go to their local registration site and access more information about the elections. We also made sure that practical information was included, such as how to get to the polling station. That was the 'act' part. Because we are Spotify, we also created new playlists to soundtrack our listeners' voting experiences. We teamed up with some first-time voters' favourite artists and influencers to build new playlists that could entertain listeners throughout the election process.

Almost two million users visited *Play Your Part* in the run-up to the 2020 elections, demonstrating the willingness of our users to stay informed and receive content on issues they care about. The positive results confirmed our view: a company that identifies an important societal issue that is in line with its purpose and core values can have a positive impact on employee engagement and on customers' experience with its products.

GLOBALISATION

The positive outcome of the first iteration, together with the conclusions we could draw from user data, led us to make our *Play Your Part* hub available globally. Each market decides if and how they will use it based on their local needs.

The work on *Play Your Part* also confirmed that initiatives of this kind – if they are to have real impact – can't be the side project of a few team members. They must span the entire company, with a focus on finding a solution to important issues.

As part of Spotify's global commitment to climate change and sustainable development, a new *Play Your Part* was launched on Earth Day 2021 with the same format: *Engage, Learn, Act.* It features podcast playlists created by guest creators on the following themes:

- Knowledge is power – listen to scientists and experts getting to the bottom of some of the major challenges facing the planet.

- Voices for change – hear activists describe how they make their voices heard in order to make a difference.

- How to make an impact – small steps you can take in your everyday life to help make our world a better place.

Through the platform, users can access other sites, such as *Time for Climate Action*,[15] where they can find more information on what they can do to make a difference. The climate site provides our users and employees with a wide range of topics to learn about: energy saving, ways to reduce your carbon footprint at home and at work, and much more.

STAY FOCUSED FOR CONTINUED IMPACT

At Spotify, we believe in transparency and ongoing conversations with our employees and this also applies to sustainability. Here, we have a dialogue about which priorities are the most important, so as not to make the mistake of trying to tackle all problems at once. The key to success is to stay focused and constantly assess the impact of an initiative before making a decision on whether to invest in it. During the *Play Your Part* journey, we learned to focus on the solution ('how can we be part of the solution?'), evaluate options, collect feedback from our users and employees and, finally, share our lessons learned externally and globally.

Global Workplace Services – creating the workplace of the future

What do we mean by Global Workplace Services (GWS)? If your company has one or more people working on physical workplace issues (office and real estate procurement, negotiation, architecture, office design and maintenance, etc.), this is the team we're referring to. However, in your case, you probably don't call these teams GWS and they may not even be based in the same function. In many organisations, they are not part of or close to HR. Almost comparable would be a *Facility management* and/or *office management* team but they wouldn't typically include all property-related work.

This final chapter of the book looks at how you can take a holistic approach to the topic, explaining why we pull this team together under the GWS umbrella and why that sits within the People Constituency close to HR.

The first reason to note is that it's a powerful way to increase employee efficiency and productivity while strengthening the culture and sense of community. The GWS team should, first and foremost, be service-oriented by:

- Serving your employees so that they can perform at their best, no matter where they work. This can be about employee safety and security. It can also be about ensuring that your

IT systems work flawlessly, no matter where your employees choose to work.

- Talking to different internal stakeholders to understand the needs of those who will use the premises. There is a big difference between *needing* and *wanting* – so the team will need to show integrity and courage.

- Serving those who visit your offices, such as partners, customers and candidates, by creating spaces that are welcoming, inclusive and inspiring. The meeting room and the space should 'breathe' (reflect and strengthen) your culture and your business.

- Enabling efficiency and well-being by taking care of the offices, which includes everything from choosing the right property to the important daily work of keeping them clean and providing the right equipment and digital systems.

- Ensuring a good and safe physical workplace that is relevant and functional for employees.

The work of this team is never static – employees come and go, technology evolves and needs change over time. With these changing needs, the GWS team's delivery must evolve, aligning with the organisation's overall business strategy and culture.

It's not always obvious that the GWS team (or whatever you choose to call it) should be part of the People Constituency. Your GWS work may be split across many parts of the business, or you may, for example, place the real estate part in the finance department. From our perspective, it makes the most sense for the People organisation to cover everything in GWS. If a team is going to provide service in all five ways mentioned above, and benefit from the HR team's knowledge and expertise in human behaviour and needs, then the People Constituency is a natural home base. After all, this is where the focus is securely fixed on finding the right balance between the needs of the business and the needs of the employees.

When you place GWS close to HR, you gain a lot of synergies. You can make your offices accessible to more people and design them in such a way that you contribute to a sense of belonging and community that works, both externally and internally – for sustainability, for the employer brand and for the consumer brand.

A close relationship between GWS and HR means you can make the best use of your premises.

For example, you can question old truths about how people should work and how the workplace should be designed. You can also save energy and money and, more importantly, shape the workplace to suit your culture and the needs of your employees. This is where HR can contribute a lot through its knowledge of people's needs and behaviours.

In short – enabling HR and GWS to work closely is key to the workplace of the future. This is especially true if you agree that the interface between people, environment and technology is both what has held back development and what is now driving new ways of working – the new world of work. In this 'marriage', employees are given the freedom to decide for themselves what supports their way of working, with the support of two professions – HR and GWS – collaborating closely. The office – the node, or the hub, if you will – should be a creative and dynamic place, which the employee chooses to be in and which encourages collaboration and meetings. It should be a place where the individual's focus, performance and creativity can be further strengthened and where the power of a 'we' becomes tangible.

The office and the employer brand

Ideally, your physical offices embody the employer brand. The office is a place where employees, visitors, partners, customers and others can see and interact with the company's identity, profile and image.

If your employees work full-time in the office, the office becomes their strongest link to the employer brand. In other words, when they think of you as an employer, they will think of the office. If you offer a hybrid solution when you think of the office, you need to think beyond a physical location. If an employee can choose to work entirely remotely, then you have another challenge.

We have found that the office becomes even more important if many employees work remotely. We therefore don't believe in closing all offices – not if you care about the well-being and health of your employees and your employer brand. Even if most people work from home (or from all sorts of other locations), it doesn't make sense not to have an office. Instead, consider the office as a social space, or even an exclusive club which your people are members of. With their 'membership cards' they are admitted to the 'clubhouse', where they can work, socialise, have fun, collaborate, learn, plan and so on.

A distributed work model is where most or all employees base themselves in the location that works best for them and are rarely in the same office, on the same floor, or even in the same city, country or time zone. Presenting these offerings provides freedom and flexibility. It's also attractive to many gig workers (perhaps especially people who work creatively to create content and don't want to be locked into working for one specific employer and in one physical location or city). It can help you find a 'virtual talent pool', which is also decentralised and global. This creates an incredible opportunity to strengthen your employer brand and attract people who would otherwise not consider you as a viable employer. If you offer remote work, you can reach a group that doesn't see themselves as employees in the traditional sense. They are 'digital nomads', or at least free spirits who don't necessarily want to be part of a community that is tied to a specific location and submit to all the trappings of employment. It's great to be able to access talent all over the world without having to physically move them to the country or city where your office is located. Whether your physical workplace is for employees who are in the office every day, or for people who come in occasionally (or are just visible in the background of a colleague's screen during video calls), it plays a very important role. The office can act as a hub, a fixed point, and strengthen the sense of community. It is key to create a sense of belonging in your offices and all the properties the GWS team manages. You want your employees to feel that their needs are met, that they are heard and seen.

The office as a hub

In order to allow for a distributed working model – and an office that fully supports your employees' needs – you need to really *know* your business and understand what your employees want and need. It is unlikely that employees from two different companies will have exactly the same needs. Don't assume a rigid or predetermined variant, such as a 3-2-2 solution (three days in the office, two from home, two off) will work. As always, never copy what someone else has done; use your knowledge of the business and employees and find your own way.

At Spotify, when we switched to our *Work from Anywhere* approach (which we will describe in more detail at the end of the chapter), we wanted to create a dynamic workplace that would be flexible and sustainable, enable a sense of belonging, and create conditions for spontaneous unplanned interactions. It would also allow for silence, concentration and reflection. We redesigned all the common spaces and tried to get away from the more static, fixed desks and meeting rooms.

We also wanted to create a social, 'collaborative' environment in the office. If your office is a space for a distributed workforce to meet, it should be a place for interaction. That, along with your workforce planning, influences your choice of real estate. How many people come into the office, why they come in, what tools they use, how they interact, and how they want to use the office, is part of what influences office planning and design. Imagine trying to map out all of this (and more) as a GWS team without knowing the company's workforce planning strategies, recruitment numbers, where employees have chosen to work from, what the business goals are, and so on. You need to consider who is using the space, as well as the local culture and business needs.

As always, what works well in a particular country, market or culture may not work as well elsewhere. So use what you believe in, your culture and values and your brand, to create *consistency* in your workplaces, no matter where your employees choose to be.

An important aspect here, and something that contributes greatly to creating a sense of belonging, is to make inclusion and belonging a central element of your office design.

The right property and the right office design

Our strategy has been to ensure that our offices are in the best possible location, wherever we are in the world. Not least because it makes us more attractive as an employer. It should be easy to commute to work, the office should be centrally located and the place should feel safe for employees, visitors and others. The building itself should ideally feel 'right' and show who we are and what we do.

We don't normally shout out where we are with a bunch of logos, but the building should 'breathe' Spotify by representing what we stand for, what we do, who we are and what we want to achieve. The real estate team is always on the lookout for suitable buildings and works with the design team to make sure the end result 'feels like Spotify'. The culture should be visible in the design of the office. It should also be designed in such a way that helps to drive the culture forwards.

When it comes to office design, it's hard to please everyone. You have a much better chance of doing so if you involve both employees and visitors as much as possible in the process. You need to understand the needs of those who will be using the office (employees, partners, visitors and others) in order to create an environment that supports them in their work, provides them with a positive experience and contributes to new meetings, collaborations, ideas and opportunities. It's a difficult balancing act to gather input from the teams that use the office today to create a generic toolkit for different environments, allowing employees to freely choose which environment suits them during the day, without designing specifically for any individual's needs. It's worth the effort to create a global 'office language' that both promotes inclusion during the process itself and then becomes embodied in your offices.

With a dynamic design, you will be able to respond more quickly to changing business needs. Moreover, building smaller and using more flexible solutions is often more sustainable. This doesn't mean that any building will work. You still need to put effort into getting the right property purchase/lease. A good understanding of who will use the space and how, together with a thorough analysis of both architectural and economic aspects, will help you choose the right building in the right location. Designing responsibly and building sustainably and practically, while ensuring that the office has many different types of rooms and other spaces, will support most ways of working in a multifaceted business. When you add your corporate identity and brand, your office should stand out and not be just another fancy office in any company. This contributes to a sense of community and pride – and a better user experience – and helps you with that sense of 'clubhouse' and 'membership' we mentioned earlier.

Here too, when designing your office space, you must be prepared to challenge old truths and fight the impulse to copy other companies. Challenge these assumptions:

1. EVERYONE WORKS IN THE SAME WAY

People function differently, have different strengths, different routines and different ways of working. A research & development department works in a completely different way than a business department, which in turn works in a completely different way than a support department. There is no right and wrong. Create reference groups that work alongside HR to develop the office design – and make sure you involve as many people as possible. Encourage them to give you feedback.

2. EVERYONE MUST HAVE THEIR OWN DESK

This is not true! When we keep pushing in more desks, we also lose space that could be used for meeting rooms (there are, of course, some examples of people who need to have a desk or other equipment because of the technology they work with, or because of a disability).

There is a limit to how many people can be accommodated in an office, taking into account ventilation and fire safety. If you design for everyone to have their own desk, as you grow, you will have to move to larger premises just to accommodate the desks that have a daily utilisation rate of no more than 30-60%. Measure yourself and you'll see!

For a company like Spotify, providing everyone with a desk is not sustainable, especially if you want an office in a great location. Space is a luxury and should be used wisely. When employees work remotely or hybrid (a few days a week in the office), it is less important for them to have their own desk in the office. The desk isn't out of the picture yet though – it has just moved to the employees' homes. The desk is also still an important element of an office landscape, and a mix of desks that anyone can use, as well as meeting spaces in an open-plan environment, provides greater convenience – and better acoustics.

3. A DISTRIBUTED WAY OF WORKING REDUCES THE SENSE OF COMMUNITY

Many global companies have employees who frequently travel between offices.

This means that they rarely use 'their' desks, which results in them often being empty. Companies like Spotify, who offer their employees the opportunity to work remotely, will see a lot of empty desks. Not only is this a huge waste, it's quite sad for those who are actually there. Those who sit and work with an empty desk as their nearest neighbour get the feeling of working in an empty office.

We have learned from interviews with our staff that they find it somewhat uncomfortable to sit at someone else's desk in a foreign office. It makes them feel rootless when they're travelling. So, if you can, create offices that are easy to reconfigure as needed, giving each team a dedicated space (a 'neighbourhood') where they can work and feel at home. Having to look for your closest colleagues or for a place to sit every time you enter the office is neither efficient nor very pleasant.

4. INCLUSION CAN BE 'PLUGGED IN' TO AN EXISTING DESIGN

No, it can't – inclusion has to be holistic. The sense of belonging is greatly influenced by the shape of the physical spaces, and there is certainly a lot to consider. It's not just about modernising, but about really wanting to make a positive change. You need to design *fully inclusive offices*. That starts with the building you choose. Is it accessible to everyone and will everyone feel included? As for your existing offices: evaluate them carefully. Install hearing loops in reception and event spaces, make sure wheelchair users can access all rooms and floors, and use gender-neutral signage for all toilets. These are just a few examples.

When it comes to office design, neurodiversity is also important. Our brains work in different ways and this affects, for example, how we learn new things, handle sensory input, understand social situations and orient ourselves in physical environments. Facilities should be easy to find and it should be clear what different rooms and spaces are used for. There should also be rest rooms and quiet spaces. New research is emerging all the time, so being open to learning, adapting and engaging with employees with special needs is of paramount importance.

5. WORK ONLY HAPPENS AT DESKS AND IN MEETING ROOMS
If you think like this, you don't use the whole office. Employees can work in more places if you create the conditions for it. With the old formula of an open plan office plus meeting rooms, there's no room for other types of meetings. It won't allow for a relaxed conversation on a couch, for a meeting around a dining table, or for sitting on your own and focusing, which may be exactly what employees need to feel good and perform at their best. Think again, make the most of your space and create a more flexible working environment, where the focus is on comfort and choice.

The workplace of the future

The office should be a place for meaningful experiences, where employees can 'feel' the culture and what the company wants and stands for. They should be able to interact in ways that have unexpected positive effects. Create a strong partnership between HR and GWS and figure out together which model is best for your business and your people. How do you find the optimal solution for you? By identifying what is most important in your business and building a customised workplace based on that. If you have an open mind and a growth mindset, the possibilities are endless. It allows you to evaluate how the office is actually being used, while imagining what happens if you tear up everything you think you know and start from scratch about what defines a workplace and what is required there. It is this kind of thinking and similar exercises that gave us the embryo of our dynamic workplace.

If you decide to follow our advice, your offices are likely to change dramatically. Be prepared to pull out your change management tools. A drastic change in the physical environment requires action from employees – they may have to think and work in a new way. This will inevitably create some uncertainty, reluctance and resistance. If you can keep your business and your employees' needs at the forefront of your workplace of the future, you will be able to innovate, or at least move forwards. You'll be able to create a place where your employees want to be and where they can do their job in the best possible way.

THE WORK FROM ANYWHERE PROGRAMME

'What does the future of work look like?' This is a question the Spotify HR team has asked ourselves many times. Globalisation and digitalisation mean that employers must be able to offer greater flexibility. The new generation of talent that wants a more personalised work experience has taken over the labour market.

At Spotify, we hadn't really defined how we would approach this in practice. Then the pandemic struck. Overnight, everyone was forced to work from home. It was a real test of our culture, our values and our ways of working. It forced us to reflect on what leadership and work should really look like in the future. During this test, we confirmed that we do have a solid foundation and thus had more opportunities to review what we wanted to do going forwards. Even before the pandemic, we'd been discussing a more flexible approach to where work should be done and now we had the chance to make a more permanent change – just a little earlier than we'd originally expected. We also knew from previous initiatives that our employees appreciate flexible solutions, which is in line with our culture.

We spent a lot of time understanding what our employees wanted in order to create a sustainable model that would work for the majority. We had to deal with some conflicting data, such as employees wanting freedom and flexibility in terms of office presence, whilst missing the sense of belonging and social interaction in the office when they take advantage of that freedom. The majority of our employees stated that they were happy to *have their cake and eat it too*, where they could spend most of their time in the office but were free to work from home when it suited them. This is one of many examples of when things can be 'both/and'. A smaller group preferred fully remote work. They wanted to spend more time outside the traditional office environment and work elsewhere.

This gave us a great opportunity to try something new, to let employees choose the solution that suits them best. Of course, it was risky – truly a 100% trust-based approach! It's also risky to stand still and hold on to old self-chosen truths. We also realised that there were many questions we still didn't know the answers to and that there is no real research in this area – yet. For example: What does all this freedom do to employees' sense of belonging and community? How does it affect their mental health? What about collaboration, creativity and innovation? Can we do without all the positive things that can happen when people meet face-to-face in everyday life?

We chose not to let these questions stop us and thus took the step towards becoming a *distributed* company, rather than a fully *co-located* one. We listed our key beliefs as guidelines when developing the programme:

- Work is not a *place*, it is something you *do*.

- Efficiency cannot be measured by the number of hours employees spend in the office. Giving them the freedom to choose where they work will increase efficiency.

- Greater flexibility allows employees to achieve a better work-life balance and also makes us more attractive as an employer to certain groups of interest, while allowing us to retain our existing employees.

- Being a distributed organisation will create better, more efficient working methods with more thoughtful use of communication and collaboration methods, processes and tools.

Within our Work From Anywhere (WFA) programme, we offer flexibility in two dimensions: workplace and geographic location. The first, *My Work Mode*, allows employees to choose between working full-time from home, full-time from the office, or a mix of both. The second dimension of flexibility allows employees to choose which country and city they are based in.

Moving towards an everyday life where employees can work in this way requires trust-based leadership, not control-based leadership. You have to let go of traditional yardsticks and stop keeping track of when employees arrive and leave the office, or how many hours they spend at their desks. Instead, the focus needs to be on what employees do – the impact they have on business performance. As described earlier, our Manager Manifesto asks our managers/leaders to lead with purpose and trust as a guiding principle. They should want and dare to lead in both good and bad times, to build and lead healthy teams and understand that leadership is a team sport. None of this argues against investing in a more flexible way of working.

When the pandemic struck, many organisations started experimenting with remote work and discussing hybrid work of various kinds, such as solutions where only some employees spent a lot of time in the office and others worked from home. There are many arguments against a hybrid model. No sensible organisation wants to create an *in-group* and an *out-group*, or an A and B team. Having multiple employer-created groupings or cultures within the company cannot be a positive for anyone. Does this mean that a hybrid solution is always wrong?

At Spotify, we are careful not to get stuck in 'either/or'. Therefore, we offer freedom and flexibility, a working model where employees can choose a *home mix* or an *office mix*. However, this comes with some challenges, perhaps the biggest of which is that the sense of belonging and community must be built in more ways than through the physical meeting in an office. This is important – our ambition is to reduce the 'friction' in the collaboration between those working in offices and those working elsewhere. We want to create conditions for ways of working where it doesn't matter where an employee is.

Our managers don't have the task of controlling their employees and the execution of their work. We've realised that, whether everyone came to the office or not, effectively, we were already distributed the moment we no longer fit into one space, one floor, one office, one country and one time zone.

It's better to find solutions for the new world of work than to work against it. This is what helped us to decide to move forwards with the new WFA programme.

STRATEGY OPERATIONS AND HR

We're able to unleash much greater productivity quicker due to Spotify operating digitally and being a distributed company. Until the COVID-19 pandemic hit, most ways of working and workflows were based on face-to-face and other non-digital interactions, even if Spotify is a digital-native company. While some could easily be replaced with technology interfaces and tools, others suffer.

To be an efficient company with a distributed workforce requires a heavy focus on the change management and investments needed to nudge employees to work with a distributed mindset, taking into account how work is done best when people are spread out. This is necessary for the sake of effectiveness. The only way to be successful in this new world was by covering two flanks – what work looks like (which sits with traditional HR) and how work is done (which sits with strategy operations). The close relationship that existed, and strategy operations being part of the people function, set us up in a great place to be able to make the decision in the way that was right for our people and our business.

The move to a fully distributed model has had a big impact on employees' daily lives and we needed to rethink how the offices were structured. The flexible, personalised approach needed to be reflected in the design of the offices, to ensure we offered an environment that supported the new way of working. The office went from being a place to do all your work in, to a space for meetings, socialising and team building. Employees should be able to come to the office and work in the way that suits them and their team best, in a way that is environmentally and economically sustainable. In short, we needed to develop our premises – and we needed to do it together.

The shift from an office-based to a distributed company is a major change management project, among the largest an HR department can initiate and be responsible for. To do this successfully, we needed to redefine the nature of the employer-employee relationship. It was also necessary to look at how we can make the transition to a new way of working as smooth as possible, how we onboard new employees, how and what training we offer to our employees and whether distributed ways of working place different and new demands on leadership and teamwork. What role will the office play in the future? How should it be designed? To be successful, all teams needed to be able to work together smoothly.

This part of the future work environment, office and way of working has been greatly simplified with HR, Strategy Operations and GWS sitting together and working together for the good of the organisation.

Learning along the way

We choose to end the book by talking about our Work from Anywhere programme because in so many ways, it reflects the way we work and what we believe in. At the heart of our strategy for attracting, developing and retaining talent is our flexible approach and willingness to try something new. It's based on trust, communication, collaboration and community. We want our employees to feel a sense of belonging when they come to the office, and also when they don't. We believe we can strengthen this feeling by taking into account that people are different. Our people have different needs, are motivated by different things and have different ways of switching their mindset to let go of old truths, think in new ways and discover what's right for our business.

Allowing employees to work from home because a pandemic requires it is one thing. Making such a solution permanent in a global company with thousands of employees spread across the world is another. Especially when so much of the work is based on teamwork and the feeling that we're doing this together. We need to find ways of working that suit the new era, where employees can be just as agile and innovative as before, receive just as much support from their managers and feel just as safe with each other – even if they rarely see one another.

The 'controlled chaos' that is part of our DNA helps here. We never underestimate what our people have to deal with in terms of constant change. As we've said many times in the book, we're also careful not to get stuck in a rut and do things in the same way just because we don't have all the answers yet. Instead, when we see something we believe in, we want to take the plunge, even if it means learning along the way and occasionally correcting our course. In some cases, we get it right from the start, like when we launched our *Global Parental Leave* programme in 2015, or the *Global Flexible Holidays* approach, which we mentioned earlier in the book.

With our Work From Anywhere programme, as with previous launches of global programmes involving all of our circa 10,000 band members (at the time), we took the plunge, whilst well aware that we would probably have to make adjustments down the road. Just over a year after launching this ongoing experiment, we observed significant improvements in our recruitment process. The time to hire has notably accelerated and we have successfully reduced staff turnover compared to the pre-pandemic period. Additionally, we've been able to tap into new talent pools, which has greatly promoted diversity within our workforce.

Playing safe and slow is not our thing, and neither is fast and wrong. In this new era, we know what we can do, we make no apologies for our central role and we contribute to the business, the organisation and the people.

Final words

In the introduction to this book, we talked about the 'HR palette', which is said to contain 171 different colours. This is just another way of saying that HR work is complex and our profession is constantly evolving. Many people have different opinions about the function of HR and what we do. We can listen to these opinions, but we also need to be confident in our expertise. We need to be clear about what we bring to the table and what skills we have, so that we can make a real difference. In other words, we should aim to master the colours and feel comfortable with all of them – whether they are garish, subtle, innovative, or whatever they are. Maybe if we even dare to mix colours, we could be better placed to contribute to the development and growth of individuals, teams and the organisation as a whole.

In this new era, we need to listen even more to our employees and treat them with even more respect. Everything we do in HR can be done well or badly. That doesn't make us particularly unique; it's true for most professions. In our industry, however, there is a lot we can do with excellence, character and worth – or without. We can behave with or without integrity.

In this new era, it's also important to be able to act quickly – and sometimes boldly. At Spotify, we believe in getting down to business – *doing* – rather than sitting around drafting fancy wording and spending hours, days or weeks describing, explaining, documenting, revising. This doesn't mean that we never document anything, or that we don't have well-functioning processes. It just means that we don't spend the majority of our time on administration, updating processes and guidelines. We *do* first and then document. In the best-case scenario, we *do* and document simultaneously!

When you do a lot – well, sometimes you make mistakes. Both big and small mistakes. It's inevitable. You have to own them, learn from them, correct them and then – on you go again. If you hide behind your keyboard and only do exactly what's expected of HR, so as not to risk being questioned, then you may end up with nothing more than a perfect employee handbook, well-polished processes and an endless amount of neat and well-crafted PowerPoint presentations.

At Spotify, we are far from sitting down at a table that has already been laid. Those of us in HR still have regular discussions about what the menu should look like – we cook together, set the table together and eat together. Sure, the kitchen can get messy at times and things aren't always where you left them, but we have a shared vision of the end result and we take the journey together. It's a way of working that doesn't suit everyone, but it works for us.

We have the most exciting job in the world – if we dare to let it be. The fun is often the difficult and challenging part. Don't ever give up the fun parts! It's all too common to bring in consultants when things start to heat up in the organisation, when it's really exciting – when it's about culture and value journeys, employer branding, employee value proposition or reorganisations – in contexts where we can do the most good with our skills, when we can come into our own. For goodness sake, do this work yourself.

When you do undertake these challenges – dare to think new. Radically new. You owe yourself and your whole organisation something better than a legacy of slow, bureaucratic processes that you can't explain and that no one really understands or finds particularly effective. Rethink, redo, reorganise. Find new, relevant ways to get out of the starting blocks and fly over the obstacles. There will be difficulties and you will have to clear the path.

In this book, we've tried to describe how we think and do things at Spotify and we hope it will inspire you. Don't get hung up on our words and think our way is the only way. Challenge our truths, just as you should challenge others' and your own. In the areas where you feel you don't have enough knowledge or experience, try to change that. Don't let it be a reason not to step into this new era. Be open to change, including your own.

The contributors from Spotify

KATARINA BERG

I, Katarina, am the CHRO at Spotify and oversee all aspects of the strategic HR work. I am responsible for developing and implementing the People Strategy in support of Spotify's overall business plan. At the time of writing, I am also responsible for Spotify's global teams in Strategy Operations, Workplace Services and Equity & Impact. My voice is heard throughout the book and perhaps especially in the sections on employer branding and EVP, culture and core values, Talent Intelligence, Strategy Operations and Global Workplace Services, where I am the sole author.

My co-authors and collaborators:

ALEXANDER WESTERDAHL

Alex is Head of HR for Product and Technology at Spotify. He has contributed predominantly to the chapters on attrition, departure and onboarding, global workplace services, and culture and retention. He is particularly knowledgeable about HR work in large technology departments. If his thoughts in the book resonated with you, you'll be pleased to know that you can often get the chance to hear him speak at HR conferences around Europe. Alex is part of the 'A-Team' (Anna & Alex), who designed and launched Spotify's *Work from Anywhere* programme in early 2021.

ANNA LUNDSTRÖM

Anna, Head of HR for Business at Spotify, is the second part of the A-Team. Her invaluable insight and knowledge of HR, which she enjoys sharing with colleagues and others in the industry, makes her a key part of Spotify's HR leadership team and this book. She has led the writing of the chapter on change management and straightened out all aspects of Spotify's *Work from Anywhere* programme.

ARVID HEDMAN

Arvid, Global Head of Total Compensation & HR Insights, is most visible in the chapter on compensation and benefits. One of the most exemplary practitioners and strategists of the new HR era, he brings fresh, logical and lateral thinking to what is often seen as a rigid subject.

DINA GABRIEL, LAUREN S. WURGAFT AND EBBA GRYTBERG

Dina, Global Head of Equity, Diversity & Impact, joined Spotify as a senior HRBP with proven DIB experience. She is a great example of internal mobility and contributes to the chapter on diversity, inclusion, equity and belonging. Dina brings valuable expertise and actionable efforts to this highly debated area. Lauren takes credit for the social impact input and the pioneering work within this space, while Ebba is the source of knowledge regarding sustainability.

GARY MUNRO

Gary is Head of HR Insights (People Analytics & HRIS) at Spotify. His logical and effective approach to using data and ensuring the entire HR team has access to HR data that can drive business decisions is reflected throughout the book, as it is key in the new era. With the launch of *Disco & Bounce*, Spotify's advanced people analytics platform, Gary has made a strong impact on HR innovation and HR tech. You can read more about it in his chapter on people analytics and in the chapter on psychometrics that he co-authored with Jon.

JOHAN SELLGREN

Johan, HRBP at Spotify, is one of the team's most resilient members. He connects the past with the present and what will happen in the future. He explores how to make strategic workforce planning more pragmatic in the chapter on just that.

JOHANNA BOLIN TINGVALL

Johanna is Global Head of Learning & Development (GreenHouse), Talent Growth and CommunityX. Johanna has contributed extremely valuable content to the whole book. She has written the chapters on onboarding, learning and leadership, and performance development, and also co-authored the introduction to the section on culture and retention. Johanna is co-author of the Swedish edition of this book. She co-edited the English edition. Without Johanna, there would be no book(s).

JON SINGEL (NO LONGER WITH THE BAND)

As Global Head of Talent Acquisition, Jon is really good at operating talent acquisition to respond to fast-paced organisational needs. Any company in hyper growth relying on an in-house team to act as a strategic HR 'recruitment muscle' should have a Jon. He has written the chapter on TA and shared his and Spotify's views on the broad and controversial topic of psychometrics.

LINN CALDAS

Linn is responsible for the company's mental health work: Heart & Soul. Linn, with her extensive know-how and internal networking, contributed significantly to the chapter on mental health, drawing upon her role as our Heart & Soul expert.

MATTIAS STÅLHAMMAR AND SONYA SIMMONDS (SONYA NO LONGER WITH THE BAND)

Mattias (Global Head of GWS) together with Sonya (Architect and Global Head of Design & Build) contributed their expertise and insights to the final chapter. This dynamic duo played a big role in driving our culture through our physical presence – so our offices are more than just premises.

MICHAEL KIM

MK, who serves as Spotify's Head of HR in the JAPAC and SAMEA regions, wrote the chapter on crisis management and helped set the stage by answering the question 'Global HR – what is it?' in the book's introduction. MK is better than anyone at demonstrating the importance of clear, consistent and compelling communication during crises and is the originator of the Spotify Global Parental Leave Policy, launched in 2015.

MIKAEL BÄCKSTRÖM (NO LONGER WITH THE BAND)

As Head of HR Specialist and Senior HRBP at Spotify, Micke used his broad HR expertise to write the chapters on labour law and HR technology. His superpower is that he can make sure that simple things stay simple and that the work is firmly rooted in reality.

DR TOMAS CHAMORRO-PREMUZIC

Our external partner, Tomas, contributes thoughts based on his vast experience as an opinion leader and writer in the industry. He has peppered the book with introductions to the sections on attracting and recruiting the right people and the core of HR work. Tomas is a good friend of the team who is always testing the limits of every 'truth', especially in the areas of assessment and leadership, but also in everything related to behavioural science.

SALLY WHATLEY

Our project manager and English editor has worked side by side with Katarina and the team throughout the writing process. With her communication skills and years of experience in the Spotify HR team, she has coached every author and influenced the chapters. You readers may be more grateful for that than you think (while others are less pleased) – she has removed probably more than 95% of the 'Katarina-isms' that were in the text from the beginning.

Thank you!

by Katarina Berg

Writing this book with an entire team has been every bit as difficult as you would expect – and more rewarding than I could ever have imagined. The truth is that we have started writing three times and we would probably never have finished without the curse and blessing that COVID-19 proved to be. Due to the pandemic, we managed to find some of the missing pieces of the book's puzzle – and the time and focus we didn't have before the forced work from home period of 2020–2022. The co-authors have been highly involved in each chapter. As long as we have worked together, they have always shown true dedication and commitment to the amazing profession and mission we all share. Getting wild ideas in batches (which I am most guilty of) and then turning them into a book is as difficult as it sounds. Completing it has been both challenging and rewarding.

To all the people I have had the opportunity to lead, be led by, or observe as a remote leader: thank you for being the inspiration and foundation of the new, bold era of HR.

I am particularly grateful to Johanna Bolin Tingvall for reading, proof-reading, editing and contributing in many other ways during this co-creation process. I am also indebted to Sally Whatley, who has provided editorial assistance, for her tireless support in breathing new life into the writing as the book was first written in English, then translated into Swedish and then back to English again, thus having to be rewritten a few times over.

A special thank you to my dear friend, the ever-enthusiastic Professor Tomas Chamorro-Premuzic, who immediately agreed to write half of all the introductory theory sections and who is a great thinker in HR, leadership and recruitment selection. I am enormously grateful for Tomas's inspiration and collaboration – and for his being so relentlessly provocative and not always agreeing with us.

Of course, I have to thank all those who have been closest to me during this voyage: Johanna Bolin Tingvall and Anna Lundström, Alexander Westerdahl, Arvid Hedman, Gary Munro, Michael Kim, Mikael Bäckström, Jon Singel, Johan Sellgren, Preeti Singh and Per Larsson. They have been instrumental in what this team has and does on a daily basis. Not to mention the subject matter experts: Isa Notermans, Travis Robinson, Elizabeth Nieto, Lauren Wurgraft, Ebba Grythberg, Linn Caldas, Emil Falsen, Mattias Stålhammar, Nina Hammarström and Sonya Simmonds. I am amazed daily that you never say no and are always open to new ideas and opportunities. I am eternally grateful for each of you, for all your work, your perseverance, your integrity and your professionalism. Thank you for your drafts, long and short, and for trusting me to rewrite and edit. You have been as important in getting this book done as in what we accomplish every day, side by side and always better together. Thank you so much for the laughs, the tears, the successes and the failures – you are simply the best. I am so happy and proud of every day I get to work alongside you.

Thank you to everyone who has contributed to what we do at HR, Strategy Operations & GWS on Spotify, you are simply amazing! Special thanks to my boss Daniel Ek, who when I asked him if I could write two books (cliffhanger!) replied "yes", after his usual: "Why and what problem are you trying to solve?" Thank you for being a leader I trust, honour and respect! I took the position to make this journey for and with you.

To Tessa McIver, our patient and encouraging editor: We liked her immediately; she had us at hello. She worked tirelessly and with speed. Thank you Marta Bartnicka, Agnieszka Adaszewska, Anita Rochalska, Ewa Szmidt and Wojciech Karkoszka, the team at Virtualo/Empik. Magda Dziewguc & Google Cloud Summit and Nette Lövgren – the best cover designer we could ever imagine. A special thanks to Lena Hegg, who was my boss (and more importantly, my role model) in HR during my internship at Volvo Trucks. Thank you for introducing me to the idea of 'there are only two ways to do things: good or bad, worthy or unworthy' and showing me how this notion colours the entire company culture and becomes a guiding principle in everything you do. Also for showing me, rather than telling me, how really difficult situations really define who you are and what your legacy as a leader will be. The world is a better place because of people who want to develop and lead others. What makes it even better is people who dare to be radically different and share their way of thinking, acting and learning. Thank you to everyone who wants to develop and help others to develop.

To everyone in the People Constituency at Spotify, for all you contribute, for our community and shared vision – and for daring to trust me. It is an honour to be on this journey with you. Thank you for letting me serve you and be part of our incredible company. Thank you for always being there and creating an environment where innovative and driven individuals can do their very best.

I want to thank EVERYONE who has ever said something positive to me or taught me something. I heard every word and it always had meaning. To those of you who did the opposite – you are forgotten and the team and I used your negativity and uncertainty as fuel to drive us forwards. Together.

Without all the experiences and support from my team at Spotify, this book would never have existed. Once again, I have been blessed with the best team ever. You have given me the opportunity to lead an amazing group of individuals – leading great leaders is a blessed role to have. Thank you Gustav, Alex, Dawn and Paul – I love you!

Although the years at Spotify have given me highlights of wisdom (aka grey hairs), I see them as a bonus: silver and glitter. My time at Spotify has been worth it.

Finally, I want to thank my father, who never taught me about leadership but rather showed me. On a total institution – a ship – he was the undisputed captain of the seven seas. He was always there at the helm, day and night. He was faithful to his values and his team, with an analytical mind and a warm heart.

O Captain! my Captain! our fearful trip is done;
The ship has weathered every rack, the prize we sought is won;
The port is near, the bells I hear, the people all exulting,
While follow eyes the steady keel, the vessel grim and daring.
But O heart! heart! heart! (Carpe Diem).

WALT WHITMAN[16]

References

1 Briggs, K., Briggs Myers, I. & McCaulley, M. (1987). *Myers-Briggs Type Indicator: Form G.* California: Consulting Psychologists Press.

2 Tim Ambler and Simon Barrow defined *employer brand* in 1996 as: "The package of functional, economic, and psychological benefits provided by employment, and identified with the employing company".

3 Bassi, L. & McMurrer, D. (2007). Maximising Your Return on People. *Harvard Business Review*, March 2007, see https://hbr.org/2007/03/maximising-your-return-on-people.

4 Tupes, E.C. & Christal, R.E. (1992). Recurrent Personality Factors Based on Trait Ratings. *Journal of Personality*, 60(2): 225–251.

5 Arcus, S. (2015). Talentism is the New Capitalism. *New Zealand Management*, 15 June 2015, see https://management.co.nz/article/talentism-new-capitalism.

6 Myers, V. (2022). *Diversity Doesn't Stick Without Inclusion.* 25 February 2022, see www.vernamyers.com/2017/02/04/diversity-doesnt-stick-without-inclusion/.

7 Dweck, C. SurveyMonkey Goldie Speaker Series, 20 June 2017, see https://www.linkedin.com/pulse/chat-professor-carol-dweck-how-growth-mindset-can-drive-rhisa-muse/.

8 Mohr, T.S. (2014). Why Women Don't Apply for Jobs Unless They're 100% Qualified. *Harvard Business Review*, 25 August 2014, see https://hbr.org/2014/08/why-women-dont-apply-for-jobs-unless-theyre-100-qualified.

9 McKinsey & Company (2020). Diversity Wins. How Inclusion Matters, see www.mckinsey.com/~/media/mckinsey/featured%20insights/diversity%20and%20inclusion/diversity%20wins%20how%20inclusion%20matters/diversity-wins-how-inclusion-matters-vf.pdf.

10 Drucker, P. (1959). Work and Tools. *Technology and Culture*, 1(1): 28–37.

11 De Saint-Exupéry, A. (2012). *Airman's Odyssey*. Translated by Lewis Galantière, Stuart Gilbert. Boston: Houghton Mifflin Harcourt, p. 39.

12 Edelman (2020). 2020 Edelman Trust Barometer, see www.edelman.com/trust/2020-trust-barometer.

13 McKinsey (2012). How Companies Capture the Value of Sustainability: Survey Findings, 28 April 2021, see https://www.mckinsey.com/business-functions/sustainability/our-insights/how-companies-capture-the-value-of-sustainability-survey-findings.

14 UN (2022). *The 17 Goals*, see https://sdgs.un.org/goals.

15 Spotify. 'Time For Climate Action', see https://tfca.earth/ALL_us/spotify.

16 Whitman, W. (1888). *O Captain! My Captain!* Walt Whitman Papers: Literary file, see https://www.loc.gov/item/mss77909008/.

KATARINA BERG is the CHRO at Spotify and is responsible for initiating
and implementing the organisational, leadership and employee strategy
for the development of Spotify's overall business plan.

Other co-authors:
Alexander Westerdahl, HR Unit Lead, R&D; **Anna Lundström**, HR Unit
Lead, Business; **Arvid Hedman**, Global Head of Total Comp & HR
Insights; **Gary Munro**, Head of HR Insights (People Analytics & HRIS);
Johan Sellgren, Global HRBP; **Johanna Bolin Tingvall**, Global Head of
Learning & Development (GreenHouse), Talent Growth and CommunityX;
Jon Singel, Global Head of Talent Acquisition; **Linn Caldas**, Global Lead,
Heart & Soul; **Michael Kim**, Head of HR JAPAC and SAMEA; **Mikael
Bäckström**, HRBP & Global Head of HRS; **Mattias Stålhammar**, Global
Head of GWS; **Sonya Simmonds**, Global Manager for Design & Build;
Dina Gabriel, Global Head of EDI; **Lauren S. Wurgaft**, Global Head of
Social Impact; **Ebba Grytberg**, Global Sustainability Lead; **Dr Tomas
Chamorro Premuzic**; and **Sally Whatley**, Project Manager and Editor.

An organisation that doesn't continuously invest in its people will stop
growing and stop developing. Any organisation that doesn't bring in
the right people at the right time, into the right services, and adjust its
organisational design accordingly, will lose momentum and competitive
advantage. This is the era of the employee.

At Spotify, from the very beginning, we have strived to create an
environment where innovative and creative employees can be their
best selves. It has been, and continues to be, incredibly exciting – and
challenging – to try to create a truly global culture during constant and
rapid growth.

It's absolutely essential that we (the Spotify HR team) understand what
makes the organism Spotify live and thrive and move forwards, that we
understand the business and know the core business inside and out,
and that we are integrated into the business rather than 'visiting'. It also
makes our work more fun, and both more tactical and more strategic.